D0970222

The Romance in America

The Romance in America

STUDIES IN COOPER, POE,
HAWTHORNE, MELVILLE,
AND JAMES

By JOEL PORTE

WESLEYAN UNIVERSITY PRESS

Middletown, Connecticut

Library of Congress Catalog Card Number: 69-17795

Manufactured in the United States of America

FIRST EDITION

Romance, who loves to nod and sing,
With drowsy head and folded wing,
Among the green leaves as they shake
Far down within some shadowy lake,
       To me a painted paroquet
Hath been—a most familiar bird—
       Taught me my alphabet to say,—
To lisp my very earliest word
While in the wild-wood I did lie
A child—with a most knowing eye.

. . . .

. . . even the graybeard will o'erlook
Connivingly my dreaming–book.

EDGAR ALLAN POE,
"Romance" (1831)

CONTENTS

PREFACE

THANKS to a series of major critical studies that have appeared in the past decade and a half, it no longer seems necessary to argue for the importance of romance as a nineteenth-century American genre. Students of American literature—notably Richard Chase—have provided a solid theoretical basis for establishing that the rise and growth of fiction in this country is dominated by our authors' conscious adherence to a tradition of non-realistic romance sharply at variance with the broadly novelistic mainstream of English writing. When there has been disagreement among recent critics as to the contours of American fiction, it has usually disputed, not the existence per se of a romance tradition, but rather the question of which authors, themes, and stylistic strategies deserve to be placed with certainty at the heart of that tradition.

Thus, for example, Charles Feidelson (*Symbolism and American Literature*) sees the symbolic or symbolistic imagination as the typically American mode; his major exemplars among American fictionists are Poe, Hawthorne, and Melville. (He mentions Cooper not at all and James only in passing.) For R. W. B. Lewis (*The American Adam*), on the other hand, the presence of the Adamic myth or archetype is the determining factor, to be found notably in the works of Cooper, Hawthorne, and Melville. (Poe is excluded, as he is—totally and inexplicably—from Richard Chase's *The American Novel and Its Tradition*.) Harry Levin's valuable *The Power of Blackness* locates an American tradition in the configurations of symbol and theme suggested by that title; its principal centers of interest are Poe, Hawthorne, and Melville. By far the most comprehensive recent study as regards the range of writers treated is Leslie Fiedler's *Love and Death in the American Novel*, but the obsessive thesis of this book—that American writing is notable for its failure to deal with "adult heterosexual love"—makes its argument curiously constricted as compared to the wide scope of its materials. Finally, Daniel Hoffman (*Form and Fable in American Fiction*) sees a tradition of new world writing characterized almost exclusively by the use of "folklore, myth, and ritual"; and his treatment excludes Cooper, Poe, and James.

It will be obvious to my reader—and I am happy to acknowledge—that the present study could hardly have been written without a knowledge of and dependence on these six major works of synthesis. But the essay that follows differs from them importantly, I believe, in emphasis and intent. My object has been to demonstrate the existence of a fictional tradition running throughout the nineteenth century and including Cooper and James, as well as Poe, Hawthorne, and Melville—a tradition of fictional themes, materials, and treatments that suggests the unity in variety of all five authors.

I have attempted to show that all these writers created, partially or completely, according to a theory of stylized art—heavily dependent on the use of conventional, or archetypal, figures and on symbol, parable, dream, and fantasy—in order to explore large questions (and this list is not exhaustive) about race, history, nature, human motivation, and art. Particularly from Poe to James, I have tried to suggest that the American romance is characterized by a need self-consciously to define its own aims, so that "romance" becomes frequently (as I have had occasion to note particularly of *The Scarlet Letter*) the theme as well as the form of these authors' works. American romancers, Daniel Hoffman remarks, "have all taken the role of the artist to be the discoverer and revealer of truth," and it is a curious but important fact that our writers have consistently tried to fulfill that role by reflexively questioning their own assumptions within their books. As R. W. B. Lewis has noted, comparing contemporary fiction with that of the American nineteenth century, in both cases (for somewhat different reasons) "literature doubles back on itself and becomes obsessed with the task of exploiting its own tribulations." I have addressed myself in part to exploring why this should be so and what significance it has.

One further word of explanation, or apology, may be in order. Several friendly critics who took the trouble to read this work in manuscript have commented on the oddity of a study of American romance that fails to deal with *Moby-Dick* and indeed urged strongly that I include a section on Melville's masterpiece. At the proverbial risk of attempting to produce a *Hamlet* without the Prince, I have not taken their advice—probably out of diffidence. But perhaps something more positive may be said in defense of my omission. First, the amount of expert commentary already available on *Moby-Dick* is impressive and somewhat intimidating. (Harry Levin has wittily and justly remarked that the production of such criticism seems almost to have "taken the place of whaling among the industries of New England.") More to my point, however, although I would insist that *Moby-Dick* belongs squarely in the tradition of American romance that I explore in this study, there is a problem here for the critic of form or genre, since the book is a romance *within* (following Northrop Frye) an anatomy, to say nothing of Melville's excursions into dramatic or even operatic writing. In addition, since the scope and variety of Melville's writing career dictated limitation, I became interested—for reasons which will appear—in examining his prose fiction of the crucial years after 1851.

Indeed, the substantial—in most cases, prodigious—output of all five authors treated in this book made limitation mandatory, and I have not hesitated to be selective according to my own tastes and concerns. Yet I believe that the main argument of my study has validity beyond the material chosen for examination here and that it will prove illuminating for certain other works and authors as well.

I owe a debt to undergraduate and graduate students at Harvard and Radcliffe who have explored the American romance with me, criticizing my ideas and offering many of their own. Friends and colleagues also made numerous wise suggestions, for my not following more of which, alas, nothing but authorial stubbornness is to blame. I am grateful to Harvard University for providing the research leave in 1966–67 during which the bulk of this study was completed. Throughout an unusually cold year, first in Nervi, on the Italian Riviera, and then in Jerusalem, my dauntless and undiscourageable wife stoked the furnace, stroked the cat, and sustained my labors with both pasta and patient understanding.

J. P.

Cambridge, Massachusetts
August 1968

The Romance in America

I

COOPER

1. *"The Aboriginal Indian Vision"*

IT has become customary, in any attempt to write about Cooper's imaginative vision, to begin with a nod in the direction of D. H. Lawrence, and this gesture is decidedly not to be seen as simply another example of the usual scholarly or critical courtesy extended to the man who got there first. In a very real sense, Lawrence did not have to *get* there at all. For his essay on Cooper (surely the best of the individual chapters in *Studies in Classic American Literature*) seems to owe its peculiar acuteness to the fact that he and Cooper shared the same feeling about the American continent—a feeling for its terrifying grandeur and cruel power.

An extremely suggestive corroboration of this identity of view is afforded by an earlier passage in *Studies*, in which Lawrence comments on Crèvecoeur's observation of nature red in tooth and claw:

> It is the rudimentary American vision. The glimpsing of the king-birds in winged hostility and pride is no doubt the aboriginal Indian vision carrying over. The Eagle symbol in human consciousness. Dark, swinging wings of hawk-beaked destiny, that one cannot help but feel, beating here above the wild center of America. You look round in vain for the "One being Who made all things, and governs the world by His Providence." [Franklin's creed]
>
> "One species pursue and live upon another." [Crèvecoeur]
>
> Reconcile the two statements if you like. But, in America, act on Crèvecoeur's observation.[1]

---

1. *Studies in Classic American Literature*, reprinted in *The Shock of Recognition*, edited by Edmund Wilson (New York, 1955), p. 931.

3

In Cooper, to be sure, one often hears the deistic accents of a Franklin, as when Natty Bumppo insists that the forest will never deceive, "being ordered and ruled by a hand that never wavers." But if, overlooking such patent mouthing of pious doctrine, we "trust the tale" (as Lawrence would have it[2]) and observe Cooper in moments of great imaginative power, we find him closer to Crèvecoeur than to Franklin, impelled like Lawrence by the force of the "Eagle symbol." One such moment occurs in *The Pioneers*, as Cooper attempts to convey a sense of the impressiveness of seasonal change in America, when the earth, "like a victim to contention," becomes literally a battleground for the mortal combat between winter and approaching spring. Winter, the hoary ruler of the seasons, dies hard in America, and late in April "still a dark and gloomy covering concealed" the waters of Lake Otsego. Flocks of wild geese passed over, looking for a resting place, but "on finding themselves excluded by the chill covering, [they] would soar away to the north, filling the air with discordant screams, as if venting their complaints at the tardy operations of nature."

Then Cooper finds the perfect symbolic referent for the reluctant departure of the powerful season:

> For a week, the dark covering of the Otsego was left to the undisturbed possession of two eagles, who alighted on the center of its field, and sat eyeing their undisputed territory. During the presence of these monarchs of the air, the flocks of migrating birds avoided crossing the plain of ice, by turning into the hills, apparently seeking the protection of the forests, while the white and bald heads of the tenants of the lake were turned upwards, with a look of contempt. But the time had come, when even these kings of birds were to be dispossessed.

The ice finally breaks up, "the lingering remnant of winter" is expelled, and "just as the last sheet of agitated ice was disappearing in the distance, the eagles rose, and soared with a wide sweep above the clouds." But this glimpse of what Lawrence called the "king-birds in winged hostility and pride" suggests only a temporary dispossession; for in truth, as Lawrence insists, the American eagle shrieks, "We are the masterless."[3]

---

2. *Ibid.*, p. 909.
3. *Ibid.*, p. 912.

The wilderness is not to be tamed or domesticated so easily, and anxiety for renewed cruelty—the return of winter—will always be present.[4]

The centrality of this "rudimentary American vision" to Cooper's scheme in the Leatherstocking Tales is further suggested by an important episode in *The Deerslayer*, when the newly named Hawkeye wins his right, ritually as it were, to use the fabulous weapon Killdeer. The target is a high-flying eagle—indomitable, proud, scornful of man's petty attempts to limit it—which both Natty and Chingachgook fail to bring down with ordinary weapons. As the seemingly charmed bird flies even higher, "looking down, as if in contempt, at his foes," causing the usually sagacious Indian to comment on the impossibility of the task, Hawkeye calls for the uninitiated Killdeer, exclaiming "with glistening and delighted eyes, 'we'll see if Killdeer isn't Killeagle too!'" In Natty's hands, of course, Killdeer is Killanything, and the young scout brings down the bird forthwith, at once establishing his claim to the weapon and his mastery over the American wilderness, represented by the enormous bird. Fittingly, however, after killing the eagle, Natty is seized by great remorse, for it is as much the spirit of the great forest as he is, and the death of the bird makes him meditate lugubriously on his own end.

But Cooper approximates even more closely Lawrence's "aboriginal Indian vision" in *The Prairie*, using imaginative materials strikingly consistent with those we have already noticed. The scene is that of a desperate combat between the Pawnees and the Sioux in which an aged Sioux warrior, Bohrecheena, weak and wounded and greatly afraid of being left behind to be scalped ignominiously by the Pawnees, begs a young Sioux—the fiercest of his fierce tribe and appropriately named "the Swooping Eagle"—to carry him back to the village. The Swooping Eagle agrees, "answering to the appeal with a stern look of inflexible resolution." Placing himself and Bohrecheena on his horse, he sets off at great speed, but the Pawnees give chase, and the pair are in grave danger

---

4. Thomas Philbrick suggests the dependence of Cooper's description of the reluctant departure of winter on James Thomson's *Spring*. But Philbrick admits that Cooper's "method is more complex and subtle than Thomson's," especially as regards Cooper's symbolic use of the two eagles. (See "Cooper's *The Pioneers*: Origins and Structure," *PMLA*, LXXIX [1964], 585 ff.) Cooper, writes John T. Frederick, "had a violent and unaccountable predilection for the eagle" ("Cooper's Eloquent Indians," *PMLA*, LXXI [1956], 1010).

of being overtaken. "Stop," cries Bohrecheena, "the Eagle of my tribe must spread his wings wider. Let him carry the white hairs of an old warrior into the burnt-wood village!"

> The Swooping Eagle threw himself from the back of the horse, and assisted the other to alight. The old man raised his tottering frame to its knees, and first casting a glance upward at the countenance of his country-man, as if to bid him adieu, he stretched out his neck to the blow he himself invited. A few strokes of the tomahawk, with a circling gash of the knife, sufficed to sever the head from the less valued trunk. The Teton mounted again, just in season to escape a flight of arrows which came from his eager and disappointed pursuers. Flourishing the grim and bloody visage, he darted away from the spot with a shout of triumph, and was seen scouring the plains, as if he were actually borne along on the wings of the powerful bird from whose qualities he had received his flattering name.

Perhaps at no other place in the Leatherstocking Tales (except the de-scription of the slaughter at Fort William Henry) does Cooper succeed as well in creating a sense of those "dark, swinging wings of hawk-beaked destiny" that Lawrence felt palpitating "above the wild center of Amer-ica." In this passage, the familiar Cooperesque images of Indian, eagle, vast space, and bloody death coalesce to form a memorable picture of the continent in all its violence and cruelty. Cooper, at his best, seems far less interested in reconciling Franklin and Crèvecoeur than in creating, to quote Richard Chase, "a world where nature is dire, terrible, and beauti-ful, where human virtues are personal, alien, and renunciatory, and where contradictions are to be resolved only by death."[5]

2. *"An Original Conception of the Life of Man"*

In his *The Popular Book in America*, James Hart reports that the Bos-ton publisher Samuel Goodrich "estimated in 1820 that three-quarters of the books Americans bought were of English origin."[6] If this was true,

---

5. *The American Novel and Its Tradition* (New York, 1957), p. 7. Marius Bewley offers an extremely perceptive analysis of Cooper's uncanny feeling for "violence and psychological terror"—his "sense of the imponderable nature of reality"—in *The Spy* and *The Water-Witch*. (See *The Eccentric Design* [New York, 1963], pp. 74–77, 315–316.)

6. *The Popular Book in America* (New York, 1950), pp. 67–68.

it would certainly justify the celebrated contemporary challenge that Sydney Smith scornfully thrust at his provincial cousins across the sea: "In the four quarters of the globe, who reads an American book?" If Americans themselves were scarcely reading American books, one might remark, who else should have been reading them? But Smith's question can usefully be paraphrased, so as to reduce it from a supercilious vaunt to an intelligible statement of precisely the kind of problem that faced such a writer as Cooper in 1820: In the four quarters of the globe, who knew what a really American book was?[7] If, along with Lawrence, we can put aside our impatience at the frequent unreality of Cooper's vision and accept the Leatherstocking Tales as "a kind of yearning myth"[8] of the New World, we can begin truly to measure Cooper's achievement as an American writer.

In this context, Richard Chase's definition of "myth" is particularly helpful. He calls it "a way of sanctioning and giving significance to those crises of human experience which are cultural as well as personal: birth,

---

7. For a discussion of the contemporary crusade launched by the *North American Review* for a native American literature, see Gregory Paine, "Cooper and the North American Review," *Studies in Philology*, XXVIII (1931), 267–277. In his review of *The Spy* (published in the *NAR* in July, 1822) W. H. Gardiner praised Cooper for having "laid the foundations of American romance." In Marcel Clavel, *Fenimore Cooper and His Critics* (Aix-en-Provence, 1938), pp. 82–91, there is an interesting discussion of Gardiner's review, which, according to M. Clavel, "Cooper never forgave." When *The Pioneers* was published in 1823, one American journal (*Niles' Weekly Register*) pointedly responded to Sydney Smith by saying that Cooper's third book would "be read by tens of thousands even in Great Britain" (*Ibid.*, p. 147).

The Smith controversy and its significance in relation to Cooper were well summarized by William Gilmore Simms some two decades later: "The success of the 'Spy' was very great, and it at once gave Mr. Cooper reputation in Europe. It may be said to have occasioned a greater sensation in Europe than at home;—and there were good reasons for this. At that period America had no literature. Just before this time, or about this time, it was the favourite sarcasm of the British Reviewers that such a thing as an American book was never read. Mr. Irving, it is true, was writing his sweet and delicate essays; but he was not accounted in England an American writer, and he himself,—no doubt with a sufficient policy—his own fortunes alone being the subject of consideration—took no pains to assert his paternity. The publication of the 'Spy' may be assumed to have been the first practical reply to a sarcasm, which, since that day, has found its ample refutation" (*Views and Reviews in American Literature, History, and Fiction*, edited by C. Hugh Holman [Cambridge, Mass., 1962], p. 265).

8. *Studies in Classic American Literature*, p. 953.

initiation into life, ideal friendship, marriage, war against man or nature, death." Cooper was compelled to be a romancer in the Leatherstocking books because he tried, however imperfectly, to define and explain certain "mythic" aspects of the American experience—call them crises or, perhaps better, cruxes—that could not be dealt with in the realistic novel as he knew it, with its attention limited mainly to detailed description and analysis of the motions and motives of (usually) polite society. It is "the very abstractness and profundity of romance," as Chase sees it, that "allow it to formulate moral truths of universal validity." Here, of course, the "universe" is America, and whatever Cooper may lack in profundity, the earnestness and singularity of his mythopoeic effort are notable. Surely Chase is right in insisting that there emerges from Cooper's work in the Leatherstocking Tales "an original conception of the life of man and its significance"[9] in America that was to be of lasting importance for all serious American authors—and, one should add, for American culture at large.

It is of course notoriously difficult, in attempting to describe the nature of Cooper's achievement as an American romancer, to decide just which themes, and their treatments, are most peculiarly and particularly American. But two of Cooper's consistent concerns deserve at least nomination to this difficult category: race and women. Cooper's handling of these themes offers an especially apt illustration of that Manichean sensibility which Yvor Winters, Richard Chase, and others have felt to be so characteristic of the American literary imagination.

The importance of race as a theme in the literature of a country whose lands were wrested from the hands of non-whites should hardly seem surprising, but one must add that Cooper commenced his writing career at a point when the notion of race began to have special interest for an American writer. He was, of course, thoroughly versed in the theoretically egalitarian beliefs of European and, more particularly, American eighteenth-century thinkers. But in the first decades of the nineteenth century these fine theories were being put to hard practical tests in America. (On the Indian question, for example, Samuel Eliot Morison notes that "Jefferson professed benevolent principles toward them, but coveted their lands in order to encourage western migration and keep the United States agricultural."[10]) And the resettlement of the Indians largely undertaken

---

9. *The American Novel and Its Tradition*, pp. 53, xi, 45.
10. *The Oxford History of the American People* (New York, 1965), p. 380.

in the 1820's made that period one of great bitterness in white-red relations.[11] This national mood must have contributed significantly to awakening Cooper's profound interest in race, which is certainly one of his great themes. For it was surely not, as Leslie Fiedler would have it,[12] exclusively a concern over miscegenation that compelled Cooper on this topic, but rather a desire to come to clarity on a great human question. The notion of race ultimately became for Cooper, as we shall see, a way of meditating on good and evil.

As for women, their undeniable, if oblique, importance in Cooper's fiction can only be accounted for in a more complicated fashion. There is first of all the idea that, as Fiedler puts it, with "the fatherland abandoned, the Pope rejected, the bishops denied, the king overthrown—only the mother remained as symbol of an authority that was one with love" for the "fatherless" American.[13] This special significance of the woman is easily observed in nineteenth-century American writing: Cooper's Elizabeth Temple, like an American Madonna, acts as a gentle mediatrix for the harsh legal judgments of Judge Temple, as does Hawthorne's Phoebe for those of Judge Pyncheon. But the general notion of the American male's rebellion against authority also suggests some of the hidden complexities of Cooper's treatment of women. In Lewis Mumford's view:

> The hope of making a fresh start in this new land explains the constant note of rebellion that underlies our greatest literary expressions: rebellion against the political state, against the caste system, against property, against religious ceremony and ritualism, even, in Huckleberry Finn, against tidy routine and mechanical punctuality, as against every kind of cowed conformity.[14]

If Mumford's formulation begins, in agreement with Fiedler, by positing the idea of rebellion against masculine authority, it ends by suggesting (however innocuously in its mention of Huckleberry Finn) an ultimate flight from a new tyranny—women.

We are faced with the paradox of an American who fled the Old

---

11. On the question of Indian removal and resettlement, see Roy Harvey Pearce, *The Savages of America* (Baltimore, 1953), pp. 53–75, and Francis Paul Prucha, *American Indian Policy in the Formative Years* (Cambridge, Mass., 1962), pp. 213–249. For Cooper's interest in and knowledge of the Indians, see Gregory Paine, "The Indians of *The Leatherstocking Tales*," *Studies in Philology*, XXIII (1926), 16–39.

12. Cf. *Love and Death in the American Novel* (New York, 1960), p. 202.

13. *Ibid.*, p. 49.

14. *The Golden Day* (Boston, 1957), p. xxi.

World to escape the "father" and replace him with the image of "woman," only to find that the woman could ultimately become a worse and more subtle tyrant: not only the gentle guardian of religion and culture, but simultaneously an incitement to license and desire—at once demanding respectful love and obedience and inspiring lust. Fiedler is certainly right in saying that "in Cooper's America, the attribution to the female of all moral authority had turned her into a super-ego figure, the embodiment of civilization itself"; but he is wrong in insisting that "marriage for Natty [Bumppo] would therefore have represented a turning from the id to the super-ego,"[15] since he overlooks Cooper's manifestly dual attitude toward women. In *The Deerslayer* Natty pointedly rejects an offer of marriage from the convincingly attractive Judith Hutter (he himself calls her "wonderful handsome, and enticing") specifically because she is, not the "super-ego," but an openly sexual woman. Natty Bumppo, the archetypal American hero, runs off to the forest to escape, neither the superego per se nor carnality per se, but rather the awful implications of mixing good and evil (religion and sex, as it were) as they are represented by the confusing single image of woman. She confronts him with a morally equivocal situation, and it is the fruit of *this* tree—this kind of knowledge—that Natty spurns. And surely Fiedler misleads when he insists that the American hero escapes to the woods so that he can indulge his id in homoerotic fantasy (Natty and Chingachgook, Huck and Jim). The aim is a flight from temptation—a quest for the purity of moral simplicity—and not self-indulgence.

Ultimately in Cooper, whether we are dealing with the question of race or of women, the American hero is simply facing his own duplex nature—the light and darkness within himself—and the duplex nature of experience generally. In the first of the Leatherstocking books, *The Pioneers*, Cooper creates a moment beautifully symbolic of the underlying problem of his series when the young Oliver Edwards, walking in the moonlight, alternates his glance between the aged Chingachgook (here cast in the role of the dissipated John Mohegan), whose "dark, fiery eyes . . . told a tale of passions unrestrained, and of thoughts free as air," and the "gentle countenance" of the clergyman's daughter, Miss Grant, whose eyes "rivalled the soft hue of the sky." Oliver is thereby "led to consider the difference in the human form," says Cooper; but the question,

---

15. *Love and Death in the American Novel*, p. 209.

here in its simplest and earliest mode, that Cooper really seems to be suggesting is, how can humans be at once wild and heavenly? (At another point in *The Pioneers*, John Mohegan himself will state the problem neatly: "John is a Christian beast.") Later Cooper will probe more deeply into the possibilities of wild and heavenly Indians, as well as wild and heavenly women, as the strange antinomies of human nature appear everywhere.

3. *The Red and the White*

"You must know, Sarpent," affirms Natty Bumppo in *The Deerslayer*, "that the great principle of Christianity is to believe *without* seeing; and a man should always act up to his religion and principles, let them be what they may."

> "That is strange for a wise nation," said the Delaware, with emphasis. "The red man looks hard, that he may *see* and understand."

This impressive interchange between the two philosophers of the forest gives unintended meaning to Mark Twain's comic allegation that "Cooper's eye was splendidly inaccurate. . . . He saw nearly all things as through a glass eye, darkly."[16] The echo of I Corinthians reminds us that Cooper, as a religious author (and Natty, as his Christian hero), frequently views things with the abstractness of white Christian vision. But whatever his principles and however inaccurate his eye for actuality, Cooper was at least not color-blind—blind, that is, to the dangerous possibility that men of a different race (and therefore conviction) may see things not only differently, but at least occasionally even more profoundly than white men. Chingachgook's remark, clearly endowed by Cooper with peculiar significance, suggests that however blind the Indian may be to eternal things, he perceives the things of this world with uncommon steadiness and clarity. The red man and the white man differ, not only in their beliefs, but in their ways of knowing and, most importantly, in the things they know.

Cooper's interest in these matters appears in the first volume of the Leatherstocking Tales through the person of John Mohegan, who is in

---

16. "Fenimore Cooper's Literary Offenses," reprinted in *The Shock of Recognition*, pp. 586–587.

the advantageous position, at least theoretically, of being both a red man and a Christian. As, in moral terms, a kind of borderline case, John is able to comment shrewdly on the ambiguities of human nature. Thus he is one of the few characters in the book licensed to make insinuations about the character of the sacrosanct Judge Marmaduke Temple. Apropos of the apparently accidental wounding of Oliver Edwards by the Judge, John observes: "The children of Miquon [William Penn; Judge Temple is a Quaker] do not love the sight of blood, and yet the Young Eagle has been struck by the hand that should do no evil!"

> "Mohegan! old John!" exclaimed the Judge, "thinkest thou that my hand has ever drawn human blood willingly? For shame! for shame, old John! thy religion should have taught thee better."

"The evil spirit sometimes lives in the best heart," replies John with the diabolical insight of the Indian, whereupon the clergyman, Mr. Grant, intervenes and John is made to eat his words. But the portrayal of human character in the book tends to confirm John's belief in the ambivalence of our nature. Judge Temple himself, for example, is shocked and dismayed by wanton destruction of life, exemplified by the wholesale slaughter of pigeons and fish in Templeton as a kind of sport, yet he joins in with gusto; just as Oliver Edwards, although extremely distressed by Natty Bumppo's crucial killing of a deer out of season, is himself "inflamed beyond prudence" by the excitement of the chase. Again, when the eyes of the normally placid Old John begin glaring "with an expression of wild resentment," the author tries to excuse him by explaining that the Indian (the recipient, we should notice, both of the white man's Christianity and of his rum) "was not himself." But the true burden of Cooper's tale is that every man has a capacity for radical doubleness—for being a "Christian beast."[17] Although the clergyman, while equivocating in Cooper's best Enlightenment style ("Do not mistake me, I beg, for it is not color, nor lineage, that constitutes merit"), insists that it is Oliver Edward's supposed descent from the Indians that accounts for his "revengeful principles," we learn finally that Oliver has no Indian blood at all. And the ultimate word of truth is left, as always, to John Mohegan: "Is there

---

17. In *The Savages of America* Roy Harvey Pearce astutely suggests how paradoxical it was that even while civilization and Christianity were considered indispensable for the salvation of the Indian, the removal of the Indians to the Western territories was being justified with the argument that contact with "civilized" and "Christianized" white men was corrupting and destroying the Indians.

difference below the skin? No." As distinct from the clergyman (whose spirit clearly influences the choice of an epitaph for the Indian's tombstone: "his faults were those of an Indian, and his virtues those of a man"), Mohegan affirms that all men have a touch of, not whiteness, but blackness (or redness) beneath the skin.[18]

Natty Bumppo, of course, as he himself never tires of asserting, is "a man without a cross"—"pure white," in Lawrence's phrase. It is largely Natty's function in his tales to maintain and demonstrate the absoluteness of the distinction between paleface and redskin, between the "wild" man and the Christian (for it is "oncreditable," Natty insists, "for a white man not to be a Christian"). Set amid the enormous dangers and temptations of the American forest—man alone in the wilderness—Natty is burdened with the great task of proving that the integrity of his whiteness is complete, and that this dark, mysterious aboriginal continent cannot force him (as it does many a Hawthorne character) into moral collapse. Along with most Unitarian and Transcendental thinkers, Cooper believed ideally that the white man, transferred from the Old World to the New and therefore washed clean of the corrupting influences of an ancient civilization, would demonstrate his natural moral goodness.[19] Thus if Natty fails to prove that his whiteness is absolute and innate, the American experiment in this sense could be said to be a failure; or, at least, his failure would suggest that America could not hope to survive the decline of a

---

18. In "Cooper's *The Pioneers*: Origins and Structure," pp. 589–590, Thomas Philbrick suggests how central to *The Pioneers* is the notion of repressed human passions that continually threaten to break through into violent action. Edwin Fussell writes: "As early as *The Pioneers*, Cooper introduces, but does not really activate, his conception of the Double Indian—Delaware vs. Mingo—as an obvious allegorical equivalent for the good and evil to be found in all men" (*Frontier: American Literature and the American West* [Princeton, 1965], p. 38). Kay Seymour House, *Cooper's Americans* (Columbus, Ohio, 1965), pp. 47–71, contains an interesting discussion of Indian doubleness, especially as exemplified by Saucy Nick/Wyandotté in *Wyandotté*.

19. See Frank M. Collins, "Cooper and the American Dream," *PMLA*, LXXXI (1966), 79–94, on Cooper's belief in the possible flowering of man's natural goodness in America. But Collins finally stresses Cooper's ambivalence on just this point. Apparently overwhelmed by a vision of universal evil at the end of his life, Cooper would say in his last work that "even in the forest and the most secluded dales of the country" the evil urge could be found. It now appeared to Cooper, writes Collins, "that what was 'true in the old world' would, 'in the end, be found to be true here.'" Cf. A. N. Kaul, *The American Vision: Actual and Ideal Society in Nineteenth-Century Fiction* (New Haven, 1963), p. 112.

wary Calvinism, which, forewarned of its depravity, had therefore been forearmed.[20]

Yet, as the creation of an author with a strongly eighteenth-century mentality, Natty is also forced in his utterances to let his "observation with extensive view/Survey mankind from China to Peru," finding, with Dr. Johnson, as he does so that human nature is everywhere the same. As Natty explains patiently to Judith Hutter, "You find different colors on 'arth, as anyone may see, but you don't find different natur's." On this level Natty is committed to a kind of ethical relativism—influenced, on Cooper's part, by Enlightenment egalitarianism—that would tend ultimately to undermine the validity of making moral distinctions between races. As a consequence, the depravity and bestiality of the redskin would have to be seen either as the result of the influence exerted on his character by the American wilderness, or as an innate human propensity potentially existing in all men. In either case, the paleface in America would be equally subject to depravity and bestiality.[21] To combat the impeccable logic of this argument (of which Cooper was thoroughly aware) Natty is therefore allowed to have, on another and perhaps deeper level, a primitive racial consciousness—a firm commitment to the absolute nature of his whiteness. Thus Natty Bumppo was set by his creator in a condition of permanent tension, stretched between what might be called a submerged Manicheism, which sees the world in archetypally strict black and white terms, and a liberal rationality that tends to insist on the complexity of moral questions and the consequent danger of simplistic views. As Cooper says of Natty, sympathetically but somewhat apologetically exposing his contradictions, "he possessed every disposition to hear reason, a strong, innate desire to do justice, and an ingenuousness that was singularly indisposed to have recourse to sophisms to maintain an argument, or to defend a prejudice. Still, he was not altogether free from the influence of the latter feeling."

---

20. The American dream of innocence, writes Frank Collins, "could exist only as the kind of fantasy which passes easily into nightmare: the more apparently inviolable the sanctuary the greater the shock of invasion and transformation. In what has become the characteristic American nightmare, the corruptive invaders acquired, as they drew nearer, features disturbingly familiar, even familial."

21. Roy Harvey Pearce argues convincingly in *The Savages of America* that the image of the Indian in much late eighteenth- and nineteenth-century American writing functioned to warn civilized white men of the ubiquitous dangers of savagism.

The essential falsity of Natty's claim to sweet eighteenth-century reasonableness on the question of race can be seen in the several important places in the Leatherstocking Tales where an attempt is made to distinguish between "gifts" and "nature." The quick-witted Judith Hutter is rightly confused by Natty's distinctions and asks for clarification. Natty explains that "natur'" is what is innate in a person, the "wishes, wants, idees, and feelin's" that are born in him. "This natur' never can be changed in the main, though it may undergo some increase or lessening." But gifts, he continues, "come of sarcumstances." Thus, in good eighteenth-century relativistic terms, Natty affirms that "natur'" (human nature) is everywhere the same but that "gifts" (habits and customs) are environmentally determined. On earth, he finely insists, we find "different gifts, but only one natur'." This lovely liberal theory, however, the action of *The Deerslayer* perfectly refutes.

Even on a purely theoretical level, we can observe Natty taking the opposite position in *The Pathfinder*. There, when he insists at one point to the incredulous Cap that such things as scalping are only "skin-deep," depending as they do on "edication," he immediately adds, mixing his terms and thereby muddying his theory, that they also depend on "nat'ral gifts." Earlier in the book, he had already shown his hand more clearly. "As for the raal natur'" of the white man and the redskin, Natty says, "it is my opinion that neither can actually get that of the other." Cap then assumes the position of the eighteenth-century man of reason:

> "And yet we sailors, who run about the world so much, say there is but one nature, whether it be in the China-man or the Dutchman. For my own part, I am much of that way of thinking too; for I have generally found that all nations like gold and silver, and most men relish tobacco."

Natty's response is swift and certain:

> "Then you sea-faring men know little of the red-skins. Have you ever known any of your China-men who could sing their death songs, with their flesh torn with splinters and cut with knives, the fire raging around their naked bodies, and death staring them in the face? Until you can find me a China-man, or a Christian-man, that can do all this, you cannot find a man with a red-skin natur'."

Here, of course, Natty is praising the Indian for his bravery and endurance, but the burden is still that the redskin's nature is inherently ferocious, by implication inhuman. Later in the book Natty will assert dogmatically the absolute and, in his view, fortunately unbreachable gap between the nature of a "Christian" and that of a red man: "no christianizing will ever make even a Delaware a white man; nor any whooping and yelling convart a pale-face into a red-skin." Natty's profound need to believe that "whiteness" is an eternal principle forces him into the odd position of implicitly denying the possibility of Christian conversion, whereby we see that "whiteness" for him is a category that transcends Christianity. It is part of an archetypal distinction between good and evil on which the moral being of the American hero itself seems to depend. The voice of eighteenth-century rationalistic relativism is again heard in *The Prairie* in the person of Dr. Obed Battius, who affirms the dangerous heresy that "color is the fruit of climate and condition, and not a regulation of nature." Whereupon Natty enlists the aid of the child of darkness, the Indian himself, to intone the immortal truth: "The Wahcondah . . . fashioned his children with care and thought. What he has thus made, never alters!" And the old trapper adds his own amen: "Ay, 'tis in the reason of natur' that it should be so."

The disparity in Natty between what he frequently says and what he actually seems to believe or by his action demonstrates on the question of race is nowhere more beautifully illustrated than in *The Deerslayer*, the last of the Leatherstocking Tales, where Cooper opposes the true American hero in the wilderness, Natty, to the frontiersman who lacks the one thing really needful, moral fibre. The latter figure is here represented by Hurry Harry March (Cooper had already suggested this opposition in the person of Ishmael Bush in *The Prairie*). March is a perfect racist:

> "Here's three colors on 'arth; white, black, and red. White is the highest color, and therefore the best man; black comes next, and is put to live in the neighborhood of the white man, as tolerable, and fit to be made use of; and red comes last, which shows that those that made 'em never expected an Indian to be accounted as more than half human."

Natty responds in the organ tones of an apparent humanitarian liberalism: "God made all three alike, Hurry." March cries out, incensed: "Alike! Do you call a nigger like a white man, or me like an Indian?"—inadvertently suggesting the danger lurking in the liberal argument: that a white man might harbor "redskin" tendencies. Natty replies, invoking his standard distinction between "gifts" and "nature," that God undoubtedly had his own reasons for coloring men differently: "Still, he made us, in the main, much the same in feelin's; though I'll not deny that he gave each race its gifts. A white man's gifts are christianized, while a red-skin's are more for the wilderness." And as examples of the "cruel" gifts that are specifically an Indian's, Natty mentions the scalping of the dead and the ambushing of women and children.

When this important discussion is resumed later in the chapter, with March trying to convince Natty that Indians are not human and Natty resolutely maintaining that they are, it begins to resemble the hilarious argument about Frenchmen between Huck and Jim in the "Was Sollermun Wise?" chapter of *Huckleberry Finn* (suggesting that Mark Twain actually learned something from Cooper!). March insists:

> "Now, skin makes the man. This is reason; else how are people to judge of each other? . . . You know a bear from a hog, by his skin, and a gray squirrel from a black."
>
> "True, Hurry," said the other, looking back and smiling; "nevertheless, they are both squirrels."
>
> "Who denies it? But you'll not say that a red-man and a white man are both Injins?"
>
> "No; but I *do* say they are both men. Men of different races and colors, and having different gifts and traditions, but, in the main, with the same natur'."

These truly fine sentiments of Natty's certainly seem to carry the day, and Cooper intrudes in his own voice to inform us, if we have missed the point, that March is a racist ("Hurry was one of those theorists who believed in the inferiority of all the human race who were not white"). But we should notice the ambiguity that the tale actually demonstrates. Hurry Harry March exhibits the "gifts" of a redskin: he scalps, ambushes women and children, and would even (as Judith Hutter claims) marry a squaw, "provided she was a little comely." March's *actions* thus show that a paleface *can* harbor redskin traits, thereby undermining his dogmatic assertion that color is an absolute determinant of nature. Natty, on the other hand, when he is invited to participate in March's savage escapades, responds firmly: "My gifts are not scalpers' gifts, but such as belong to my religion and color. . . . I'll not unhumanize my natur' by falling into ways that God intended for another race." Thus, by being what he is,

Natty proves that the nature of a true white man *is* fundamentally and absolutely different from that of an Indian: acting like a redskin would "unhumanize" him.[22]

Cooper's racial dialectic would be incomplete, however, without the redskin point of view, and he offers this sporadically throughout the Leatherstocking Tales. We have already seen how, through John Mohegan in *The Pioneers*, Cooper suggests the Indian's special insight into the human heart and the ambivalence of human nature. In *The Pathfinder* he allows another Indian to comment briefly on the white man's character: "Yengees too greedy—take away all hunting-grounds—chase Six Nation from morning to night; wicked king—wicked people. Pale-face very bad." Mabel Dunham, who hears this complaint from the lips of the Tuscarora June, wife of the sly Arrowhead, sees the truth in June's opinion and "felt the justice of the rebuke . . . too much to attempt an answer." In *The Deerslayer* it is again a woman, this time the simple Hetty Hutter, who is lectured by Rivenoak on the disparity between the paleface's actions and his Christian Bible:

> "If he is ordered to *give* double to him that asks only for one thing, why does he *take* double from the poor Indians, who ask for *no* thing? He comes from beyond the rising sun, with his book in his hand, and he teaches the red-man to read it; but why does he forget himself all it says? When the Indian gives, he is never satisfied; and now he offers gold for the scalps of our women and children, though he calls us beasts if we take the scalp of a warrior killed in open war."

One might perhaps accuse Cooper here of simply putting into the mouth of an Indian a Christian parson's Sunday sermon on hypocrisy and backsliding, but in the context of the racial discussions which permeate the Leatherstocking books, Rivenoak's words clearly serve to suggest that "red" bestiality is to be found in "white" natures. Hetty, at least, is "sorely perplexed" and driven to insisting that "no, no . . . there can't be two sides to truth." But Cora Munro, the knowledgeable dark lady of *The Last of the Mohicans*, who is similarly lectured by Tamenund, *knows* that truth is double and can only reply in shame, "It is so." As for why it is usually a woman who is forced to listen to the Indian's complaint, the

---

22. Marius Bewley discusses the March-Bumppo racial theorizing at length, stressing, however, what he calls Natty's "poetry of tolerance" (*The Eccentric Design*, pp. 93 ff.).

answer may be that Cooper, by portraying the female as either completely perplexed or else apologetic and repentant at the Indian's harsh words of truth, is trying to salvage the white woman from the dark notion of pale-face duplicity.

Cooper's most impressive presentation of the question of race from the redskin point of view is put, oddly enough, into the mouth of Magua, the villain of *The Last of the Mohicans* (as if to suggest that his evil-doing is partially due to, and perhaps justified by, race hatred):

> "The Spirit that made men colored them differently.... Some he made with faces paler than the ermine of the forests: and these he ordered to be traders; dogs to their women, and wolves to their slaves. He gave this people the nature of the pigeon; wings that never tire; young, more plentiful than the leaves on the trees, and appetites to devour the earth. He gave them tongues like the false call of the wild-cat; hearts like rabbits; the cunning of the hog ....With his tongue, [the white man] stops the ears of the Indians; his heart teaches him to pay warriors to fight his battles; his cunning tells him how to get together the goods of the earth; and his arms inclose the land from the shores of the salt-water to the islands of the great lake. His gluttony makes him sick. God gave him enough, and yet he wants all. Such are the pale-faces."

"They are devils incarnate!" says Harry March of the Indians, "and understand a man as well as they understand a beaver." If it takes diabolical insight to analyze white character so devastatingly, Magua, the arch-devil of them all, is specially suited for the job.

Whites are abject to their wives, heartless to their servants, capitalists by nature (thus grasping and acquisitive), cowardly, deceitful, and rendered disgusting by their appetites and desires. Since these are for Cooper secret truths almost too terrible to be uttered, they are entrusted to the care of the darkest and most savage of all Cooper's savages, an Indian whose slyness and irrational malice should suffice officially to call into question anything that he says. And yet the eulogy of his own kind that Magua delivers after his bitter diatribe against the whites is spoken with all the accents of poetic truth that Cooper can muster:

> "Some the Great Spirit made with skins brighter and redder than yonder sun ... and these did he fashion to his own mind. He gave them this island as he had made it, covered with trees, and filled with game. The wind made their clearings; the sun and rains ripened their fruits; and the

snows came to tell them to be thankful. What need had they of roads to journey by! They saw through the hills! When the beavers worked, they lay in the shade, and looked on. The winds cooled them in summer; in winter, skins kept them warm. If they fought among themselves, it was to prove that they were men. They were brave; they were just; they were happy."

Cooper's ambivalence on the question of race is nowhere better illustrated than in Magua's performance here.[23] It exhibits Cooper's disgust with his own race and his deep yearning to unite in himself the best qualities of the white man and the beau ideal of the redskin—his yearning, that is, to exchange his "humble self" for Natty Bumppo. And in the book that portrays the death of that splendid example of noble whiteness, Cooper insinuates a suggestion that the race itself is doomed: "Your warriors think the Master of Life has made the whole earth white. They are mistaken. They are pale, and it is their own faces that they see." This proclamation by the magnificent Pawnee-Loup Hard-Heart echoes the impressive warning of the patriarch Tamenund in the earlier *Last of the Mohicans*: "Let them not boast before the face of the Manito too loud. They entered the land at the rising, and may yet go off at the setting sun." Cooper's complicated attitude toward opposing racial claims seems almost to issue finally in a chilling prophecy of the ultimate decline of paleface supremacy.

4.   *A Paradise for Bachelors*

WHEN we think of Cooper's treatment of women in the Leatherstocking Tales, our first impulse usually is to share Mark Twain's scorn for the woodenness of Cooper's "females," or perhaps to remember James Russell Lowell's couplet: ". . . the women he draws from one model don't vary,/All sappy as maples and flat as a prairie." Unfortunately, the verse is catchier than it is accurate, and suggests that Lowell had not read Cooper's books very attentively. Cooper offers many examples of clever, buxom, and passionate brunettes to balance his sexless and silly

---

23. "If Cooper seems nearly to espouse Magua's view," writes Edwin Fussell, it is because he is "bent on deriving from this tragic and elegiac action as many ominous ambiguities as he can" (*Frontier: American Literature and the American West*, p. 43).

blonde ingénues, establishing, as Leslie Fiedler says, "once and for all the pattern of female Dark and Light that is to become the standard form in which American writers project their ambivalence toward women." But Cooper achieved more, in his treatment of women, than simply to set for future American writing two invaluable archetypes. The dark and fair ladies function in the Leatherstocking Tales as an essential part of the myth of the American Adam, Natty Bumppo.

These archetypal females make their appearance in purest form in *The Last of the Mohicans*, where they are represented by Alice Munro and her half-sister Cora—the two aspects of woman. Alice, notably blonde and blue-eyed, is first seen riding through the forest, when she "artlessly suffered the morning air to blow aside the green veil" that covers her face. She is young (just adolescent enough to be believably nubile) and markedly without guile (since cunning, as we shall see, always implies sexuality), and she suffers no one but nature (*innocent* nature, symbolized by her green veil) to touch her purity. Cora, on the other hand, conceals her charms with "care" and is "rather fuller and more mature" than Alice. The fair sister is simply frightened by the evil Magua, but Cora looks at him with "pity, admiration, and horror" combined, "as her dark eye followed the easy motions of the savage. The tresses of this lady were shining and black, like the plumage of the raven. Her complexion was not brown"—she is not *literally* a squaw—"but it rather appeared charged with the color of the rich blood, that seemed ready to burst its bounds." As we should expect, she has a "dark, thoughtful eye" (she is described as "more thoughtful" than Alice) and is ripe, almost rampant, with female carnality.

Between Cora and her sister there exist officially all the requisite love and devotion, but we are made aware of a barely suppressed sense of rivalry—the yearning felt by a presumably experienced woman to return to the pristine state of the innocent virgin. (" 'That I cannot see the sunny side of the picture of life, like this artless but ardent enthusiast,' she added, laying her hand lightly, but affectionately, on the arm of her sister, 'is the penalty of experience, and, perhaps, the misfortune of my nature.' ") By clear implication a fully sexual woman, Cora harbors a not-so-secret sympathy for the darkly attractive savage—officially contradicted, of course, by her public statements of horror whenever Magua mentions marriage—and it is she who is forced to bear the "fierce looks," "wavering glances," and other expressions "that no chaste female might endure" of the lustful savage. Even the reserved and noble Uncas is committed by nature to showing a preference for Cora: he treats Alice with "sufficient courtesy," but when faced with Cora, "his dark eye lingered on her rich, speaking countenance."

What Cora's countenance utters, of course—even, as Cooper would have it, in spite of her conscious intentions—is the dark secret of human sexuality. (Cora's slight admixture of Negro blood, received from a slave ancestress from whom she is "remotely" descended, surely is intended as a kind of folk-shorthand for establishing her claim, not to Negro racial identity, but to passion. However, one cannot absolve Cooper of hedging on the question of female sexuality by trying to convince us—and himself—that it is a "Negro" characteristic and thus not to be thought of in connection with the blonde Alice or any pure white woman.) It is not just the evil Indian, Magua, who is attracted to Cora, but theoretically any Indian, for sexuality in Cooper's mythic scheme of things is the "redskin" element in human nature—an element which, as we have seen, Cooper cannot help but discover in the paleface also.

The universality of this mythos reveals the narrowness of Fiedler's notion that miscegenation is the "secret theme" of *The Last of the Mohicans* and of the Leatherstocking Tales generally.[24] Despite Cooper's obvious interest in and horror of racial mixing, the not very secret theme of *The Last of the Mohicans* seems more truly to be the Miltonic one, that sex brought and brings death into the world, with all our woe and loss of Eden. Magua/Satan (the connection is made explicitly by Cooper) brings about the destruction of Uncas/Adam and Cora/Eve, to say nothing of his turning all of Fort William Henry into a fallen world of death and desolation. The only ones really exempt from the effects of sin are Natty and Chingachgook, who have substituted ideal friendship and devotion to manly duty for the baser passions, and seal their compact of purity with almost religious zeal (a firm handshake and scalding tears) over the monitory grave of Uncas, who was noble but tainted by desire.

The archetypal blonde and brunette appear again, this time in a slightly comic form, in *The Deerslayer*, where they are incarnated in the Hutter sisters, Hetty and Judith. With a show of wit that improbably combines a conventional Elizabethan conceit and Indian insight, Chingachgook names the girls, respectively, the Drooping Lily and the Wild Rose:

---

24. *Love and Death in the American Novel*, pp. 202 ff.

"Drooping" for Hetty, because she is simple-minded, a wilted version of the normally alert and strong-willed blonde heroine; and "Wild" for Judith, because with her reputation for looseness she is a kind of wood nymph, a sylvan version of the normally (but usually covertly) passionate dark lady.

Hetty, "a subdued and humble copy" of her sister, is so far removed from the notion of sex that she is scarcely described by Cooper at all, except for his saying that she is "guileless, innocent, and without distrust." Judith, however, is convincingly presented as a delicious morsel, fit "only for a man whose teeth show the full marks." She is a woman who "has had *men* among her suitors, ever since she was fifteen," and the brutally masculine Hurry Harry March waxes eloquent over her endowments: "The hussy is handsome, and she knows it. Boy, not a tree that is growing in these hills is straighter, or waves in the wind with an easier bend, nor did you ever see the doe that bounded with a more nat'ral motion." Natty's reaction to March's tempting description of Judith is defensive— "For my part, I feel more cur'osity about the feeble-witted sister than about your beauty"—and his warning to March makes an interesting suggestion about this passionate creature: "I would think no more of such a woman, but turn my mind altogether to the forest; *that* will not deceive you, being ordered and ruled by a hand that never wavers."

For Natty the fundamental choice is between women, with their blandishments, and the innocent forest. But his way of stating this truth clearly suggests that, whereas the forest is God's creation, the dark lady is not. She is the devil's child, associated, as we should expect, with cleverness and redskins. ("Judith," reveals March, "is as full of wit, and talk, and cunning, as an old Indian orator.") For as Natty insists, "the Evil Spirit delights more to dwell in an artful body, than in one that has no cunning to work upon." Here Cooper not only institutes an association of sex with the head that was to become standard in the American romance, but also combines in Natty's reaction our national ambivalence toward sexuality and what many observers consider our native anti-intellectualism.

Other important characteristics of the two women are suggested when Natty enters the Ark of the Hutter family and finds himself in the girls' bedroom. Hetty's "homely vestments" remind him of his mother (the standard connection is thus established between the fair lady and motherhood, the hearth and the heart); but on seeing Judith's fancy clothes, "he bethought himself of a sister, whose incipient and native taste for finery had exhibited itself somewhat in the manner of that of Judith." The identification between the dark lady and the figure of the sister—to be developed in the fiction of Poe, Melville, and Faulkner as the maddeningly tantalizing and forbidden incest wish—is very faint, but it is certainly present. Cooper only tells us that "these little resemblances opened a long-hidden vein of sensations; and as he [Natty] quitted the room, it was with a saddened mien." The vein of Natty's sensations is presumably one of tenderness; but since Judith and his sister are clearly associated in Natty's mind, we are free to consider the more complex implications of the passage. Is Natty forced to recall a sister who, like Judith, was also a fallen woman? Or is he saddened by being confronted, in the opposing images of mother and sister—fair lady and dark lady—with his own complicated reactions, usually submerged, to the dual figure of woman?

What is certain, in any case, is that in rejecting Judith's marital overtures at the end of *The Deerslayer*, Natty is rejecting not only the general notion of marriage but also, and more particularly, the strong suggestion of sexuality provided by Judith's escapades at the garrison. Marriage to Judith represents the threat of mixing sex and sentiment—the threat of discovering, within oneself, a moral ambiguity. Ultimately Natty flees the moral "messiness" implied by the female character itself, and chooses to push off into the forest so that he can wrestle instead, as Lawrence says, with "the American wild, as a hermit wrestles with God and Satan,"[25] in a realm where the adversary is external and the categories of good and evil more clearly delineated.

It might seem a flat contradiction of the foregoing formulation that we find Natty Bumppo in *The Pathfinder* actually offering himself to Mabel Dunham in marriage. But a close scrutiny of the story reveals no contradiction at all; on the contrary, the essential fable of Leatherstocking and Cooper's underlying intention in his treatment of women in the series are here most clearly brought to the surface. In *The Pathfinder* the belief in the essential duality of the female nature is embodied, not in the familiar two ladies, but in the two roles between which Mabel Dunham must choose in the course of the action: either the religiously devoted daughter of her father, or the sinful (because sexual) wife of a lusty young man.

---

25. *Studies in Classic American Literature*, p. 964.

The first alternative is contained, surprisingly but with a ruthless logic, in Natty's offer of marriage to Mabel. Cooper's intention should be unmistakable—to the reader, at least. Natty and Sergeant Dunham, Mabel's father, have been "tried, sworn, and constant" friends for twenty years, beginning before Mabel was born, and the idea for the match largely originates with the father. "Although necessarily much weaned from the caresses and blandishments that had rendered his child so dear to him, during the first year or two of his widowhood, he had still a strong, but somewhat latent, love for her," and he clearly intends to gratify that love by choosing a mate for her who will really be a surrogate father. When Natty exhibits diffidence at his abilities in courtship, the Sergeant reassures him by saying, "Tut, tut, man; I foresee I must do half this courting for you!"

Mabel is not slow at realizing that marrying Natty would be like marrying her father, and she receives his proposal with manifest horror: "While I esteem, respect—nay, reverence you, almost as much as I reverence my own dear father, it is impossible that I should ever become your wife. . . . a match like that would be unwise—unnatural, perhaps." And Natty himself sees the justice of Mabel's complaint: "Yes, unnat'ral—ag'in natur'; and so I told the serjeant, but he *would* have it otherwise." Yet Mabel is almost convinced to do as her father wishes:

> Trained like a woman [as a woman should be!], to subdue her most ardent feelings, her thoughts reverted to her father, and to the blessings that awaited the child who yielded to a parent's wishes.
> "Father," she said quietly, almost with a holy calm—"God blesses the dutiful daughter! . . . certainly the man is not living for whom I have more respect than for Pathfinder; not even for you, dear father."

All the while that Mabel is making this speech of holy sacrifice, her face, Cooper tells us, seems "angelic," but a practiced eye "might have traced something wild and unnatural in it." And this intimate interview between father and daughter reaches its conclusion in a climax of tears: "Mabel threw herself into her father's arms—it was the first time in her life—and sobbed on his bosom like an infant. The stern old soldier's heart was melted, and the tears of the two mingled; but Serjeant Dunham soon started, as if ashamed of himself," and Mabel goes sobbing to bed.

It is difficult to know just how conscious Cooper was of this (as it now appears) unabashed toying with the notion of incest; it surely casts a strange light on his own role as the father of daughters. But the obvious intent here is quite other: like the protagonist of a Restoration tragedy, Mabel must choose between love (passion) and honor. It is as if the Sergeant and Natty were combining in an attempt to convince women to choose a life of "purity" and renunciation, rather than the expression of their physical and emotional natures. But the implications of this situation for Natty Bumppo himself are even more interesting. It is worth noting, first, that the only time in the Leatherstocking series when Natty seems in serious danger of marriage, the danger is more apparent than real. We *know* that Mabel Dunham will never marry the Pathfinder; and we have good reason to suspect that Natty knows this too and thus has offered himself, for the first and last time, *safely*, in a situation where he does not really run the risk of being accepted (the whole episode ultimately affording Natty the acceptable emotional outlet of a shameless indulgence in self-pity). Furthermore, Natty sees very clearly just what sort of marriage offer he is making. "You're more befitting to be my daughter than to be my wife," he finally admits to Mabel; and at the very moment when he asks her to choose between himself and Jasper Western, he attempts to encourage her to speak freely by saying, "I told him [the Sergeant] that I would be a father to you, as well as a husband, and it seems to me no feeling father would deny his child this small privilege. Stand up, Mabel, therefore, and speak your thoughts as freely as if I were the Serjeant himself." Standing-in for her father, he urges her to choose him as a husband!

Natty is thus manifestly offering himself only as the most parental of spouses, since Cooper is aware that any other kind of marriage would damage Natty's mythic status. "I'm sometimes afear'd," the Pathfinder says early in the book, "it isn't wholesome for one who is much occupied in a very manly calling . . . to form friendships for women,—young women in particular." If he is to remain, as Mabel originally sees him, "above, beyond, superior to all infirmity . . . a man . . . little liable to the weaknesses of nature," he must, in Cooper's words, be "untempted by unruly or ambitious desires . . . neither led aside by the inducements which influence all to do evil." Chief among these inducements, of course, is sex. Women are a danger because, through sex appeal, they weaken the moral fibre and would make Natty give in to "evil"—would show it, in fact, to be an integral part of his nature. Desire would prove him an irretrievably fallen man. Therefore, if Natty is to marry Mabel, he can do so only as a

COOPER 🌿 27

father—a guide and protector. He must believe always in the sentimental love religion—in woman's purity, in her right to remain holy, inviolate, and unsexual. For Natty to accept Mabel otherwise would be to admit his own sexuality. Therefore, he cannot acknowledge that he has a pleasure phallus to offer a woman; Killdeer is a symbol of law, order, chastisement, and food-getting. One might say that Natty revenges himself on female sexuality by insisting on treating women unsexually. The kind of marriage he offers Mabel Dunham is a punishment for the eternal Eve in all women.

Cooper, as a matter of fact, closes *The Pathfinder* on an explicitly Miltonic note. As Mabel prepares to leave Natty and cleave unto Jasper, the young lovers look "like a pair of guilty beings":

> Jasper and Mabel sat, resembling Milton's picture of our first parents, when the consciousness of sin first laid its leaden weight on their souls. Neither spoke, neither even moved; though both at that moment fancied they could part with their new-found happiness [Eros], in order to restore their friend [Natty] to his peace of mind. Jasper was pale as death; but, in Mabel, maiden modesty [!] had caused the blood to mantle on her cheeks, until their bloom was heightened to a richness that was scarce equalled in her hours of light-hearted buoyancy and joy.

Sin and death have entered the world again, and Pathfinder/God is suffering, as is Jasper/Adam. Only Mabel/Eve/Lilith is pleased. Or, to put it another way, Natty is the old Adam confronted with a young pair who willingly "fall" all over again, and his peace of mind is accordingly disrupted. Yet Natty's anguish is a necessary component of his character. He must be continually reminded of the nearness of danger, so that he can avoid it at all costs. He knows that sin brings death and loss of Paradise, and if he would remain worthy of the American Eden, he must be careful.

"This being," Cooper tells us, with profound insight into his own creation, "in his peculiar way, was a sort of type of what Adam might have been supposed to be before the fall, though certainly not without sin." This paradox defines Natty Bumppo, the American Adam, who combines prelapsarian virtue with postlapsarian knowledge. He is aware that he can maintain his goodness in a fallen world only by means of a strict moral code, devilish cunning, and a deadly weapon. His is a goodness that takes evil tacitly into account, a militant goodness that protects its purity by being always on guard against the enemy. He believes the civilized world to be evil and separates himself from it; he is self-righteous and wary. As Cooper explains:

> The affinities of such a character were, as a matter of course, those of like for like. His associates and intimates . . . were generally of the highest order, as to moral propensities; for he appeared to possess a species of instinctive discrimination that led him insensibly to himself, most probably, to cling closest to those whose characters would best reward his friendship

—better, to cling closest to those whose characters would least endanger his position. Women, with their ambiguous natures, are of course the primary threat.

We are now in a position to spell out the essential fable of Natty's celebrated friendship with Chingachgook, the "Big Sarpent" (so called, as Natty never tires of explaining, after "a sartain sarpent at the creation of the 'arth that outwitted the first woman"). The American Adam knows intuitively how to avoid the error of his archetypal ancestor: he can only hope to retain possession of his American Eden if he makes a pact with the devil and they jointly exclude women from the virgin forest. "Where is the man to turn this beautiful place into . . . a garden of Eden for us?" Judith Hutter demands of her sister Hetty. The harsh answer is given throughout the Leatherstocking Tales: the American Eden (to paraphrase Melville) is a Paradise for bachelors only.

5. *The Lesson of Nature*

MANY critics—beginning with Balzac's now familiar observation that "never did the art of writing tread closer upon the art of the pencil" —have commented on Cooper's descriptive powers. That Cooper was committed, in some sense, to rendering the actual impression made on a responsive observer by the American landscape is easy enough to understand. At least until late in the nineteenth century Nature was one of America's most characteristic attractions and thus as predictable a subject for the American romancer as were the distinctions of society for an English novelist. The growth of American literature (and of the arts in general in our country) is intimately connected with the attempt to capture the various moods and attitudes of the American continent. We may blame Cooper for too often stopping the action of his tales while he attempts such renderings, but his achievements in this regard are noteworthy.

Cooper's affinities with the Hudson River School of painting, the first to exhibit a consistent interest in American landscape, are easy to spot. During a lull in the action of *The Last of the Mohicans*, Major Heyward stands musing over a sunset on Lake George in midsummer:

> The sun poured down his parting glory on the scene, without the oppression of those fierce rays that belong to the climate and the season. The mountains looked green, and fresh, and lovely; tempered with the milder light, or softened in shadow, as thin vapors floated between them and the sun. The numerous islands rested on the bosom of the Horican, some low and sunken, as if imbedded in the waters, and others appearing to hover above the element, in little hillocks of green velvet; among which the fishermen of the beleaguering army peacefully rowed their skiffs, or floated at rest on the glassy mirror, in quiet pursuit of their employment.

That Cooper is here trying his hand at a set piece is obvious (he even offers a one-sentence aesthetic "theory" that neatly sums up the aims of the Hudson River School: "The scene was at once animated and still").[26] But the sketch does have some relation to the human themes of the tale, nature here reflecting a general weariness of war and the normal desire of

---

26. There are many valuable articles on the pictorial element in Cooper's writings. James F. Beard, Jr., discusses Cooper's relations with the American painters of his time in "Cooper and His Artistic Contemporaries," published in *James Fenimore Cooper: A Re-Appraisal*, edited by Mary Cunningham (*New York State History*, XXXV [Cooperstown, N.Y., 1954]), pp. 480–495. Beard, who notes that Thomas Cole painted at least one scene from *The Last of the Mohicans*, stresses Cooper and Cole's joint belief in providing a "harmony of poetic coloring" (p. 489). Howard Mumford Jones's "Prose and Pictures: James Fenimore Cooper," reprinted in his *History and the Contemporary* (Madison, Wis., 1964), pp. 61–83, also discusses Cooper's relations with the Hudson River School. Jones associates Natty Bumppo's great "Tree" speech in *The Prairie* with the Hudson River School's cyclical theories of history (pp. 74–75). Cooper's affinity to the Hudson River School in *The Prairie* is noted, too, by Donald A. Ringe in "Man and Nature in Cooper's *The Prairie*," *Nineteenth-Century Fiction*, XV (1961), 313–323. In another article, "Chiaroscuro as an Artistic Device in Cooper's Fiction," *PMLA*, LXXVIII (1963), 349–357, Ringe documents the notion that chiaroscuro was characteristic of the Hudson River School, especially in the work of Durand and Cole. And in "James Fenimore Cooper and Thomas Cole: An Analogous Technique," *American Literature*, XXX (1958), 26–36, Ringe cites—discussing a passage from *Satanstoe*—the "typical elements of a Hudson River landscape . . . the long perspective downward and reaching out to a framing range of hills, the mixture of the placid and the wild, the unified multiplicity of specific details, the accomplishments of men dwarfed by the infinite expanse of nature . . . the ruins of a deserted fortress" (pp. 32–33).

both besiegers and besieged, French and English, for peace and serenity.

Whatever Cooper's interest in achieving purely pictorial effects, his tales evince what might be termed a more typically romantic concern with regard to nature: the romancer's interest in portraying nature as a character, an animistic force, in his fictional world. With Cooper, in nineteenth-century American fiction, the art of the pencil begins to tread close to the art of writing, as natural descriptions are used preternaturally to reflect or influence states of human thought or feeling. Thus in *The Last of the Mohicans*, after the ghastly, brutal massacre at Fort William Henry, the scene that only a short time before had been viewed by Heyward with so much pleasure is no longer placid and hardly resembles a canvas by Cole or Durand:

> A frightful change had . . . occurred in the season. The sun had hid its warmth behind an impenetrable mass of vapor, and hundreds of human forms, which had blackened beneath the fierce heats of August, were stiffening in their deformity, before the blasts of a premature November. . . . The crowded mirror of the Horican was gone; and, in its place, the green and angry waters lashed the shores, as if indignantly casting back its impurities to the polluted strand . . . and the northern air poured across the waste of water.

Nature is now seen as the scourge of an angry God: everything has been "scathed by the consuming lightning" or worse. Cooper himself points the moral of his grim description: "The whole landscape, which, seen by a favoring light, and in a genial temperature, had been found so lovely, appeared now like some pictured allegory of life, in which objects were arrayed in their harshest but truest colors, and without the relief of any shadowing." We have moved into the world of Poe and Ryder, where natural scenery becomes a representation of human disaster—to use a recent critic's phrase, the landscape of nightmare. The true picture of reality, Cooper suggests, is an allegory of horror, where the meaning of events is inscrutable. "The eye even sought relief, in vain, by attempting to pierce the illimitable void of heaven, which was shut to its gaze." The only voice is that of the wind, which seemed "to whisper its moanings in the cold ears of the dead." All is "wildness and desolation."

This use of natural description to suggest dark undertones of meaning is not uncommon in Cooper (we shall look at other examples in *The Prairie*). But if his use of nature reaches out to some of the techniques of later American fiction, it is also firmly joined to late eighteenth- and early nineteenth-century romantic attitudes, particularly to the nature philosophy of Wordsworth. In his own voice, to be sure, Cooper often sounds more Augustan than romantic, especially when he takes the trouble self-consciously to develop "correct" views of nature in orotund periods, intoning with Burkean sweep:

> The sublimity connected with vastness is familiar to every eye. The most abstruse, the most far-reaching, perhaps the most chastened of the poet's thoughts, crowd on the imagination as he gazes into the depths of the illimitable void. The expanse of the ocean is seldom seen by the novice with indifference; and the mind, even in the obscurity of night, finds a parallel to that grandeur which seems inseparable from images that the senses cannot compass.

The diction and thought are conventional, and the effect of Cooper's language here is to separate us, reverently but firmly, from nature, as the mind engages in theoretical discourse. The feeling is very different from that of Wordsworth's "Our destiny, our being's heart and home, / Is with infinitude, and only there," where the suggestion is clearly one of emotional union with nature rather than abstract understanding of it.

But such a passage only illustrates the transitional character of Cooper's attitude toward nature. Another kind of sensibility reveals itself when Cooper's attitudes are filtered through the mind and heart of Natty Bumppo, whose theories of nature and language are truly Wordsworthian. "By speakin'," insists Natty, subsuming a great deal of both Wordsworth and Coleridge, "I don't mean, chatterin' . . . but comin' out with . . . honest, deepest feelin's, in proper words." Honesty of sentiment, he suggests here, is intimately connected with honesty of diction; and all utterance should be poetic—that is, sincere and inevitable, phrased in language that is radically suitable. And Natty has a theory of the imagination to suggest where "proper words" may be found. Like Wordsworth, who assures us that "we can feed this mind of ours/In a wise passiveness," Natty believes that potent influences work on us unawares: "Many's the hour I've passed, pleasantly enough, too, in what is tarmed conterplation by my people. On such occasions the mind is actyve, though the body seems lazy and listless." In these moments of inspired indolence, surrounded and touched by natural objects (Natty mentions "an open spot on a mountain side" as a suitable place), we learn to think and speak truly.

David Perkins' lucid exposition of Wordsworth's "religion of Nature" is particularly helpful here. What distinguishes Wordsworth, he writes, "is his assumption that nature—mountains, lakes, clouds, winds—can become a language for the human mind. . . . He does not claim that religious knowledge or truth can be inferred from the natural world. He feels, instead, that in nature such knowledge is mediated to us as in a language."[27] Such a formulation is useful in helping us understand the religion of the forest with which Cooper has endowed Natty Bumppo. It is not simply that the forest illustrates the most fundamental truths of natural theology, although it does this, as when Natty speaks of everything being "left in the ordering of the Lord, to live and die according to his own designs and laws." Nor are we only implying, as Perkins says of Wordsworth, that "the human mind can use the forms of nature as a language for feeling." Rather, and more importantly, it is that nature itself utters the essential truth of its creation. It cannot falsify; it cannot deceive; it cannot help but say precisely what it is.

Nature thus becomes a paradigm for authentic utterance of any sort, but especially for poetry—true speech. "The woods are never silent," explains Pathfinder, "to such as understand their meaning. Days at a time, have I travelled them alone, without feeling the want of company; and, as for conversation, for such as can comprehend their language, there is no want of rational and instructive discourse." Nature serves Natty as that ideal companion who does not chatter but comes out with honest feelings in proper words. It is the realization of Emerson's dream of a realm where the word is one with the thing and there is no "rotten diction" because everything simply utters its own true name. As Perkins puts it, "in the processes of imagination by which the human mind weds itself to nature," ultimate truths are revealed because the language of nature finds its way into the vocabulary of man.[28]

Cooper makes it abundantly clear throughout the Leatherstocking Tales that Natty Bumppo was conceived of as a primitive poet, a man

---

27. See *Wordsworth and the Poetry of Sincerity* (Cambridge, Mass., 1964), pp. 91–93.

28. "*The Deerslayer*," writes Edwin Fussell, "depends on the ethics of Emerson, which in turn depend on the aesthetics of Wordsworth" (*Frontier: American Literature and the American West*, p. 61). In "Conceptual Ambivalence in Cooper's Leatherstocking," *American Literature*, XXXI (1960), 397–420, Robert H. Zoellner refers to Natty Bumppo's attitude toward the wilderness as a "pseudoreligious aestheticism" (p. 404).

whose closeness to and reverence for nature enables him to speak the true name of every created thing and thus to get as close to essential truth as man can. Natty Bumppo is Adam the namer. When Dr. Battius suggests that scientific methods of observation and naming are better than the "Indian wisdom" (to use Thoreau's phrase) of an ordinary man who has lived close to nature, Natty bursts out: "Who named the works of His hand? can you tell me that, with your books and college wisdom? Was it not the first man in the Garden, and is it not a plain consequence that his children inherit his gifts?" By "children" Cooper means, of course, only those descendants of Adam who have not been corrupted by a fallen world; Natty is speaking of himself. Dr. Bat replies that the old trapper's reading of the "Mosaic account" is too literal, thereby demonstrating that he himself lacks that active belief in the continuing power of myth which informs and dignifies Natty's own existence. For Natty is not simply repeating something that he once heard from the Moravians. He truly believes that man in the uncorrupted state of nature remains a primitive poet, a true son of Adam, and his outburst amounts to an insistence that his powers be recognized. "I'm an admirator of names," Natty states emphatically in *The Last of the Mohicans*, and he demonstrates how serious that interest is in *The Deerslayer*. The kinds of names that move him are the ones that give some insight into the essences of things.[29]

It is altogether fitting that Natty's greatest interest in names should be evinced in the book that portrays both him and the American forest in their pristine state—unspoiled, unwearied, ready to reveal the secret of their natures to a sympathetic eye. It is in *The Deerslayer* that both Natty and the majestic lake (Otsego) that provides the setting for the tale receive and justify their names. As Natty stands in front of the lake for the first time, he gazes "at the dark hills and the glassy water in silent enjoyment." Hurry Harry March has already told him, in a perfunctory manner, that this lake, like all others, is "pretty much water and land, and points and bays," but Natty is not satisfied. " 'Have the Governor's or the King's people given this lake a name?' he suddenly asked, as if struck with a new idea. 'If they've not begun to blaze their trees, and set up their compasses, and line off their maps, it's likely they've not bethought them to disturb natur' with a name.' " March replies that, far

---

29. Speaking of the American Adam, R. W. B. Lewis writes: "he was the type of creator, the poet par excellence, creating language itself by naming the elements of the scene about him" (*The American Adam: Innocence, Tragedy, and Tradition in the Nineteenth Century* [Chicago, 1955], p. 5).

from naming the lake, the government scarcely knows where it is. "I'm glad it has no name," Deerslayer continues, "or, at least, no pale-face name; for their christenings always foretell waste and destruction." The agents of civilization use names as instruments of power; their wish is to possess nature, not to know it. Natty wants to hear the name given the lake by the redskins, hunters, and trappers, for "they are likely to call the place by something reasonable and resembling." Although March knows the name given the lake by the men of the forest—"Glimmerglass" —his explanation of the name is as perfunctory as his natural description, since, as Cooper writes, "Hurry Harry thought more of the beauties of Judith Hutter than of those of the Glimmerglass, and its accompanying scenery." Nature does not speak to Hurry Harry.

Natty, however, has a true feeling for what the name implies, and it is through his eyes that we actually see the Glimmerglass in all its splendor:

> ... the surface of the lake being as smooth as glass and as limpid as pure air, throwing back the mountains, clothed in dark pines, along the whole of its eastern boundary, the points thrusting forward their trees even to nearly horizontal lines, while the bays were seen glittering through an occasional arch beneath, left by a vault fretted with branches and leaves.

Cooper tells us that, even if he was unconscious of it, Natty had the feelings of a poet, responding both to the "innate loveliness" of the scene and to the opening it provided "into the mysteries and forms of the woods." Thus, although Natty has not himself literally endowed the lake with a name, he as it were justifies the name it has been given, in-tuiting its innate rightness and providing, in his own person, a bridge between the beauties of natural forms and the human imagination.

When it comes time in *The Deerslayer* for Natty's own name to be understood, it is quite suitably nature's own child, the simple-minded Hetty Hutter, who does the asking. "What's *your* name?" she breaks out, eliciting from Natty an answer pregnant with meaning: "That's a ques-tion more easily asked than it is answered." For the identity of the Amer-ican hero, the man of the New World, has been an active concern in American writing at least since 1782, when (as Daniel Hoffman reminds us) Crèvecoeur posed "at the birth of the Republic the question of national identity which our writers have never since ceased trying to answer."[30]

---

30. *Form and Fable in American Fiction* (New York, 1965), p. 33.

One thing at least seemed clear to Cooper: nature in the New World must in some sense be both the standard and the determinant of the American's character. The American would earn his various identities by his actions as he passed through the many crisis situations imposed on him by this continent, his life being thus a continuous process of self-definition. And his final identity would be, not a discrete item, but rather the sum of all the identities honestly won. Although he is young in *The Deerslayer*, Natty already has had many names, all earned, all provisional: "My names have come nat'rally; and I suppose the one I bear now will be of no great lasting, since the Delawares seldom settle on a man's ra'al title, until such time as he has an opportunity of showing his true natur'." (If Natty's final name truly sums up his character, Cooper tantalizingly keeps this ultimate knowledge from us. When the Wahcondah calls Natty to Him at the end of *The Prairie*, we hear only the old trapper's stirring response: "Here!") And Natty does not at all contradict his avowed concern with names when he says to Hetty, "I put no great dependence . . . on names"; he is only expressing his anxiety over the danger of misnomers. "Men are deceived in other men's characters, and frequently give 'em names they by no means desarve." He has a deep commitment to finding out only *true* names, especially his own.

"Tell me *all* your names," insists Hetty, "I want to know what to think of you." Natty accordingly begins with his family name, and most readers probably feel that here Cooper misses his opportunity to explain or justify Natty's curious surname. We are told only that the name was handed down from father to son in accordance with white Christian "gifts." "Bumppo has no lofty sound, I admit," Natty states, "and yet men have bumped through the world with it." There seems to be more than a hint here that Natty, as the democratic American hero, has been endowed with a garden variety name to indicate his necessarily humble origins, but the suggestion dissolves in a bad pun. More importantly, we are being shown that ordinary paleface names, traditionally and conventionally handed down from one generation to the next, have *no* meaning, no inherent logic that unites them with the thing named.

Natty's true names have been awarded him by the Delawares, and they are all drawn from nature: first "Straight-tongue" for his truthtelling, then "The Pigeon" for his swift foot, then "Lap-ear" for his having the nose and sagacity of a hound, and finally "Deerslayer" for his prowess in using his first rifle. Hetty pronounces his present name superior to Natty Bumppo, and the Deerslayer is gratified. But this last book of the Leatherstocking series is dedicated to celebrating a great *rite de passage*, Natty's winning of his most characteristic name. The new title is conferred by the dying Loup Cervier, who has been brought down by the young scout's unerring bullet: "That good name for boy [Deerslayer]—poor name for warrior. He get better quick . . . eye sartain—finger lightning—aim, death—great warrior soon. No Deerslayer—Hawkeye—Hawkeye—Hawkeye." Natty has earned the right to be part of the cycle of life in the American forest, and he is christened into manhood with the impressive word, uttered thrice in a kind of magic incantation, of the dying Indian—the true spirit of the woods. On the shores of the lake whose name and character Natty, with his keen and sensitive eye, has helped us to understand, he himself is defined in natural terms.[31]

The centrality of nature (and of Natty) to Cooper's scheme of things in the Leatherstocking Tales is further illuminated by the underlying theme of *The Deerslayer:* time, change, and the mutability of human things. Old Tom Hutter, the supposed father of Judith and Hetty, and a sometime pirate and plunderer, presently is a squatter on Glimmerglass in his "Ark" and "Castle." After fifteen years in residence the rapacious old man claims the lake as his property. But Cooper has an object lesson in mortality to teach through the figure of Hutter. Scalped alive by the Indians whom he has consistently mistreated, Hutter dies miserably, and as he expires, Cooper has Hetty read from the seventh chapter of *Job,* beginning pointedly with *"Is there not an appointed time to man on earth?"* Old Tom clearly represents sinful man cut off in all his earthly pride. He had built himself an Ark and a Castle for safety, but unlike Noah (Natty himself makes reference to Noah when March asks about the meaning of "ark") Hutter is manifestly not a just man, and the vessel fails to save him. Moreover, the "mystery" which lies at the heart of the Castle, the chest that Judith considers a "tabooed relic," is full not of religious significance and power but of the fripperies of civilization, and

31. In the American wilderness, writes David Brion Davis, "when lakes or warriors receive a name, it corresponds exactly with the thing. Cooper succeeds admirably in conveying the delight of man in intimate harmony with nature, beholding and naming creation for the first time" ("The Deerslayer: A Democratic Knight of the Wilderness," in *Twelve Original Essays on Great American Novels,* edited by Charles Shapiro [Detroit, 1958], p. 12).

that too is finally of no avail.[32] The Castle, emblem of the Hutters' worldly hopes, was an object, Cooper tells us, "that had received its form or uses from human taste or human desires" and deformed the landscape, which was otherwise "native, and fresh from the hand of God." When Hawkeye, Chingachgook, and Uncas return to the scene of *The Deerslayer* fifteen years after Hutter's death, they find all the signs of civilization in a state of decay and the remains of the Hutters wiped out:

> The remains of the castle were still visible, a picturesque ruin. The storms of winter had long since unroofed the house, and decay had eaten into the logs. All the fastenings were untouched, but the seasons rioted in the place, as if in mockery at the attempt to exclude them. The palisades were rotting, as were the piles; and it was evident that a few more recurrences of winter, a few more gales and tempests, would sweep all into the lake, and blot the building from the face of that magnificent solitude. The graves could not be found. Either the elements had obliterated their traces, or time had caused those who looked for them to forget their position.

The works of man are evanescent, but the "magnificent solitude" of the American forest is from eternity to eternity. The three friends find the lake itself "unchanged; the river still rushed through its bower of trees; the little rock was wasting away by the slow action of the waves in the course of centuries; the mountains stood in their native dress, dark, rich, and mysterious; while the sheet glistened in its solitude, a beautiful gem of the forest."

American history may seem "to reach the mists of time" because so much has happened here; and "on the human imagination," as Cooper writes in the first sentence of the book, "events produce the effects of time." Yet (the author could state in 1841) "four lives of ordinary duration would suffice to transmit . . . all that civilized man has achieved within the limits of the Republic." It is really only the wilderness itself that is eternal, seen in "the long succession of unknown ages, in which America and all it contained existed apart, in mysterious solitude, a world by itself; equally without a familiar history, and without an origin that the annals of man can reach." And only those humans who understand the spirit of the wilderness—like Tamenund the patriarch ("a man so old

---

32. Cf. A. N. Kaul, *The American Vision*, pp. 130–131.

that few can remember when he was in his prime"), or Natty Bumppo—can participate in nature's eternity.

Natty alone in the book gets his time from nature. Hurry Harry March has a clock set solely to his animal needs ("Much as I like the sun, boy, I've no occasion for it to tell me it is noon; this stomach of mine is as good a time-piece as is to be found in the colony"). Hetty Hutter, a notch up the scale, tells time, despite her reputed simple-mindedness, by depending on her intellect ("When the mind is engaged [she was thinking of her beloved Hurry Harry], it is better than any clock"). In the Hutter Castle, as in civilization generally, time is told—inaccurately, as we should expect—through the artifice of a clock ("The clock was industriously ticking, but its leaden-looking hands did no discredit to their dull aspect, for they pointed to the hour of eleven, though the sun plainly showed it was some time past the turn of the day"). Natty depends, not on his stomach, his intellect, or the leaden aspect of mechanical contrivance, but on nature's golden face. In a dramatic episode in *The Deerslayer* he amazes the Huron chiefs by returning to their camp, precisely as agreed, at high noon, when "the sun was just entering a space that was known to mark the zenith."

As Natty tells Judith, contrasting the evanescence of human good looks with the perennial beauty of nature, " 'Arth is an eternal round"; and he himself participates in this cycle. Cooper chose for the penultimate chapter of the book an epigraph from Shelley that emphasizes his theme of the mutability and transience of human desire:

> The flower that smiles to-day
>   To-morrow dies;
> All that we wish to stay,
>   Tempts and then flies:
> What is this world's delight?—
> Lightning that mocks the night,
> Brief even as bright.

But Cooper had already corrected and balanced the pessimism of this view with the stanza from Byron's *Childe Harold* that opens the book:

> There is a pleasure in the pathless woods,
> There is a rapture on the lonely shore,
> There is society where none intrudes,
> By the deep sea, and music in its roar:

> I love not man the less, but nature more,
> From these our interviews, in which I steal,
> From all I may be, or have been before,
> To mingle with the universe, and feel
> What I can ne'er express, yet cannot all conceal.

By leaving Natty Bumppo, in the last of the Leatherstocking books to be published, shining forever in eternal youth (in a "crescendo of beauty," as Lawrence puts it) Cooper attempted to mingle his hero with the universe, in order to express his profound belief that a sinless existence passed in communion with the American forest would confer immortality.

6. *Romance as New World Epic*

WHEN Cooper, in the Preface to the Leatherstocking Tales, asserted his belief that if anything from his pen were destined to "outlive himself" it would be this series, he was making a claim to be considered ultimately and most durably as an American romancer. What this title was supposed to mean, Cooper made reasonably clear: he had taken a "poetical view" of the career of his American hero and the Indians among whom he lived, thereby elevating their characters to that *"beau-idéal"* of universal meaning which, at least according to Aristotle, rendered poetry more serious and more philosophical than history. Cooper was content to rest his case for romance on the name of Homer, arguing that the romance, like the epic—however stylized, elevated, and conventional—somehow presented the truth of human life. Like William Gilmore Simms, who in 1835 had insisted that "the modern Romance is the substitute which the people of the present day offer for the ancient epic,"[33] Cooper believed in "the power of epic to mirror the soul of a people" (the phrase is Richard Chase's[34]). This aim was clearly paramount in his mind when he shaped the two most epic-like of the Leatherstocking books. In *The Last of the Mohicans* and *The Prairie* Cooper wrote, in the broadest sense, his *Iliad* and *Odyssey*.

Cooper's attempt in *The Last of the Mohicans* to elevate his characters

---

33. This remark, made by Simms in the "Advertisement" to *The Yemassee*, is cited by Richard Chase, *The American Novel and Its Tradition*, pp. 15–16. See also Simms's *Views and Reviews*, p. xxxiv.

34. *The American Novel and Its Tradition*, p. 17.

to epic proportions is most obvious in the figure of the superbly malign, nobly evil Huron chief, Magua. But the creation of Magua owes far more to Milton than to Homer: he is an avatar of Milton's Satan (and, as in Milton's epic, much more successfully depicted than the good figures). Seeing him alone in his hut, awake through the long night, as "the low flames that fluttered about the embers of the fire threw their wavering light on the person of the sullen recluse," an observer would not have found it difficult, Cooper tells us, "to have fancied the dusky savage the Prince of Darkness, brooding on his own fancied wrongs, and plotting evil." Like Satan, Magua in his discourses (as we have seen) presents an image of magnificently heroic tribulation, and his end is equally heroic as he takes a final Miltonic plunge: "Turning a relentless look on his enemy, he shook a hand in grim defiance. But his hold loosened, and his dark person was seen cutting the air with its head downward, for a fleeting instant, until it glided past the fringe of shrubbery which clung to the mountain, in its rapid flight to destruction."

The keynote of *The Last of the Mohicans*, as of both *Paradise Lost* and the *Iliad*, is loss, and this motif is signalled by the opening epigraph chosen by Cooper from Shakespeare's *Richard II:*

> Mine ear is open, and my heart prepared:
> The worst is worldly loss thou canst unfold:
> Say, is my kingdom lost?

Although the underlying theme is common to both Milton and Homer, the framework of the book is more clearly derived from the *Iliad*. Cooper's world is divided between wily Greeks and noble Trojans (Mingoes and Delawares), and the action concerns itself with a coveted woman (Cora). Magua is specifically associated by Cooper, through epigraphs taken from Pope's *Iliad*, with the Greek leaders (both Achilles and Agamemnon); and the last chapter of the book, in which Chingachgook/Priam, along with the remaining members of his tribe, celebrates and mourns the death of Uncas/Hector, is obviously patterned after the twenty-fourth book of Homer's epic, the funeral of Hector. "Hektor's tragedy is that of Troy," writes Richmond Lattimore,[35] and the same can be said of Uncas. With his death Cooper commemorates the disappearance of his beau ideal of the Indian, the splendid Lenni Lenape. "As for me," intones the solitary Chingachgook, "the son and the father of Uncas, I am a blazed pine,

---

35. "Introduction," *The Iliad of Homer* (Chicago, 1961), p. 45.

in a clearing of the pale-faces. My race has gone from the shores of the salt lake, and the hills of the Delawares." And his mournful words are echoed by those of the aged patriarch of his tribe: "Why should Tamenund stay? The pale-faces are masters of the earth, and the time of the red-men has not yet come again. My day has been too long. In the morning I saw the sons of Unamis happy and strong; and yet, before the night has come, have I lived to see the last warrior of the wise race of the Mohicans."[36]

The Last of the Mohicans, like the *Iliad*, celebrates the heroic virtues of individuals against a background of general social disintegration. In *The Prairie*, the next of the series in order of publication, Cooper attempted, so to speak, to pick up the pieces. Like the *Odyssey*, in which Homer moves from the tragically fragmented world of his first epic to a saga of reintegration and the reconstitution of a social order, *The Prairie* moves in the direction of viable cultural myth. Its underlying purpose, like that of the *Odyssey*, is to expose and explain the assumptions of a culture. And if the hero of Cooper's epic is somewhat of an anachronism in the world that is coming to birth, he is perhaps no more so than is Odysseus himself, a king of the Mycenean age projected forward into a time of oligarchic demagoguery.[37] But it will not do to bind ourselves too strictly in paralleling Cooper and Homer; any such comparison, if it is to be useful, should be suggestive, not restrictive. The main point seems clear enough: Cooper had the notion of epic in mind as he shaped *The Prairie*.

Oddly, the setting of *The Prairie*, like that of the *Odyssey*, was conceived of by Cooper as a kind of sea, as he explains in the opening chapter:

> From the summits of the swells, the eye became fatigued with the same-
> ness and chilling dreariness of the landscape. The earth was not unlike
> the ocean, when its restless waters are heaving heavily, after the agitation
> and fury of the tempest have begun to lessen.

Cooper extends at some length this parallel between ocean and prairie, which becomes operative in the action of the book when the adventures recounted are often seen as epic voyages into an unknown waste. As the Bush family returns from having found and buried the body of Asa,

---

36. In "Myth-Maker and Christian Romancer," in *American Classics Reconsidered*, edited by Harold Gardiner, S. J. (New York, 1958), p. 79, Charles A. Brady compares the Mohicans to Trojans.

37. Cf. Cedric H. Whitman, *Homer and the Heroic Tradition* (Cambridge, Mass., 1958), especially pp. 306 ff.

for example, the hill of their settlement rises into view "like some tower emerging from the bosom of the sea." Natty Bumppo changes direction in order to elude pursuit "as a vessel changes her course in fogs and darkness to escape from the vigilance of her enemies," although "to most of the fugitives their situation was as entirely unknown as is that of a ship in the middle of the ocean to the uninstructed voyager." And when Natty meets an Indian, he spots the tribe of the warrior "by the same sort of mysterious observation, as that by which the seaman knows the distant sail," for in this world where the opposing groups "resembled so many fleets at sea" and move toward each other "as a squadron of cruisers is often seen to steer across the waste of waters," Natty must have the seaman's eye of an Odysseus if he is to succeed. In view of Cooper's persistent nautical metaphors, one might almost say that Natty, like Homer's hero, suffers "many hardships on the high seas in his struggles to preserve his life and bring his comrades home." And taking the long view, one might add that Natty, too, "failed to save those comrades, in spite of all his efforts. It was their own sin that brought them to their doom."[38]

In the world of *The Prairie*, as in that of the epic normally, it is still the age of the gods, and the air is alive with divinities, preternatural signs, and wonders. The villainous Abiram White (who should know, as his Old Testament name indicates, that he is being watched from above) steals "a furtive and involuntary glance at the placid sky . . . as if he expected to see the Almighty eye itself beaming from the heavenly vault." For when the wind swept across the prairie, Cooper tells us, it would have been easy to imagine oneself back "in the ages of fable," when the "spirits of the air" descended to participate in human events. The wind rushes and the dust eddies "as if guided by a master hand," and it is not difficult for Ishmael Bush "to imagine strange and unearthly sounds were mingling in the blasts . . . . the rushing of the wind sounded like the whisperings of the dead." Natty Bumppo himself seems of divine origin, as he steps into the book out of a stupendous sunset (he is presumably called back into one at the end), appearing as a "colossal" figure in a "flood of fiery light." To the Bush family this "mysterious object" gives

---

38. *The Odyssey*, translated by E. V. Rieu (Baltimore, Md., 1946), p. 25. D. H. Lawrence, of course, called the Leatherstocking books altogether "a sort of American Odyssey, with Natty Bumppo for Odysseus" (*Studies in Classic American Literature*, p. 952). David Brion Davis writes of Natty's "Homeric heroism" and calls him "an aged Odysseus" in *The Prairie* ("The Deerslayer," p. 2).

the "impression of a supernatural agency," and he is watched with "super-stitious awe."[39]

Besides his being larger than life and presumably having some special connection with the divine, Natty is the epic hero par excellence in other ways. Like Odysseus, he is widely traveled and knows the customs of many peoples. ("I have seen the waters of the two seas!" he boasts.) And when Duncan Uncas Middleton, not knowing to whom he is speaking, relates the past deeds of the fabled Nathaniel Bumppo (like Demodocus, at the court of Alcinous, singing the fall of Troy before the wretched and unknown castaway who was once a great hero), Natty gives himself away, as did his Homeric paradigm, in a flood of epic tears. "Boy, I am that scout; a warrior once, a miserable trapper now!" he laments, where-upon the "tears broke over his wasted cheeks, out of fountains that had long been dried, and, sinking his face between his knees, he covered it decently with his buckskin garment, and sobbed aloud." As a final touch, to parallel Odysseus' faithful dog Argos, Natty has his Hector (who, like the Homeric pet, is discreet enough to predecease his master).

But more in line with his presumably Anglo-Saxon heritage, Natty has the qualities of a northern epic hero such as Beowulf. Keenly aware of the ravaging process of time, he often speaks in the poignant accents of the *ubi sunt* motif.[40] ("Where is the herd of buffaloes, which was chased by the panther across this plain, no later than the morning of yesterday!")

---

39. "It is not accidental," writes Marius Bewley, "that Cooper has managed to suggest that Natty Bumppo steps back into the flaming heavens from which he seemed to come. The scene has a largeness and simplicity that carries the mind back to some remote heroic age, and it places a seal of consecration on Cooper's response to American society and reality" (*The Eccentric Design*, p. 112). Donald A. Ringe, "Chiaroscuro as an Artistic Device in Cooper's Fiction," notes that Cooper's way of introducing Natty in *The Prairie* "almost sanctifies him" (p. 351). Cooper seems to have connected Natty with notions of numenous power from the very first conception of Leatherstocking. In *The Pioneers*, the boat of Natty and John Mohegan materializes eerily out of the night in front of Cooper's startled heroines, eliciting a response pregnant with implication:

> " 'It appears to be supernatural!' whispered Louise, beginning to retrace her steps towards the party.
> " 'It is beautiful!' exclaimed Elizabeth."

40. Donald Darnell, "Uncas as Hero: The *Ubi Sunt* Formula in *The Last of the Mohicans*," *American Literature*, XXXVII (1965), 259–266, associates the *ubi sunt* theme and, in passing, the death of Beowulf with Uncas, the last of the Mohicans. Cf. Kay Seymour House, *Cooper's Americans*, p. 62.

And he habitually laces his speech with terse maxims, of both the *bith* and *shal* variety. ("Advice is not a gift, but a debt that the old owe to the young." "Of what use are former deeds, when time draws to an end?" "A grey head should cover a brain of reason, and not the tongue of a boaster.") He loves to recount past deeds, thereby supplying his own epic history (in more than a half-dozen asides in *The Prairie*, some of considerable length, he summarizes the plots of the two previous Leatherstocking books, *The Pioneers* and *The Last of the Mohicans*, and even manages to allude to *The Deerslayer*, still fourteen years ahead in Cooper's career). And in the very accents of a Beowulf he foresees and laments the passing of an epoch in his own decline: "I am without kith or kin in the wide world! . . . when I am gone there will be an end of my race."[41]

In addition to supplying his hero with truly heroic qualities, Cooper has observed the stylistic implications of his epic world in *The Prairie*. On the simplest level, there is free and conscious use of epic similes. Natty's smile is "like a gleam of sunshine flitting across a ragged ruin"; a "cloud, as it is about to discharge the subtle lightning, is not more dark or threatening, than the look with which Ishmael greeted the intruder"; the evil Mahtoree's smile "lighted his fierce, dark visage, as the glare of the setting sun reveals the volume and load of the cloud, that is charged to bursting with electric fluid"; and Mahtoree's amazement "burst out of his dark rigid countenance . . . like a flash of lightning illuminating the gloom of midnight." In all of these examples the similes, comparing human expressions to good or bad weather, help to supply a figurative tone for the moral qualities of the person spoken about, dividing the cast of characters broadly into light and dark figures.

But nature does more than furnish incidental imagery; it is an organic part of the scheme of Cooper's epic romance. Animals are used, for instance, as an aid in characterization, establishing a kind of human hierarchy. Ishmael Bush is described variously as an elephant, an "over fatted beast," the "Great Buffalo" (his Indian name), a prowling bear, and even, in an unusually active moment, as an "awakened lion." The Bush family generally are notable for their animality; they even think of the murdered son Asa and the hidden Inez as beasts. Dr. Bat's most amusing moments have to do with a confusion of genus; he is definitely writ down an ass when it is discovered that his great scientific find, the *Vespertilio Hor-*

---

41. John J. McAleer, "Biblical Analogy in the Leatherstocking Tales," *Nineteenth-Century Fiction*, XVII (1962), 217–235, suggests an extensive parallel between Natty Bumppo and Moses.

ribilis Americanus (American Bat!), is none other than his own *Asinus Domesticus.*

Unlike the Bush family, which comes out rather badly in a comparison with the brutes, the old trapper has known how to maintain his dignity as a man. "Men are no common objects in these empty fields," he says, "and I humbly hope, though I have so long consorted with the beasts of the wilderness, that I have not yet lost the look of my kind"; and even his dogs share this dignity and humanity. In this primitive world, where bestiality is a real danger, man can distinguish himself from the lower creation only by choosing to emphasize his specifically human qualities. "The figure of a man," Cooper asserts as Natty Bumppo stands up in front of a herd of stampeding bison, "when sustained by the firmness and steadiness that intellect can only impart, rarely fails of commanding respect from all the inferior animals of the creation."

Cooper's reliance on vegetable imagery in *The Prairie* is perhaps even more important than his use of animals. Let us consider one example: trees. We know, through constant reiteration, that it is the sound of axes and falling trees that has driven Natty Bumppo farther and farther west. Natty seems to react with almost physical pain to the destruction of trees. He watches with a "melancholy gaze" and a "bitter smile," suppressing any "more audible utterance," as the eldest son of Ishmael buries his axe "to the eye in the soft body of a cotton-wood tree."[42] The Ishmaelite then stands regarding the effect of his blow "with that sort of contempt with which a giant might be supposed to contemplate the puny resistance of a dwarf," after which "he quickly severed the trunk of the tree, bringing its tall top crashing to the earth in submission to his prowess." When his brothers "saw the prostrate trunk stretched on the ground," they advanced to level the other trees in the area, as if, says the author, "a signal for a general attack had been given."

Cooper's language clearly suggests the human struggle and loss involved for Natty in the death of the trees: they are his family in the forest. Thereafter in the book the vital connection between Natty and the trees becomes increasingly strong. (He describes himself as "a frosted pine" which "must soon be laid in the ground," and Cooper says that

---

42. Henry Nash Smith says that Cooper is so eager to make his "symbolic point [about Natty's tortured hatred of the axemen who are despoiling the wilderness] that he has Bush's sons chop down a grove of trees conjured up for the purpose in the midst of the treeless great plains" (*Virgin Land: The American West as Symbol and Myth* [New York, Vintage Books], p. 257).

"though evidently so near its dissolution, his attenuated frame still stood like the shaft of seasoned oak, dry, naked, and tempest-riven, but unbending and apparently indurated to the consistency of stone.") This connection culminates metaphorically in one way when Natty delivers his great speech affirming order and meaning in the natural world—as opposed to civilization—and relating man to this world:

> "It is the fate of all things to ripen, and then to decay. The tree blossoms, and bears its fruit, which falls, rots, withers, and even the seed is lost! . . . There does the noble tree fill its place in the forest, loftier, and grander, and richer, and more difficult to imitate, than any of your pitiful pillars, for a thousand years, until the time which the Lord hath given it is full. Then come the winds, that you cannot see, to rive its bark; and the waters from the heavens, to soften its pores; and the rot, which all can feel and none can understand, to humble its pride and bring it to the ground. From that moment its beauty begins to perish. It lies another hundred years, a mouldering log, and then a mound of moss and 'arth; a sad effigy of a human grave. This is one of your genuine monuments, though made by a very different power than such as belongs to your chiseling masonry! . . . and as though it were put there in mockery of [man's] conceit, a pine shoots up from the roots of the oak, just as barrenness comes after fertility."

The poignant elegiac note of the speech is provided, of course, by the obvious nearness of Natty's own death. Like that of the noble tree, his life and death—an existence spent close to nature by a man imbued with natural piety—are the sole proof and guarantee of meaning and inscrutable power. And the possible fruits of such a life are not to be measured by the ordinary standards of civilized man. "Tell me not of your worlds that are old!" Natty says to the uncomprehending Dr. Bat. His own life speaks of worlds of value that are forever young.

But the metaphoric connection between Natty and nature culminates more directly in the action of the tale when the sinister Abiram White, violator of both the moral and natural law, is left to hang on a solitary willow tree, of which Cooper remarks:

> As if in mockery of the meagre show of verdure that the spot exhibited, it remained a noble and solemn monument of former fertility. The larger, ragged, and fantastic branches still obtruded themselves abroad, while the white and hoary trunk stood naked and tempest-riven. Not a leaf nor a sign of vegetation was to be seen about it. In all things it proclaimed the frailty of existence, and the fulfilment of time.

Like his namesake in the Bible, who revolted against Moses and was swallowed up by the earth, Abiram is punished by that generative order of nature whose laws he has violated; and the high priest of that order, Natty Bumppo, is metaphorically seen as his executioner. Here Cooper's use of natural imagery gives form to his book in the largest sense and inspires some of his most impressive writing.

Despite Richard Chase's assertion that Cooper "is never the allegorist," there is unquestionably a major social—perhaps one should call it a sociological—allegory at the heart of *The Prairie.* Indeed, it is hard to make much sense out of the book otherwise. It is of course realistically (but not, as we shall see, parabolically) silly that the Bush family should be where it is, doing what it is doing. In its seemingly pointless abduction of Inez to the middle of nowhere, along with its insanely scrupulous attempt to keep her identity, even her existence, a total secret, the family's action looks forward to the theater of the absurd. But if Abiram's craven and foolish scheme for making money by kidnapping Inez wins him only our disgust and incredulity, Ishmael at least has the dignity of being at once the unwilling accomplice of his brother-in-law and the almost willing agent of destiny. His burden is to bear the major weight of instrumenting Cooper's social parable.

For the great theme of the book, like that of Aeschylus' *Eumenides* in reverse, is the shift from a patriarchal to a matriarchal society—in another sense, from the world of the Old Testament to the world of the New, from a harsh, primitive, brutal, aggressive world to one of culture and love. Ishmael's implicit position as the great Hebraic patriarch of the book is made abundantly clear. (He acted, Cooper tells us, "with as much composure as if the species of patriarchal power he wielded was universally recognized.") What is opposed to Ishmael is perhaps less clear, certainly more complicated, but nonetheless present in the book—surprisingly so. It is the power of woman, in the person of the beautiful Inez de Certavallos, the goddess of sex and culture.[43]

We have already noticed that Cooper's female types owe their being to a profound distinction between the light and the dark which was to be of major importance for American fiction. In *The Prairie* Ellen Wade, the blonde, blue-eyed, all-American girl, is symbolically played off

---

43. "Inez links all elements of plot," writes William Wasserstrom, and he comments on her "odor of passion" and "peculiar erotic power" ("Cooper, Freud and the Origins of Culture," *American Imago*, XVII [1960], 423–437).

against—is indeed the handmaiden of—the dark, foreign, Catholic Inez, who is a living representative of the Louisiana Purchase. The description of Inez is important and Cooper builds up to her startling first appearance in a breathtakingly dramatic moment of impending violence that savors of the forbidden:

> Her person was of the smallest size that is believed to comport with beauty. . . . Her dress was of a dark and glossy silk, and fluttered like gossamer around her form. Long, flowing, and curling tresses of hair, still blacker and more shining than her robe, fell at times about her shoulders, completely enveloping the whole of her delicate bust in their ringlets; or at others streaming in the wind. The elevation at which she stood prevented a close examination of the lineaments of a countenance, which, however, it might be seen was youthful, and, at the moment of her unlooked-for appearance, eloquent with feeling. So young, indeed, did this fair and fragile being appear, that it might be doubted whether the age of childhood was entirely passed. One small and exquisitely moulded hand was pressed on her heart, while with the other she made an impressive gesture, which seemed to invite Ishmael, if further violence was meditated, to direct it against her bosom.

Inez's gesture, which suggests the transmuting of violence into sexual energy, is a good emblem of her role. And Cooper has lost no opportunity to imbue her with a mingled air of culture and carnality, even adding to the usual characteristics of the dark lady (as represented, say, by Cora Munro) a further hint of illicit attractiveness in Inez's passionate pubescence—that additional fillip of nymphet sexuality recurrent in our literature from Poe to Nabokov. Inez's implied youthfulness by no means contradicts the usual notion of maturity characteristic of the archetypal dark lady, however, since that maturity is intended mainly to imply knowledge and experience, and Inez's beauty, as Cooper tells us in a revealing oxymoron, is both "intellectual and nearly infantile." In fact, by adding pubescence to the normal attributes of the dark lady Cooper has, however unconsciously, moved her in the direction of a fantasy figure of pure carnality in which any suggestion of Oedipal taboo (i. e., capacity for motherhood) has been removed.

It is Ellen and Tachechana who are associated with the "heart," the pure and simple joys of maternity. Ellen's beauty is "maturer" than Inez's (though not intellectual, she has an "active mind") and "more animated." In contrast to the indulgent, imperious, sybaritic dark lady,

Ellen is characterized by "assiduity and tenderness" and "frank features"—the type of the good, pure, firm American blonde. (As we should expect, both the good and bad Indians, Hard-Heart and Mahtoree, prefer Inez.)

Inez represents the fertile carnality and intellect of the Old World, the dangerous knowledge and power of a fallen race that Cooper (with the Louisiana Purchase as a historical justification) is determined to bring into the light and domesticate in the American Eden: an Eden that, in a post-Adamic world ,still tries to sustain its illusion of purity and moral superiority—a form of spiritual pride whose price is cultural barrenness. The major part of Cooper's parable is to be found in Chapter 15 of *The Prairie*, and it is worth some inspection.

After the Purchase, the author tells us, there remained the problem of blending "the discrepant elements of society"—that is, of reconciling the "active" Protestant and the "indolent" Catholic. "In attaining so desirable an end, woman was made to perform her accustomed and grateful office. The barriers of prejudice and religion were broken through by the irresistible power of the master-passion." As an example of how the "indolent" Catholic female force won over and was joined to Protestant energy, Cooper tells the story of Captain Duncan Uncas Middleton, newly arrived in Louisiana, who fell in love with Inez, beautiful daughter of the proud and stern Don Augustin de Certavallos, and managed to win her hand despite the fierce objections of her father. Besides being strongly attached to his daughter, the Don is of course distressed by Middleton's being a "heretic," and Cooper's mastery of the real issues involved in his tale is beautifully exhibited by the metaphors he uses to describe the attempted conversion of the soldier by the Certavallos family. Throughout, the possibility of Middleton's becoming a Catholic is spoken of in strongly sexual language, as the religious objective and the carnal prize are imaginatively mingled. The priest who has been working on the young Protestant declares, for example:

> While no positive change was actually wrought in the mind of Middleton, there was every reason to hope the entering wedge of argument had been driven to its head, and that in consequence an opening was left through which it might rationally be hoped the blessed seeds of a religious fructification would find their way, especially if the subject was left uninterruptedly to enjoy the advantage of catholic communion [Inez!].

On her side, the passionate bride-to-be "thought it would be a glorious consummation of her wishes to be a humble instrument of bringing her lover into the bosom of the true church," and she looked forward to her wedding "with feelings in which the holy emotions of her faith were blended with the softer sensations of her years and situation."

Thus the carnality of the dark lady literally becomes equivalent to that cultural, ethical, and social influence—Old World "Catholicism"—which Cooper feels must be mated with "American" moral uprightness. And the real (that is, parabolic) point of Abiram's abduction of Inez is clearly implied in the bride's response when Middleton asks her how he is to act: " 'Be like him [the Don] in *every* thing,' she answered, looking up in his face, with tears in her eyes, and speaking with emphasis; 'in *every* thing. Imitate my father, Middleton, and I can ask no more of you.' " It is obvious that so long as Middleton and Inez remain close to the Don, in Louisiana, the mutual attachment of father and daughter will remain too strong. The union that Cooper is advocating cannot be consummated until the woman has been removed to free and open territory—the great West—and the grip of the father has been relaxed. Cooper wants the young American hero to be subject to the fructifying influence of Inez's Catholicism without his being forced to accept (indeed, imitate) the Old World father, a symbol of that repressive authority which Protestant America was originally founded to escape.

The main outlines of Cooper's parable thus begin to emerge: old wounds must be healed and Protestant and Catholic must reunite, so that America can move forward with both energy *and* beauty into a progressive future in our fallen world. The daughter must be allowed to leave her father, so that the dangerous but necessary female force can flourish. And in this regard, the freeing of Inez serves as a pattern and excuse for Ellen Wade's own manumission from the Bush clan. Ishmael, the dethroned patriarch, along with his accursed race, withers ignobly away. And Natty Bumppo, the primitive hero who has no place in the modern world of America, a world that has learned how to compromise with what to him are "abominations"—this great figure dissolves nobly back into the natural order that brought him forth.[44]

---

44. Robert H. Zoellner in "Conceptual Ambivalence in Cooper's Leatherstocking" speaks of "Cooper's unconscious dissatisfaction with the asocial Leatherstocking as a comprehensive symbol of the American ethos" (p. 420). But, since Cooper's sympathies seem so evenly divided between approval of civilization's inexorable westward movement and disapproval of the destruction of America's virgin forest, it seems more accurate to speak—as does Henry Nash Smith—simply of "a deep tension in Cooper's mind . . . a clash of irreconcilable values" ("Introduction," *The Prairie* [New York, 1950], p. xvi). Cf. note 46, below.

In spite of the comprehensive cultural myth that Cooper gropes toward in *The Prairie*, Natty Bumppo remains at the vital center of the book. It opens and closes with Natty in center stage, and the fact that it is concerned with Natty's measured decline into death dictates the time of year—autumn—when all of the action takes place. More importantly, Natty is the touchstone for measuring human virtue in the book. The wisdom of his old age is contrasted frequently to the inexperience and rash youth of Paul Hover. The temperateness of his fatherly interest in Hard-Heart ("I never was a father, but well do I know what is the love of one. . . . My heart yearns to you, boy, and gladly would I do you good") is contrasted to the frantic possessiveness of the aged Le Balafré. And there is clearly an implied contrast between Natty's version of fatherhood and the harshness of Ishmael toward his sons. (Those sons, indeed, suspect their father of being "ready to imitate the example of Abraham, without the justification of the sacred authority which commanded the holy man to attempt the revolting office.") Though an outcast, even if by choice, Natty is eminently superior in morals and habits to the other outcast, Ishmael, who is in many ways a sad caricature of the old trapper. And what reader can forget the tedious lengths to which Cooper goes to prove Natty's superiority in wisdom to the supposedly learned man of science, Dr. Obed Battius?[45]

But let us return to what we have just noted: the fact that *The Prairie* is set in the fall of the year. An important underlying theme of the book is death, and Natty is here once again at the very center of Cooper's romance. He alone who knows how best to live is most prepared to die; and Cooper gives us many opportunities to compare Natty's nobility in this respect to other human reactions toward death. Abiram, the cowardly murderer, is craven and afraid; Dr. Bat's scientific certainty appears to desert him at the ultimate moment; and old Le Balafré tries desperately to support and perpetuate himself by adopting Hard-Heart. The noble young Pawnee Loup, Natty's symbolic son, seems to equal his father in bravery before death; but even this nobility is qualified by Hard-Heart's vehement desire for revenge on the Sioux. Only Natty, the great human soul of the virgin forest, is truly at one with the natural order that ordains a death to all living things, as his many musings in the vein of memento mori and his tranquil end make clear.

---

45. Donald A. Ringe suggests that Natty is also compared to both Bush and Bat as regards a "proper attitude toward the physical world" ("Man and Nature in Cooper's *The Prairie*," p. 317).

Natty Bumppo, through great strength and purity of intention, has seemingly redeemed himself from Adam's curse, thereby wholly and singly meriting the great unspoiled land that is his bride. Cooper's magnificent yearning myth of the ideal man of the New World is a stirring, if limited, projection of a certain human potential once available to America. And Cooper's parable of cultural growth and assimilation notwithstanding, Natty's poignant death amid the rise of alien forces casts a kind of gloom over the future possibilities of American life.[46]

---

46. Roy Harvey Pearce stresses the fact that Natty's story must be a "tragic story," for although Cooper never intended to suggest "that the civilization which sent Bumppo to a death on the prairie was thereby an evil force," he "could see that westward expansion and progress in crushing such a man as Bumppo would crush something heroic in American life" ("The Leatherstocking Tales Re-examined," *South Atlantic Quarterly*, XLVI [1947], 527).

II

POE

1. *The Secret Soul of Man*

ON the surface, it seems possible to justify Poe's claim to being an American author only by insisting on the tautology that he happened to write in America. Certainly the ease with which he has been adopted by foreign authors and readers tends to undermine any narrowly national view of his achievement (although one might argue that the nineteenth-century craze for Poe is one of the first signs of that international passion for American themes and treatments that has flowered with the full recognition of American literature in this century). But, as a matter of fact, Poe's most abiding concerns are those of the American romance generally, and none more so than his lifelong obsession with the secret soul of man. To say that Poe's manifest interest in the theme of "life in the wilderness" connects him with Cooper, while his explorations into human psychology point forward to Hawthorne and Melville, is not to indulge in one of those frequently absurd linkings of influence that are presented as literary history. For the theme of "life in the wilderness" and that of the deeper psychology are ultimately one.[1] Unsupported by the traditional social, political, and theological arrangements and explanations of the Old World, the American hero is by very definition "in the wilder-

---

1. "Perhaps in part because of his inability to master the West directly," writes Edwin Fussell, Poe "became deeply concerned with what can only be understood as a psychological—or, in the literal sense, metaphysical—equivalent of the American frontier." See *Frontier: American Literature and the American West* (Princeton, 1965), p. 170. Throughout his chapter on Poe, Fussell develops a fascinating metaphoric equation between Poe's interest in exploring "boundary" states of consciousness and a concern for the American wilderness.

ness"—"man in the open air" (as Whitman benignly saw him) or, more complexly, "the hero in space" (in R.W. B. Lewis's phrase[2]). He is free—indeed, compelled—to confront in solitude the ultimates of the universe and his own soul.

The sensibility and situation of this new hero would drive his creators to explore new possibilities in fiction—forms, as Richard Chase says, freed "from the ordinary novelistic requirements of verisimilitude, development, and continuity," and therefore capable of containing "astonishing events" intended "to have a symbolic or ideological, rather than a realistic, plausibility."[3] It is as if the absence in America of all the European social conventions and institutions—a lack seen by Henry James, in his famous statement on Hawthorne,[4] as the downfall of the American author—had instinctively been turned into a virtue by American writers, inclined to symbolistic modes by temperament and tradition and eager to explore questions or attempt treatments normally excluded from the English novel.[5]

Poe's career seems emblematic of the underlying aspiration of every American romancer to find a way of exploring the secrets of the human soul. Certainly Poe felt, as did Rousseau, that the way to undying literary fame in the modern world lay open to the man who could write and publish "a very little book," its title "a few plain words": "My Heart Laid Bare." But, added the American author ominously (in "Marginalia"), "this little book must be *true to its title*," and such a creation he considered impossible. "No man dare write it. No man ever will dare write it. No man *could* write it, even if he dared. The paper would shrivel and blaze at every touch of the fiery pen." Rousseau might boast, on the opening page of his *Confessions*, of the uniqueness of his intention to tell the unvarnished truth about a man; but despite his deliberate attempt at honesty, the result is tinged with sentimental fakery. His every wilderness is only a pastoral Paris, and the whole production turns out to be an elaborate self-justification tremulously read to a circle of friends and

---

2. See *The American Adam: Innocence, Tragedy, and Tradition in the Nineteenth Century* (Chicago, 1955), *passim*, but especially pp. 88–92.

3. *The American Novel and Its Tradition* (New York, 1957), pp. ix, 13.

4. See *Hawthorne*, in *The Shock of Recognition*, edited by Edmund Wilson (New York, 1955), pp. 459–460.

5. The question of an American symbolic or symbolistic tradition is explored by Charles Feidelson, Jr., *Symbolism and American Literature* (Chicago, 1953).

enemies. Rousseau could write his *Confessions* only because they told nothing *too* terrible to relate; for him, what is contained in the human heart is ultimately explainable and justifiable.

Poe, on the other hand—like his later disciple, Henry James's Prince Amerigo, who knew that everything *is* terrible in the heart of man— was too frightened of true revelation to believe in the possibility or advisability of simple honesty. "It is a deeply consequential error this," he asserts, "the assumption that we, being men, will in general, be *deliberately* true." Such an assumption unfortunately infects our reading habits: "We dote upon records, which, in the main, lie; while we discard the *Kabbala*, which, properly interpreted, do *not*." Poe's own romances are his attempt at writing a kind of *Kabbala*, a fantastic, esoteric literature capable of at once containing and withholding the deepest truths. For the imagination of man is not licensed "to explore with impunity its every cavern. Alas! the grim legion of sepulchral terrors can*not* be regarded as altogether fanciful; but . . . they must sleep, or they will devour us— they must be suffered to slumber, or we perish."

Thus Poe evinces simultaneously a deep interest in and a fear of exploring the underside of human consciousness. (This explains why the keynote of his fiction is so frequently evasion—why we usually see his characters trying to avoid, with diabolical cleverness, the full and final implications of what they are.[6]) This tension accounts for the fact that Poe's art is mainly a truth-telling which masquerades as trumped-up terror, hoax, exaggeration, or farce—mere grotesquery or buffoonery, a bizarre literary version of our national pastime, the practical joke.[7] It is as if Poe were insisting that since an art that would openly reveal all is too terrible to write or to read, he is forced to resort to a self-consciously artificial art which licenses the writer to say anything and the reader to believe nothing. Poe shares with other romancers what Chase calls "the penchant for the marvelous, the sensational, the legendary, and in general the heightened effect." But the important question, so well phrased by Chase, "is always: To what purpose have these amiable tricks of romance

---

6. Speaking of "Tamerlane," Edward H. Davidson writes that the "method of simultaneous concealment and revelation became . . . central to Poe's art." *Poe: A Critical Study* (Cambridge, Mass., 1957), p. 5.

7. "Poe was always great not only in his noble conceptions but also as a prankster." Charles Baudelaire, "New Notes on Edgar Poe," in *The Recognition of Edgar Allan Poe*, edited by Eric W. Carlson (Ann Arbor, 1966), p. 46.

been used? To falsify reality and the human heart or to bring us round to a new, significant and perhaps startling relation to them?"[8]

That an air of conscious falsification—trickery, prestidigitation, humbug—has always hung about the name of Poe and his productions is undeniable. The allegation of fakery is the major occupational hazard of the romancer, and Poe is a member of the breed par excellence. Even Walt Whitman's fine comment on Poe's career is tinged with a suggestion of self-indulgent unreality:

> In a dream I once had, I saw a vessel on the sea, at midnight, in a storm. . . . flying uncontroll'd with torn sails and broken spars through the wild sleet and winds and waves of the night. On the deck was a slender, slight, beautiful figure, a dim man, apparently enjoying all the terror, the murk, and the dislocation of which he was the center and the victim. That figure of my lurid dream might stand for Edgar Poe, his spirit, his fortunes, and his poems—themselves all lurid dreams.[9]

If Whitman's dream is redeemed from falsity by the accuracy of its symbolic implications, it is itself a good argument for the validity of Poe's art. Whitman's vision is a perfect emblem of Poe's meaning as an artist: he is the hero and victim of the voyage of man into himself. His world is the dark, dangerous world of our fantasies—our desires and our fears. It is a dream world, but every man dreams.

If it is true, as Yeats says, that in dreams begin responsibilities, Poe must have considered himself the most responsible of artists. Apologists for novelistic *vraisemblance* or denigrators of the romance might vilify Poe for trespassing "into the weird confines of superstition and unreality,"[10] but he would argue in his "Marginalia" that "it is by no means an irrational fancy that, in a future existence, we shall look upon what we think our present existence as a dream"—in which case, the firm distinction between reality and dream is destroyed. Poe would freely admit his great ambition to capture in words those "psychal impressions" or "fancies" that arise in the mind "where the confines of the waking world blend with those of the world of dreams," if only that he might "startle the universal intellect of mankind" into admitting that he had done "an original thing." But he must have believed that some tremendously

---

8. *The American Novel and Its Tradition*, p. 21.

9. "Edgar Poe's Significance" (from "Specimen Days") in *The Recognition of Edgar Allan Poe*, p. 75.

10. James Russell Lowell, "Edgar Allan Poe," in *ibid.*, p. 13.

important secret, for others as well as for himself, lay in such a success. He would begin with himself:

> You are not wrong, who deem
> That my days have been a dream;

and then move on to include us all:

> *All* that we see or seem
> Is but a dream within a dream

only to conclude with a terrible question:

> Is *all* that we see or seem
> But a dream within a dream?

The terms of this dialectic define Poe's peculiar power as a romancer. He was consciously devoted to exploring

> By a route obscure and lonely,
> Haunted by ill angels only,

that "wild weird clime"

> Where an Eidolon, named NIGHT,
> On a black throne reigns upright,

the "ultimate dim Thule" of man's unconscious. And the necessity of telling things slant and dreamwise—of employing indirection, paradox, and trickery—he would consider inseparable from the realm he was dealing with:

> . . . the traveller, travelling through it,
> May not—dare not openly view it;
> Never its mysteries are exposed
> To the weak human eye unclosed;
> So wills its King, who hath forbid
> The uplifting of the fringèd lid;
> And thus the sad Soul that here passes
> Beholds it but through darkened glasses.

Here, in his "Dream-Land," Poe offers us a concise exposition of the methods of the American romance generally. In the works of Hawthorne and Melville, as in those of Poe, the dream becomes the type of romance art: a surrealistic distortion of experience that manages to distill essential meaning from events and actions. Poe's definition of art—"the reproduction of what the senses perceive in Nature through the veil of the soul"—illustrates how the Aristotelian principle of mimesis has been distorted by the addition of the romancer's note of radical subjectivity. The art of the romancer is no longer, and is not intended to be, an imitation of nature, but rather an expression of the secret self.

2. *The Power of Words*

WHEN Poe speaks of the entireness of his "faith in the *power of words,*" he is simply emphasizing, in the first place, the seriousness of his devotion to literary art. But the phrase immediately begins to reverberate in other, more curious ways. What is being suggested surely is not the Yeatsian notion that "words alone are certain good"—that art (in this case, poetry) is alone of permanent and ultimate value in an imperfect world. Poe's phrase implies that with language one can do anything, bring off any *effect* (the word is a favorite of Poe's). There is present also an underlying insistence, slightly desperate in tone, that words are, not only useful to render, but potent to control experience. It is as if he were trying to convince us, and himself, that the strange matters contained in his writings owe their very existence only to the evocative power of words. He is thus in the odd position, as a romancer, of being committed at once to presenting a dark view of experience and to proving finally that it isn't so.

Everywhere in Poe's writings we are invited to believe that technique is capable of both determining and circumscribing content. It is easy—too easy—to be seduced by his "explanations" of how he goes about "constructing" a tale: having conceived "a certain unique or single *effect* to be wrought," he proceeds to invent "such incidents" and "events" as will succeed in producing his "preconceived effect." Every word is *calculated* to achieve the desired end; nothing, we might say, is left to chance or to nature. And should anyone inquire just why the author has chosen to deal in his tales with terror, passion, and horror, rather than with "Beauty," Poe replies with seeming lucidity that the latter is best treated in poetry, while the former are more suited to prose. To the reader who complains about his *"tales of effect"*—"to *play* with horror," laments Leslie Fiedler, "no matter what one's declared intent, is to pander to the lowest, darkest impulses of the mind"[11]—Poe's bland retort is: "The impressions produced were wrought in a legitimate sphere of action, and constituted a legitimate although sometimes an exaggerated interest." But the legalistic diction barely veils the flimsiness of Poe's attempt at justification. *Why*, we ask insistently, does that "interest" sometimes become "exaggerated"?

If Poe's "Philosophy of Composition" (which is not a hoax, only because it ultimately reveals whatever it was invented to conceal about "The Raven") is intended in its totality to divert our attention from serious issues, Poe's gambit could not have been better designed to be disquieting in the extreme. "Let us dismiss," he remarks with disingenuous candor, "as irrelevant to the poem, *per se*, the circumstance— or say the necessity—which in the first place gave rise to the intention of composing" such a poem as "The Raven." The reader's voice rises in dissatisfaction ("tell me truly, I implore"): what *was* the "circumstance" —worse, the "necessity"—which gave rise to the "exaggerated interest" implied by such a production? But the author intends to discuss only "artistic effect."

Analogous to Poe's insistence on the supremacy of technique—his calculated attempt to convince us that the conscious manipulations of the artist take precedence over and explain the vision of life being presented— is his insistence that reason, not passional madness, is the natural condition of man. "Man's chief idiosyncrasy being reason," he argues, "it follows that his savage condition—his condition of action *without* reason—is his *unnatural* state." It is as if we were being told that the daylight world of novelistic sanity, not the nighttime horrors of the romance, constitutes the real truth about human life. But despite the reassuring theory, the "sepulchral terrors" will have their way. Poe, of course, usually provides us with a Virgil in his Inferno, an eminently rational narrator who guides us through and explains the horrors that he presents; but we are frequently made aware, most of all by our guide's own uncertainty, that his reason is but a whistling in the dark. (And as with all whistling in the dark, the elaborateness of the tune suggests the strenuousness of the effort being made to avoid what is pressing in.) Even worse, we are often most disquieted by the strange insistence of the narrator's ratiocination; we begin

---

11. *Love and Death in the American Novel* (New York, 1960), p. 121.

to feel, uneasily, that he is *terribly* reasonable. The reader is affected by Poe's narrators as Victor Serge is by Konstantinov in Wallace Stevens' "Esthétique du Mal":

> ... "I followed his argument
> With the blank uneasiness which one might feel
> In the presence of a logical lunatic."

The rational narrator, a device which Poe uses ostensibly to convince us that reason is man's "natural state," ends up by making us suspect precisely the opposite.[12]

3. *The Haunted Palace of Art*

BEGINNING with Poe and continuing as a strong current in the works of Hawthorne, Melville, and James, the desire to test and evaluate the opposing claims of novelistic "good sense" and romance "wildness" finds expression in the very fabric of American fiction. "Art" as an implied or explicit theme and the frequent use of "artist" figures become characteristic of the American romance—indeed, are among the criteria that define it—as our authors argue out for themselves the question of daylight versus night.[13]

It might seem odd to mention "The Fall of the House of Usher" in connection with such a formulation, but this familiar tale is an especially interesting illustration of the foregoing thesis. The reader first must be asked to shift his attention slightly from the gothic horrors depicted in the story to the subtle opposition set up between the character of Roderick Usher and that of the narrator.[14] Usher is a portrait, somewhat caricatured,

---

12. Poe "often so designs his tales as to show his narrators' limited comprehension of their own problems and states of mind; the structure of many of Poe's stories clearly reveals an ironical and comprehensive intelligence critically and artistically ordering events so as to establish a vision of life and character which the narrator's very inadequacies help to 'prove.'" James W. Gargano, "The Question of Poe's Narrators," in *The Recognition of Edgar Allan Poe*, p. 309.

13. In "The Function of Poe's Pictorialism," *South Atlantic Quarterly*, LXV (1966), 46–54, Nina Baym argues cogently that most of Poe's work is concerned with exploring the nature of imagination itself.

14. In "What Happens in 'The Fall of the House of Usher'?" *American Literature*, XXXV (1964), 445–466, J. O. Bailey suggests that the narrator and Usher represent opposing aspects of Poe's own personality, the psychic and intuitive versus the rationalist.

of the artistic temperament in its most decadent—that is, romantic—
state.[15] He has a "remarkable" face, with large and liquid eyes, lips "of
a surpassingly beautiful curve," and a fine nose "of a delicate Hebrew
model." Phrenologically considered, his "finely moulded" chin shows
"a want of moral energy" (clearly suggestive of his capacity to indulge
in forbidden practices), and the "inordinate expansion above the regions
of the temple" bespeaks great intellectual powers. He is morbidly sensitive:

> The most insipid food was alone endurable; he could wear only garments
> of certain texture; the odors of all flowers were oppressive; his eyes were
> tortured by even a faint light; and there were but peculiar sounds, and
> these from stringed instruments, which did not inspire him with horror.

His emotional life is characterized by a preponderance of the darkest of
all human states, absolute *Angst*. "I dread the events of the future," he
explains lucidly, "not in themselves, but in their results." This "intolerable agitation of soul" makes every incident and experience pregnant
with unnameable terror for him. "I feel that the period will sooner or
later arrive," he confesses, "when I must abandon life and reason together, in some struggle with the grim phantasm, FEAR."

Usher is thus admirably suited by nature to exploring and giving
expression to the direst aspects of human life, and his beliefs and training
are what we should expect. He holds an opinion, we are told, concerning
the "sentience of all vegetable things": nature for him is not only a force,
animated and alive, but a source and reflection of hidden powers at work
in the world. And the titles of his favorite books—of which Poe supplies
a carefully constructed (and partially invented) list—read like a card
catalog of subjects and materials for the most lurid of romancers, apt

---

15. Many biographers and critics, including Hervey Allen, Killis Campbell, and
Arthur H. Quinn, have remarked on the similarities between Usher and Poe himself. J. O. Bailey (*ibid.*, p. 446) cites Allen to the effect that Roderick represents "the
most perfect pen-portrait of Poe himself which is known." A. H. Marks, "Two
Rodericks and Two Worms: 'Egotism; Or, The Bosom Serpent' as Personal
Satire," *PMLA*, LXXIV (1959), 607–612, sees Hawthorne's tale as an attack on Poe,
suggesting that Hawthorne viewed Roderick Usher as a possible portrait of what he
considered Poe's twisted personality. In a larger vein, Charles Feidelson, Jr., describes
the subject of "Usher" as "aesthetic sensibility" and says that "behind the whole
story is the conception of an antirational art . . . [Usher] is the artistic mind *in ex-
tremis*" (*Symbolism and American Literature*, pp. 39, 41). And Maurice Beebe, in
his *Ivory Towers and Sacred Founts: The Artist as Hero in Fiction from Goethe to Joyce*
(New York, 1964), pp. 117–128, discusses Usher as the prototypal artist in the ivory
tower tradition, who emphasizes "internal consciousness."

illustrations of the notion that there are more things in heaven and earth than are dreamt of by the most sagacious of novelists. Usher reads "the Heaven and Hell of Swedenborg; the Subterranean Voyage of Nicholas Klimm of Holberg"; several volumes of "Chiromancy"; the "Journey into the Blue Distance of Tieck; and the City of the Sun of Campanella," as well as a volume on the Inquisition by a Dominican friar. Most suggestive of all, perhaps, "there were passages in Pomponius Mela, about the old African Satyrs and Œgipans, over which Usher would sit dreaming for hours," while "his chief delight" was in perusing the "rare and curious . . . *Vigiliae Mortuorum secundum Chorum Ecclesiae Maguntinae.*" Usher's favorite fantasy material—undoubtedly connected, any psychoanalytically inclined reader would say, with his excruciatingly intense anxieties—is a combination of sexuality and death.

As an artist—he is at once poet, painter, and musician—Usher adheres strictly to the school of the fantastic and the extreme. His guitar impromptus are either perverse variations on familiar tunes or "wild improvisations." And his paintings and poems, at least judged by the two detailed examples that Poe supplies, are the very type of the romancer's art: lurid symbolism verging on hideous allegory, or ominous allegory heightened by weird symbolism. Roderick's creations hint at the terrible secret about the House of Usher, presenting an intolerably dark view of human nature.

Into this house of horror enters Poe's narrator, the sort of man who in happier days and more cheerful circumstances might have written the novels of Anthony Trollope. Although by no means unemotional or unfeeling, he is an eminently, even doggedly, reasonable person with a great need to make sense of his experiences, or at least to believe that everything ultimately is capable of some rational explanation. Strange occurrences fascinate him—he is the kind of man who is frequently tempted to peer over the brink of an oddity—but he is finally disturbed enough by the inexplicable to want only to avoid it. His speech is formal, complicated, and intricately logical, as if to express a hope that the coherences of grammar might make up for the incoherencies of life.[16]

---

16. One example: "While the objects around me—while the carvings of the ceilings, the sombre tapestries of the walls, the ebon blackness of the floors, and the phantasmagoric armorial trophies which rattled as I strode, were but matters to which, or to such as which, I had been accustomed from my infancy—while I hesitated not to acknowledge how familiar was all this—I still wondered to find how unfamiliar were all the fancies which ordinary images were stirring up."

He is intelligent, but his intelligence is more often used to protect himself from knowledge than to explore the unknown.[17]

Numerous concrete instances of all these characteristics are provided by Poe throughout the tale. When the narrator first sees the House of Usher, its melancholy aspect depresses and unnerves him, and that he should be so affected strikes him as "a mystery all insoluble." He is assailed by "shadowy fancies," and to escape them resorts to what we learn is his usual expedient, an attempt at rational explanation: "I was forced to fall back upon the unsatisfactory conclusion, that while, beyond doubt, there *are* combinations of very simple natural objects which have the power of thus affecting us, still the analysis of this power lies among considerations beyond our depth." The explanation, admittedly "unsatisfactory," offers the appearance rather than the substance of intellectual acuteness, but it at least temporarily allays the narrator's fears and protects him from a darker conclusion—that the capacity for *Angst*, seemingly groundless and unreasoning fear, is part of everyone's human makeup. Later, when the narrator finds Usher in just such a state, he can only term it "anomalous"—that is, abnormal and unwarranted. And toward the end of the tale, when he himself is finally infected with the "incubus of utterly causeless alarm," his only resource is to attempt to shake it off "with a gasp and a struggle," since the sentiment is "unaccountable yet unendurable." Our narrator has no power against the "unaccountable," and his "yet" is beautifully characteristic; that a horror without an apparent cause should be unendurable (indeed, worse than an explainable horror) makes no sense to him. He has not learned to accept the awful truth—Usher's truth—that the world's worst horrors are unendurable *because* they are unaccountable.

The narrator perpetually shies away from the suggestion of inexplicability and ultimate mystery in human affairs. Disturbed by his first

---

17. Darrel Abel calls the narrator "Anthropos" ("uncharacterized, undescribed, even unnamed") and terms him "an habitual naturalist resisting urgent convictions of the preternatural" ("A Key to The House of Usher," in *Interpretations of American Literature*, edited by Charles Feidelson, Jr., and Paul Brodtkorb, Jr. [New York, 1959], p. 52). Abel comments on the narrator's "matter-of-fact" mentality (pp. 61–62). Charles Feidelson, Jr., notes: "The gentleman who comes riding up to the House of Usher is the personification of rational convention. Like all Poe's narrators, even the most unbalanced, he would like to cling to logic and to the common-sense material world. But he has set out on a journey which is designed to break up all his established categories; reason is deliberately put through the mill and emerges in fragments" (*Symbolism and American Literature*, p. 35).

vision of the house, he attempts to calm himself by resorting to the "somewhat childish experiment" of observing, instead of the house itself, its reduplicated image in the tarn. The experiment fails, his nervousness is only increased, and he feels compelled to explain: "There can be no doubt that the consciousness of the rapid increase of my superstition—for why should I not so term it?—served mainly to accelerate the increase itself. Such, as I have long known, is the paradoxical law of all sentiments having terror as a basis." He is content to rest in a general "law," no matter how paradoxical, and to account himself a victim of "superstition," rather than confront a profound personal puzzle. But his solicitude extends beyond himself to the reader. His explanations are clearly meant to reassure us, and he avoids exploring the ambiguous, we may understand, mainly for the sake of our peace of mind. The "equivocal hints" he receives from Usher concerning the latter's mental state which relate to "certain superstitious impressions" about the house are, we are told, "conveyed in terms too shadowy here to be re-stated." Usher's strange theory of vegetable "sentience," especially in regard to the malign influence exercised over him by the very stones of the house, is brushed aside: "Such opinions need no comment, and I will make none." And whatever the narrator may have learned from Usher's "few words" about the "sympathies" existing between himself and his sister, he is not eager to go beyond reporting that they were "of a scarcely intelligible nature." Poe's main purpose in all of these instances is, of course, to heighten the sense of implied horror by being suggestive rather than explicit. And the narrator serves this purpose splendidly, in spite of himself, since his attempt to allay our fears by overlooking the "anomalous" only increases the air of the sinister. As with his first vaguely disquieting impression of the house, the narrator prefers consistently to shake off the inexplicable intimations that he believes "*must* have been a dream" and turn his attention to the "real aspect" of things, hopefully to dispel the atmosphere of unreality.

"The naked Senses," Poe wrote in "Marginalia," as if he were thinking of his narrator, "sometimes see too little—but then *always* they see too much." The narrator of "The Fall of the House of Usher" has a "noticing" eye which, clearly in defiance of his conscious intention to enlighten and demystify, weaves a pattern of surrealistic detail that contradicts any common-sense view of reality. What he sees, without apparently being fully aware of it, is a barely definable similarity between the house and its master.[18] The "minute fungi" which cover the exterior of the house (and which play a part in Usher's theory of sentience) overspread the building, "hanging in a fine tangled web-work from the eaves," while Roderick's hair, "of a more than web-like softness and tenuity," had been "suffered to grow all unheeded" and floated wildly about his face. The house gives the impression of a "wild inconsistency between its still perfect adaptation of parts and the crumbling condition of the individual stones"; likewise, in Roderick's behavior, the narrator is "at once struck with an incoherence—an inconsistency." The atmosphere reeking from the mansion is that of a "pestilent and mystic vapor, dull, sluggish, faintly discernible, and leaden-hued"; Roderick's voice is "leaden," and from his mind "darkness, as if an inherent positive quality, poured forth upon all objects of the moral and physical universe in one unceasing radiation of gloom." ("A sense of insufferable gloom pervaded my spirit," reports the narrator as he first approaches the house.) And, worst of all, "perhaps the eye of a scrutinizing observer might have discovered a barely perceptible fissure, which, extending from the roof of the building in front, made its way down the wall in a zigzag direction, until it became lost in the sullen waters of the tarn." That "scrutinizing observer" is of course our narrator, sharp enough to perceive, and willing to report, this obscure sign of inherent instability in the house, but not eager to divine for himself, or convey to us, that "oppressive secret" which is the parallel cause and sign of instability in the decaying Roderick.[19] "The eye," says the narrator entering Usher's room, "struggled in vain to reach the remoter angles of the chamber." Some things are too dark even for his scrutinizing eye.

The nightmarish view of reality suggested by the resemblance of house and master defies the narrator's explanations and discourages him from attempting to draw any conclusions, but we are not ultimately left to rest contentedly in his limited point of view. Instead, we are offered Roderick Usher's own artistic productions as oblique elucidations of

---

18. Resemblances between Roderick Usher and the house are discussed by Darrel Abel, Maurice Beebe, and E. Arthur Robinson in "Order and Sentience in 'The Fall of the House of Usher,'" *PMLA*, LXXVI (1961), 68–81.

19. Marie Bonaparte remarks that the fissure in the house symbolically "recalls the 'cloven body of woman,' of which Zola speaks" (*The Life and Works of Edgar Allan Poe: A Psycho-Analytic Interpretation* [London, 1949], p. 240). In my reading of the tale, Usher's "oppressive secret" is a sexual problem relating to his sister Madeline.

the mysteries everywhere adumbrated in the tale. Usher's poem, "The Haunted Palace," seems to be a flat allegory, with an "under or mystic current" of meaning, as the narrator suggests, insinuating "the tottering of his [Usher's] lofty reason upon her throne." The verses do equate a reasonable head that has gone bad with a "Radiant palace . . . In the monarch Thought's dominion" which has been assailed and captured by "evil things, in robes of sorrow." (The palace once had "banners yellow" for fair hair, "two luminous windows" for eyes, a "pearl and ruby" door for teeth and lips, and a king full of "wit and wisdom" for sanity.) But it is worth noting that the loss of reason is signalled by a shift from "Spirits moving musically/To a lute's well-tuned law" to "Vast forms that move fantastically/To a discordant melody"—the shift from "lawful" music to the "wild fantasias" of Usher's improvisation. The poem thus represents Usher's fate as a romantic artist: he may begin in joy and gladness, but he inevitably moves to despondency and madness as his vision darkens and he becomes aware of the "evil things" in himself and others—truths that cannot be overlooked by the artist who descends into the human depths.[20] The narrator's visit to the House of Usher is not only a visit to the soul of Roderick Usher but a glimpse into the "Haunted Palace" of the romancer's art itself.[21]

As an example of the kind of experience necessarily encountered in the realm of romance, we are offered one of the "phantasmagoric conceptions" painted by Roderick Usher:

> A small picture presented the interior of an immensely long and rectangular vault or tunnel, with low walls, smooth, white, and without interruption or device. Certain accessory points of the design served well to convey the idea that this excavation lay at an exceeding depth below the surface of the earth. No outlet was observed in any portion of its vast extent, and no torch or other artificial source of light was discernible; yet a flood of intense rays rolled throughout, and bathed the whole in a ghastly and inappropriate splendor.

Looking ahead to Hawthorne's *Marble Faun*, we might wish to name this

---

20. Darrel Abel sees the movement from "well-tuned" music to "discordant melody" as representing a general shift from "Life-Reason" to "Death-Madness" ("A Key to the House of Usher," p. 58).

21. "The House of Usher *is*, in allegorical fact, the physical body of Roderick Usher, and its dim interior *is*, in fact, Roderick Usher's visionary mind," observes Richard Wilbur ("The House of Poe," in *The Recognition of Edgar Allan Poe*, p. 264).

painting "Subterranean Reminiscences." But by itself it sufficiently suggests that realm of the submerged—the underside of human consciousness—which is the peculiar province of romance. Ordinarily dark and inaccessible, it is now exposed and illuminated by the "ghastly" light of the romancer's imagination.[22]

In the tale the picture adumbrates the dungeon-tomb reserved for Roderick's sister, Madeline, and thus suggests that the particular kind of underground experience which lies at the heart of this (and, as it turns out, most other) romance art involves the darkest aspects of sexuality. Roderick Usher's secret subject, with an obvious but unacknowledged borrowing from Byron, concerns what can be called the Manfred Syndrome: the artist-brother's illicit and finally murderous passion for his twin-sister, usually identified—as in Byron's poem—with Astarte, the eastern Venus.[23] (Ultimately, as in Melville's *Pierre*, the underlying suggestion is drawn out that the artist's narcissistic love for his female mirror image symbolizes his infatuation with his own psyche—a destructive involvement with his own unconscious which is at once the romancer's inspiration and his undoing.)

Since Poe's tale is, at its deepest level, a kind of fictional debate which argues for the seriousness of romance as a way of exploring the secret soul of man (Roderick's point of view), it is altogether fitting that the awful truth about the House of Usher should be most fully revealed by a romance within the larger romance: "the 'Mad Trist' of Sir Launcelot Canning." Poe underlines the narrator's common-sensical obtuseness and his imperviousness to the serious implications of the romance form by having him choose to read to Usher, in order to calm him, a tale which exacerbates him to the point of madness and, ultimately, death. The narrator himself at first calls the tale one of Usher's "favorite romances," and then adds, characteristically, that he was joking, "for, in truth, there is little in its uncouth and unimaginative prolixity which could have had interest for the lofty and spiritual ideality of my friend." In fact, the "Mad Trist" is a highly imaginative symbolic representation of the sordid

---

22. "All this underground vault business in Poe," writes D. H. Lawrence, "only symbolizes that which takes place *beneath* the consciousness. . . . He was an adventurer into vaults and cellars and horrible underground passages of the human soul" (*Studies in Classic American Literature*, reprinted in *The Shock of Recognition*, pp. 981, 984).

23. On Poe and Byron, see Edmund Wilson, "Poe at Home and Abroad," in *The Recognition of Edgar Allan Poe*, p. 146.

reality of Usher's psychosexual nature. And it is Usher himself who spells out its meaning for the bewildered narrator, as the incidents read out of Canning's tale coincide with the final events of Poe's tale in one final ghastly demonstration of the power and living truth of romance.

The "Mad Trist" relates an episode in which the hero Ethelred comes upon and slays a "scaly and prodigious" dragon, with "fiery tongue" and "pesty breath," which has been polluting the precincts of a golden and silver "palace." While the narrator reads, the details of this last horrible night in the house mingle with those of the "Trist" as the ravished and dying sister Madeline makes her way, with many a clinking and clanging, up to the chamber containing Usher and his friend. The tortured, terrified Roderick himself makes the connections: "Ethelred—ha! ha! . . . the death-cry of the dragon, and the clangor of the shield!—say, rather, the rending of her coffin, and the grating of the iron hinges of her prison, and her struggles within the coppered archway of the vault!" In Roderick's version of the "Mad Trist" (the wonderfully ambiguous title suggesting both insane sorrow and a mad love meeting)—and here we must gather up the repetitive elements of the fantasy woven throughout Poe's tale—the sexually tempting sister is the "dragon" that has infested and corrupted the "palace" of his soul. Roderick's own haunted palace can be restored to its pure use only by the slaying of this evil thing "in robes of sorrow" ("the lofty and enshrouded figure of the lady Madeline" appears at the end with "blood upon her white robes"). For Madeline, of course, the sexual dragon is her lustful and attacking brother.

But the assigning of blame is ultimately of no importance. Since Roderick and Madeline are twins—that is, one person—Ethelred/Roderick's confrontation with the dragon/sister represents a symbolic confrontation with his own sexuality.[24] It is an awareness of his own secret and forbidden desires that has darkened the imagination of the artist, and the romancer can never return to the "pure" state when he was free of such knowledge. Roderick's determination to slay the dragon/sister coincides with his own death. Illicit sexuality, for Roderick Usher, is inseparable from life.

For Poe's narrator, however—the rational man of daylight sensibility, whose experience of the self is blissfully free of such dark knowledge—

---

24. J. O. Bailey (see note 14 above) presents an ingenious argument for viewing Madeline as a vampire. He suggests that the final embrace of brother and sister is "violently erotic," as in vampire stories, and perhaps incestuous.

the revelation in the House of Usher is not a truth about human existence but a bad dream that can be shaken. He arrives there on a "dark" and "soundless" day, having traveled into the "shades of evening." His first ghastly impression of the House seems to him the "after-dream" of an opium eater. It "*must* have been a dream," he insists. He sees the lady Madeline for the first time with a "sensation of stupor" and listens to Roderick's wild guitar "as if in a dream." He can scarcely believe the strange world he has entered, and yet he finds it difficult not to be affected by and caught up in it: "I felt creeping upon me, by slow yet certain degrees, the wild influences of his [Usher's] own fantastic yet impressive superstitions."

The danger of being permanently infected by so dark a vision increases with time; long dreams are hardest to forget. And so he must rouse himself with a violent effort to escape the horrors he has viewed, fleeing "aghast" "from that chamber, and from that mansion," and thereby releasing himself cataclysmically from the grip of nightmare: "—my brain reeled as I saw the mighty walls rushing asunder—there was a long tumultuous shouting sound like the voice of a thousand waters—and the deep and dank tarn at my feet closed sullenly and silently over the fragments of the 'House of Usher.' " For the narrator, the ghastly world of romance is dissolved as the dark waters of night close over the fragments of his shattered dream. But for the reader, and for Poe, this world continues to live.[25]

4. *The Pleasures of Imagination*

The vitality of the world of dream is the true underlying theme of Poe's "Ligeia." And here the "spirit which is entitled *Romance*" is specifically associated with a representative of dark erotic fantasy, "Ash-

---

25. "*The Fall of the House of Usher* is a journey into the depths of the self," writes Richard Wilbur. "All journeys in Poe are allegories of the process of dreaming, and we must understand . . . *Usher* as a dream of the narrator's, in which he leaves behind him the waking, physical world and journeys inward toward his *moi intérieur*, toward his inner and spiritual self. That inner and spiritual self is Roderick Usher. . . . [He] is a part of the narrator's self, which the narrator reaches by way of reverie. We may think of Usher, if we like, as the narrator's imagination, or as his visionary soul. Or we may think of him as a *state of mind* which the narrator enters at a certain stage of his progress into dreams. . . . Usher is an allegorical figure representing the hypnagogic state" ("The House of Poe," p. 265).

tophet of idolatrous Egypt"—the numen who presided over the "ill-omened" marriage of the narrator with his fantastic Ligeia.

Like the narrator of "The Fall of the House of Usher," the speaker of "Ligeia" is without a name; it is the world, not of social existence, but of private fantasy that is the subject of the narration. Unlike that of the narrator of "Usher," however, the voice that tells "Ligeia" manifestly does not belong to a reasonable man of normal tastes and desires. The speaker (and protagonist) of "Ligeia" is a fantast, a man who willingly commits himself to the world of subjective vision—a man, we might say, who is determined to live a life of romance. More accurately, he is a romancer who believes that the dusky world of his fantasies can be *made* real, if only he wills it into reality fervidly enough. Poe, in fact, sets about demonstrating in "Ligeia" that the will to believe associated with fantasy is so strong that it is capable of making fantasy the truest reality for the private imagination. Romance is true if we wish it to be; horribly so, is the sinister corollary insisted on by Poe.

That the mysteries and perversities of the will are a major concern in "Ligeia" is signalled by the epigraph, supposedly taken from Joseph Glanvill:

> And the will therein lieth, which dieth not. Who knoweth the mysteries of the will, with its vigor? For God is but a great will pervading all things by nature of its intentness. Man doth not yield himself to the angels, nor unto death utterly, save only through the weakness of his feeble will.

Like the narrator's frequent protestations regarding the angelic, heavenly, and holy nature of his beloved Ligeia, the mention of God here is patently deceptive. For although His name is mentioned, what is being suggested is the possibility of man's attaining a god-like omnipotence to work his will over the creation. The quotation is used three times in the tale, and the last two times only the final sentence is stressed, asserting man's presumed power to hold the forces of both light and darkness at bay while he lives on in a state of extended wish-fulfillment. The apparent will, suggested by the quotation, to triumph *over* death and corruption, becomes in the tale a desire to be omnipotent *in* death and corruption—to make the corrupt dream come true.

In the world of omnipotent desire—the world of fantasy—there is no more powerful ruler than our narrator, whose perfervid imagination has conjured up the voluptuous Ligeia as the agent and example of his invincible will. That she is a figment, however vivid, of the narrator's mind is made sufficiently clear. Ligeia has no surname, no family connections or social history—only a first name of incantatory force. The narrator, who excuses his poor memory on account of "much suffering," cannot recall when he first met her: "She came and departed as a shadow," making her way into his "heart by paces so steadily and stealthily progressive that they have been unnoticed and unknown." She is a kind of gothic visitation that came to him "first and most frequently in some large, old, decaying city near the Rhine." Seated in his "closed study," he would become aware of her presence only through "the dear music of her low sweet voice" and the pressure of her "marble hand" upon his shoulder. Her beauty "was the radiance of an opium-dream—an airy and spirit-lifting vision . . . wildly divine."

"The price of pure idealism," Daniel Hoffman remarks, "is the extinction of reality, as Poe acknowledged in 'To Helen,' transforming his beloved into a statue."[26] In this case, however, the idealism of Poe's narrator is almost purely erotic. For all the associations of ethereality and spirituality with which he attempts to surround Ligeia (these indeed are a crucial sign of the narrator's skittishness about revealing directly the true nature of his fantasy world), she is clearly the perfection of erotic dreaming. In a single sentence the narrator speaks at once "of her purity, of her wisdom, of her lofty, her ethereal nature," and "of her passionate, her idolatrous love"! For us, of course, Ligeia is the familiar archetype of the dark lady. Her "raven-black" tresses are "glossy," "luxuriant," and "naturally-curling"; her eyes and lashes are pure jet. She is surrounded by the usual suggestions of intellect and Eastern voluptuousness. Her nose is somehow Hebraic, bespeaking, we are told, "the free spirit"; her lips are "heavenly," which is to say "voluptuous" (the heaven that the narrator has in mind, as he lets fall, is that which includes the "Houri of the Turk"); and her lofty, prominent forehead implies great mental powers. But the true nature of the "metaphysical investigation" into which she introduces the narrator is delicately insinuated by Poe in a sentence which is a masterpiece of sly hinting and ambiguous suggestion:

> With how vast a triumph—with how vivid a delight—with how much of all that is ethereal in hope—did I *feel*, as she bent over me in studies but little sought—but less known—that delicious vista by slow degrees ex-

---

26. *Form and Fable in American Fiction* (New York, 1965), p. 212.

panding before me, down whose long, gorgeous, and all untrodden path, I might at length pass onward to the goal of a wisdom too divinely precious not to be forbidden.

The narrator's "passionate wife" Ligeia is the Lilith of every Adam's most febrile dreams, who offers the fruit of infinite pleasure and gratification ordinarily reserved to the gods. The path opened up by her knowledge traditionally leads, of course, to death. But in the world of the narrator's erotic imagination, "death" means no more than the *petite mort* of sexual climax, to be overcome by the will to renewed potency. Man need not "yield himself to the angels" (goodness and purity) "nor unto death utterly" (that eternity of unpleasure which is the result and further end of indulgence) "save only through the weakness of his feeble will."

It is made clear that the major mystery of the will with which "Ligeia" concerns itself is the subjective omnipotence of the desire for sexual fulfillment. This is the principle taught the narrator by the "fierce spirit" of his Ligeia. Her will is purely erotic, a "gigantic volition" which exhibited itself only by her "*intensity* in thought, action, or speech." This intensity of action is not evidenced by ordinary outward signs or activity: Ligeia was "outwardly calm . . . ever-placid." Inwardly, however, she was "violently a prey to the tumultuous vultures of stern passion." Her "wild desire for life, . . . *but* for life," could be seen mainly in her "more than womanly abandonment" to love.

But Ligeia, however much a woman, is still *only* a woman, destined to be devoured by the "vultures" that stir her passion. Her capacity for gratification is subordinate to the phallic supremacy of the attacking male; the culmination of her desire brings her "death," and she can be brought back to "life" only by her partner's invincible sexual will. The dark lady, in short, is dependent for her erotic capabilities on the imagination of the dreamer who brings her forth and endows her with sexual power. The narrator of Poe's tale must be taught that the life of his fantasy depends on the power of his will.

Ligeia's plight is revealed covertly in a poem "composed by herself" not long before her "death" and read out, at her behest, by the narrator-lover. The composition is superficially a simple allegory in which "an angel throng," sitting in a theater, watches "mimes, in the form of God on high," act out "the tragedy, 'Man,' " whose "hero" is "the Conqueror Worm." Thus the drama of human events, seen *sub specie aeternitatis*, presumably ends with the triumph of death. But there are complexities in the poem worth noting. First, Ligeia's verses do not exhibit the events of human life as being under divine guidance or control. The mimes are

> Mere puppets . . . who come and go
> At bidding of vast formless things
> That shift the scenery to and fro,
> Flapping from out their Condor wings
> Invisible Wo!

In this vision of life, the powers of darkness are in charge, and "the soul of the plot" is "Madness," "Sin," and "Horror." Its central incident images a

> . . . Phantom chased for evermore,
> By a crowd that seize it not,
> Through a circle that ever returneth in
> To the self-same spot.

Ligeia's poem does not really suggest an allegory of human life at large. It is rather a ghastly symbolic rendering of the dark lady's internal being—the eternal midnight quest for erotic gratification. The climax is reached in the next to the last stanza:

> But see, amid the mimic rout,
> A crawling shape intrude!
> A blood-red thing that writhes from out
> The scenic solitude!
> It writhes!—it writhes!—with mortal pangs
> The mimes become its food,
> And seraphs sob at vermin fangs
> In human gore imbued.

The angels, "all pallid and wan," might well weep to see the "heavenly" Ligeia destroyed in this thinly disguised allegory representing a nightmarish phallic orgy.[27] From Ligeia's point of view, the play is the tragedy "Woman" and its hero the conquering male organ. The dark lady has been provisionally annihilated in the culmination of the narrator's erotic fantasy.

With the temporary collapse of his dream world, the narrator leaves "the dim and decaying city by the Rhine"—the Germany of his soul—

---

27. Lawrence calls Ligeia's poem "the American equivalent for a William Blake poem" (*Studies in Classic American Literature*, p. 975).

and travels to "fair England," as if to atone for his orgy of Teutonic fantasy indulgence by exiling himself to Northern reality. Having glutted his imagination on the dark lady, the narrator now turns, as we might expect, to the archetypal fair maiden. The "fair-haired and blue-eyed Lady Rowena Trevanion, of Tremaine," whom he marries "in a moment of mental alienation," becomes the agent of chastising reality. But the narrator, in whom the pleasure principle is invincible, is able to turn his union with the icy Englishwoman to all sorts of good uses. His sense of enraged frustration, and possibly self-revulsion, over the lost Ligeia can conveniently be worked off on the Lady Rowena. "She shunned me and loved me but little," he admits, adding—with a suggestion of how he is able to convert his punishment into a source of perverse satisfaction— that it gave him "rather pleasure than otherwise." Forcing his pure bride to cohabit with a husband she dreads, and forcing himself to live with a woman he loathes "with a hatred belonging more to demon than to man," gives a special fillip to the "unhallowed hours" of his first month of marriage.

Not surprisingly, the Lady Rowena declines rapidly, falling before long into a totally moribund state. Indeed, the narrator seems to have planned this from the start, when he led her to the bridal couch "of an Indian model, and low, and sculptured of solid ebony, with a pall-like canopy above," in a room each of whose angles was decorated with "a gigantic sarcophagus of black granite." One might be tempted to say that the fair maiden dies of fright engendered by the lurid decorations, were it not for the strong suggestion that the narrator himself does away with her by poisoning her wine. Like so many of Poe's heroes, the narrator seems to prefer his women dead or cataleptic, so that he can use their bodies in his favorite fashion—as raw material for his erotic fantasies.

Poe offers the Lady Rowena's decline and subsequent transformation as a supreme example of the mysteries and powers of the will—in this case, the narrator's will to fantasy gratification. Although he has married the fair lady of cold reality, he is not barred in his mind from re-creating the dark lady of his warm imaginings. Through sheer strength of will he *subjectively*—that is, to his own perceiving—converts the blonde Rowena into the raven-haired Ligeia. It is surely a misreading of the tale to speak, as one critic does, of "the powerful climax when the soul of Ligeia returns from death to seize the body of her successor and reclaim her place by her husband's side, through the sheer determination to live."[28] The determination is the narrator's; and the tale is concerned, not with the singularly odd case of an actual revenante, but with the more earthly (and no less odd) case of a fantast's subjective triumph.[29]

Poe takes some pains to make it clear that the narrator, after his marriage to Rowena, does everything in his power to remind himself of Ligeia. The bridal chamber is decked out in gorgeous and fantastic Eastern style, with the bridal couch, as we have noticed, devoted to darkness and death. Particular details of the room are clearly designed to recall that "circle of analogies" mentioned by the narrator at the beginning of the story as being suggestive of Ligeia's eyes and expressive glance: "a rapidly growing vine...a moth, a butterfly, a chrysalis, a stream of running water." The underlying principle is movement and metamorphosis, and his chamber in the English abbey is designed with the same notion in mind. There is a vine, "which clambered up the massy walls of the turret," and a huge censer of Saracenic pattern "so contrived that there writhed in and out...as if endued with a serpent vitality, a continual succession of parti-colored fires." There is a massive tapestry "spotted ...with arabesque figures...of the most jetty black," which "by a contrivance...were made changeable in aspect." The effect was "heightened by the artificial introduction of a strong continual current of wind ...giving a hideous and uneasy animation to the whole." In such a setting the narrator, his imagination spurred on by opium, gives himself up night and day to calling aloud upon the name of Ligeia, "as if, through the wild eagerness, the solemn passion, the consuming ardor of my longing for the departed, I could restore her to the pathway she had abandoned."

Certainly he can, if only to his own hallucinatory satisfaction. Once the Lady Rowena has apparently expired, he devotes himself doggedly to imagining that the corpse is really Ligeia: "I sat alone, with her shrouded body, in that fantastic chamber.... Wild visions, opium-engendered,

28. Arthur H. Quinn in *The Literature of the American People* (New York, 1951), p. 301.

29. "Ligeia," says Roy P. Basler, "seems both aesthetically and psychologically more intelligible as a tale, not of supernatural, but rather of entirely natural, though highly phrenetic, psychological phenomena" ("The Interpretation of 'Ligeia,'" in *Poe: A Collection of Critical Essays*, edited by Robert Regan [Englewood Cliffs, 1967], p. 52).

flitted, shadowlike before me." He glances at "the pallid and rigid figure upon the bed," and then has "a thousand memories of Ligeia." Through the night, "with a bosom full of bitter thoughts of the one only and supremely beloved, [he] remained gazing upon the body of Rowena." Soon he begins to imagine that the corpse has indeed come to life, but he is not sufficiently prepared, and the impression vanishes, whereupon he again gives himself up "to passionate waking visions of Ligeia." The cycle is repeated many times, with each incipient transformation of the fair Rowena calling forth from the narrator renewed and increased efforts at intense dreaming about the longed-for erotic object, Ligeia. Finally, with a "mad disorder" in his thoughts, a "tumult unappeasable," and "inexpressible madness," the triumphant fantast sees the dark lady before him as his dream reaches its climax in an orgy of necrophilic omnipotence. In the obscure and private world of his imagination the narrator takes possession of his wish. Here the will to pleasure reigns supreme, and all fair ladies are dark.[30]

5. *"Dream Delivers Us to Dream"*

THE protagonist of "Ligeia" is singular among Poe's narrators for the relative openness with which he exhibits his commitment to the romance world of secret desire. Far from being shocked by the dark wishes that lurk in daylight reality, he embraces them, eagerly transforming his blonde Rowena into a raven-haired Ligeia. More typically, however, Poe's heroes pretend, even to themselves, to be firmly devoted to daylight: consciously they choose sanity over madness, reason over passion, sentiment over sex. Yet, seemingly inexplicably, they are undermined by ambivalence, pursued by the very forces they have apparently done their best to avoid. Tenderly dreaming of fair ladies departed, like the hero of "The Raven," they are assailed by ebon-winged messengers of evil portent. Chastely devoted to the life of the mind, like Egaeus in "Berenice," they are incomprehensibly subverted by precisely that devotion. The "sunlight of . . . reason," in Egaeus' phrase, somehow becomes a midnight of obscene passion.

---

30. In "Poe's 'Ligeia' and the English Romantics," *University of Toronto Quarterly*, XXIV (1954), 8–25, Clark Griffith argues persuasively that "Ligeia" is at once "an allegory of terror" and "the subtlest of allegorized jests." He sees in Ligeia and Rowena grotesque parodies of the dark and fair ladies of gothic and romantic tradition.

It is not usual to think of the protagonist of "The Raven" as being in conflict over the opposing forces of light and dark; it is perhaps even less usual to consider the poem in connection with the two archetypal ladies. The poem's too great familiarity has certainly bred, if not contempt, at least carelessness in most readers' reactions; and Poe's own attempt to explain the meaning and the circumstances surrounding the composition of "The Raven" has not helped matters. "The Philosophy of Composition" is one of his trickiest pieces of writing, yet it is ultimately a great aid in reading the poem. The manifestly contrived way in which he tries to convince us that the poem was written almost mechanically, with the cold-blooded intention of producing an "effect," in itself strongly argues for deeper intent. And though his "explanation" of the poem's meaning is demonstrably disingenuous, it does hint at the real meaning. In perhaps his only totally serious paragraph in "The Philosophy of Composition," Poe argues for "some amount of complexity" and "some under-current, however indefinite, of meaning" in a work of art. The statement is worth heeding.

The essential complexity of "The Raven" lies in the suggestion of emotional ambivalence in the student-lover who is the narrator. Bereaved by death of "the rare and radiant maiden whom the angels name Lenore" —blonde by implication here and explicitly so in Poe's poem "Lenore"— the evidently high-minded young scholar has attempted vainly to drown his endless sorrow in study. He is *luxuriating* (Poe's term) in the tenderness of his sentiment for the departed maiden and one feels the intensity of his capacity for pure devotion. He is apparently expecting to feel no other emotion. Then comes the Raven, seating itself permanently on the bust over the door. Poe's comment on the bird and statue is a splendidly typical combination of subterfuge and revelation:

> I made the bird alight on the bust of Pallas, also for the effect of contrast between the marble and the plumage—it being understood that the bust was absolutely *suggested* by the bird; the bust of *Pallas* being chosen, first, as most in keeping with the scholarship of the lover, and, secondly, for the sonorousness of the word, Pallas, itself.

If the mention of "contrast" is at least initially an attempt to divert our attention to the frivolities of interior decoration, the emphasis implied by that word finally points to something more serious: the major light-dark opposition embodied in the two objects. Bust and bird do absolutely suggest one another; they represent the inseparable polarity that forms the

crux of the poem. And Poe gives us a further hint, fragmentary and
partially obscured by the talk about "sonorousness": the bust of Pallas
was chosen "as most in keeping with the scholarship of the lover." It is
also, we should add, most in keeping with his presumed devotion to
defunct virgins. The bust of Pallas, in short, is the perfect emblem of the
fair lady, the permanently untouchable object of the lover's holiest
dreams.

Onto *this* venerated figure settles the ominous and obscene Raven,
whose color and "fiery eyes" with "all the seeming of a demon's that is
dreaming" suggest a nightmare version of the dark lady. Thus the lover,
reveling in emotions of supposed religious purity directed toward the
fair Lenore, paradoxically finds himself faced with a symbol of diabolic
darkness whose responses—provoked by the lover himself—telling him
that the dark visitation has permanently taken the place of the fair maiden,
give him a "frenzied pleasure." That "most delicious because the most
intolerable of sorrow" provided by the bird's replies is equivalent to
the exquisitely unacceptable knowledge that his fair dreams have given
birth to foul nighttime visions.

Poe admits that in the two concluding stanzas the presumably "real"
Raven becomes "ideal"—i. e., "emblematical"—thereby casting back
on the rest of the poem a shadow of underlying meaning. But his own
reading of the bird's meaning is patently false. The whole conclusion to
"The Philosophy of Composition" is worth close inspection:

> "Take thy beak from out *my heart,* and take thy form from off my door!"
> Quoth the Raven, "Nevermore!"

> It will be observed that the words, "from out my heart," involve the
> first metaphorical expression in the poem. They, with the answer, "Never-
> more," dispose the mind to seek a moral in all that has been previously
> narrated. The reader begins now to regard the Raven as emblematical—
> but it is not until the very last line of the very last stanza that the intention
> of making him emblematical of *Mournful and Never-ending Remembrance*
> is permitted distinctly to be seen:

> And the Raven, never flitting, still is sitting, still is sitting,
> On the pallid bust of Pallas just above my chamber door;
> And his eyes have all the seeming of a demon's that is dreaming,
> And the lamplight o'er him streaming throws his shadow on the floor;
> And my soul *from out that shadow* that lies floating on the floor
>   Shall be lifted—nevermore.

Poe is clearly playing with us. The reader certainly has begun to regard the Raven as emblematical previous to the penultimate stanza, and Poe's deceptive suggestion to the contrary is partner to the obvious falsehood that the phrase "from out my heart" constitutes the poem's first metaphor. There are many metaphors in "The Raven" (beginning with "And each separate dying ember wrought its ghost upon the floor"), and the most complex and revealing one of all is the bird itself—manifestly not emblematical of *"Mournful and Never-ending Remembrance,"* since that would reduce the poem and its supposed climax to a mere tautology. We know from the start, as does the lover, that the beloved is permanently lost and that his mournful remembrance will never end ("vainly I had sought to borrow/From my books surcease of sorrow—sorrow for the lost Lenore . . . Nameless *here* for evermore").

What the Raven startlingly and horribly comes to represent is that "human thirst for self-torture," mentioned by Poe in the essay, which compels the student to conjure up, in the midst of his tender sorrow for the fair maiden, an image of dark violence that drives her purity from his heart. What he learns from the Raven is the secret of his own emotional ambivalence, and from out the shadow of *that* knowledge his soul shall be lifted—nevermore![31]

The lesson in the ambiguities of human nature and desire implied by "The Raven" is learned explicitly by the narrator of "Berenice," whose opening paragraph expresses his sorrowful and perplexed recognition, after the fact, of human duplexity. Speaking of the multiformity of man's wretchedness, he uses the figure of the rainbow, and then notices that his own rhetoric itself implies how strangely mixed in him are the antinomies of experience: "How is it that from beauty I have derived a type of unloveliness?—from the covenant of peace, a simile of sorrow?" He had apparently tried hard to keep things apart and distinct: dreams of reason from dreams of passion, religion from deviltry, light from darkness. But the imagination of man is a strange place.

"Dream delivers us to dream, and there is no end to illusion," says Emerson in a sentence that unintentionally defines a major premise of romance. Egaeus is by his own admission a fantast, a man who has always

---

31. "The young man in 'The Raven' will never recover his 'soul' or his acceptance of the coherence of things after his terrible insight, not only into his own madness, but into the madness of the universe itself" (Edward H. Davidson, *Poe: A Critical Study*, pp. 133–134).

lived in the "regions of fairy land," the "palace of imagination": "The realities of the world affected me as visions, and as visions only, while the wild ideas of the land of dreams became, in turn, not the material of my every-day existence, but in very deed that existence utterly and solely in itself." He would have us and himself believe, however, that his time spent in the "wild dominions [the adjective is ominous] of monastic thought and erudition" is proof that his dreams were chaste and scholarly. He reads many religious books. Engrossed by Tertullian's "*De Carne Christi*," he spends "laborious" weeks puzzling over the paradox "*Mortuus est Dei filius; credibile est quia ineptum est; et sepultus resurrexit; certum est quia impossibile.*" And yet we learn by the end of the tale that his meditations in the "wild dominions" of religious theorizing were a paradoxical sign of fascination, not with Christ, but with the flesh. Tertullian's "*sepultus resurrexit*" issues horribly in "a violated grave . . . a disfigured body enshrouded, yet still breathing—still palpitating—*still alive!*"—the narrator's carnal outrage on the body of the prematurely entombed Berenice.

The dark process that leads to Egaeus' madness is outlined by Poe with that fearfully accurate eye for the logic of nightmare that only a romancer such as he could possess. Like so many of Poe's narrators, Egaeus is a fierce devotee of reason. Reason is his goddess, his Pallas Athena, his guide and protectress in a world where the dangers of feeling —the ambiguous, the primitive, the potentially violent—lurk everywhere. Reason is his only passion. Indeed, as the impeccable logic of the tale finally demonstrates, he is possessed (to use Valéry's fine phrase) by a "delirium of lucidity."[32] For he learns ultimately that reason can turn into its opposite, that reason can betray. His romance of reason becomes a romance of sex and death.

Not surprisingly, we learn at the outset of the tale that the enormous temptation from which Egaeus' hypertrophied attachment to the mind was designed to protect him is the familiar dark lady in the person of his cousin Berenice. "Agile, graceful, and overflowing with energy," she beckoned to him from the hillside; but Egaeus, "addicted, body and soul, to the most intense and painful meditation," had no time for her "gorgeous yet fantastic beauty." Later he explains, in the odd tones of a man desperately trying to convince himself that he is speaking the truth, that her sexual attractiveness meant nothing to such a chaste and serious scholar as he:

---

32. Cited by Harry Levin, *The Power of Blackness* (New York, 1958), pp. 135–136.

During the brightest days of her unparalleled beauty, most surely I had never loved her. In the strange anomaly of my existence, feelings with me, *had never been* of the heart, and my passions *always were* of the mind. . . . I had seen her—not as the living and breathing Berenice, but as the Berenice of a dream; not as a being of the earth, earthy, but as the abstraction of such a being; not as a thing to admire, but to analyze; not as an object of love, but as the theme of the most abstruse although desultory speculation.

Soon Berenice is seized by a mysterious disease which causes her beauty to decay, and Egaeus experiences a sympathetic intensification of his own strange malady, giving Poe a chance to exhibit his superb psychological insight.[33] We should normally expect, in a man who has been consistently denied—or has denied himself—a clearly desired sexual object, an intense exacerbation of fantasy gratification as the desired object disappears from view. Egaeus, to be sure, does experience an enormous increase in mental activity as Berenice declines; this, in fact, is the nature of his "monomaniac" disease. But he takes great pains to assure us, however guardedly, that his fantasy life was "primarily and essentially distinct and different" from the usual sexual dreams "indulged in by persons of ardent imagination":

> In the one instance, the dreamer or enthusiast, being interested by an object usually *not* frivolous, imperceptibly loses sight of this object in a wilderness of deductions and suggestions issuing therefrom, until, at the conclusion of a day-dream *often replete with luxury,* he finds the *incitamentum,* or first cause of his musings, entirely vanished and forgotten. In my case, the primary object was *invariably frivolous,* although assuming, through the medium of my distempered vision, a refracted and unreal importance. Few deductions, if any, were made; and those few pertinaciously returning in upon the original object as a centre. The meditations were *never* pleasurable; and, at the termination of the revery, the first cause, so far from being out of sight, had attained that supernaturally exaggerated interest which was the prevailing feature of the disease.

Egaeus' explanation requires considerable decoding. The daydreams of the normal sexual fantast ("*often replete with luxury*") begin with an object "*not frivolous*"—that is, with an image of recognizable sexual

33. "A monomania he paints with great power," writes James Russell Lowell. "He loves to dissect one of these cancers of the mind, and to trace all the subtle ramifications of its roots" ("Edgar Allan Poe," p. 14).

meaning—which leads to a connected fantasy that may carry the dreamer far from the original image but never away from the general notion of sexuality. Egaeus' fantasies, in contrast, are clear examples of displacement: they take the place of the sexual dreams which would normally be expected. The *incitamentum* of Egaeus' fantasies is *"invariably frivolous"* —that is, not logically connected with the sexual need which is their underlying cause. His fantasies are expressions of hidden sexual anxiety, invested in apparently pointless obsessive images, for which reason his "meditations were *never* pleasurable." Egaeus cannot allow himself to admit a sexual need, or grant himself a sexual gratification, by permitting the emergence of erotic fantasies. Instead, this exceedingly mental young man becomes subject to a "morbid irritability" of the *"attentive"* properties of the mind which defies "anything like analysis or explanation."

Presumably Poe has his narrator develop this theory of frivolous *incitamenta* in order to account somehow for the seemingly inexplicable obsession with teeth by which Egaeus is soon to be possessed. But the logic behind that obsession is flawless. Let us return to Berenice. Now that her beauty has been so thoroughly destroyed by disease that she is no longer apparently a darkly passionate, sexually attractive—and therefore forbidden—woman, Egaeus feels safe in asking her to marry him. But one afternoon shortly before their marriage, when Berenice appears before her prospective husband in his library, he notices with "a sense of insufferable anxiety" that she has undergone a further transformation:

> The forehead was high, and very pale, and singularly placid; and the once jetty hair fell partially over it, and overshadowed the hollow temples with innumerable ringlets, now of a vivid yellow, and jarring discordantly, in their fantastic character, with the reigning melancholy of the countenance . . . the thin and shrunken lips . . . parted; and in a smile of peculiar meaning, *the teeth* of the changed Berenice disclosed themselves slowly to my view. Would to God that I had never beheld them, or that, having done so, I had died!

The horror is that this seemingly pure young scholar, who has devoted himself completely to intellectual pursuits and whose passions *"always were* of the mind," has come to be *passionately* obsessed by mental images— in this case, the "excessively white" teeth of Berenice: "In the multiplied objects of the external world I had no thoughts but for the teeth. For these I longed with a frenzied desire." Yet Egaeus still cannot bring himself to admit that his passions have finally and actually been engaged. The teeth, he insists, were present only "to the mental eye" and had become the "essence" only of his "mental life." They are, after all, only *ideas*. But this is precisely why Egaeus desires them:

> I . . . seriously believed *que tous ses dents étaient des idées. Des idées!*— ah, here was the idiotic thought that destroyed me! *Des idées*—ah, *therefore* it was that I coveted them so madly! I felt that their possession could alone ever restore me to peace, in giving me back to reason.

The narrator's obsession is an extremely lucid expression of the fundamental truth of his psychosexual life. For him, seemingly nonsexual ideas have always taken the place of forbidden sexual emotions; that is, his sexual desires have apparently been displaced into a mental concentration on ideas. Now the underlying truth is exposed: *ideas for him are sexual objects*, which he covets "madly" and must possess. But the full explanation of the narrator's obsession lies in Poe's use of the female archetypes. Egaeus has tried to avoid true passion, represented by his sexually desirable cousin Berenice, the dark lady, and can agree to marry her only when she has ceased to be a sexual threat. What, then, must have been his horror to discover this very archetype of purity, a blonde and therefore presumably desexualized Berenice, calling to him with "a smile of peculiar meaning" which discloses thirty-two erotically cathected *ideas*, her shining teeth. The ghastly truth about his supposedly *pure* passion for ideas is pushed up toward consciousness by this curiously apposite manifestation of the outwardly fair maiden's innate sexuality. Egaeus' passion for the mind has come to haunt him in the mouth of his cousin. And the logic of his intense need to extract Berenice's teeth is clear enough: he must remove those teeth (ideas) that make the blonde maiden attractive, resolving her ambiguous coalescence of sex and purity, and thus restoring himself to peace by symbolically desexualizing his cherished reason.

But although Egaeus' madness has its own logic, his method of removing the sexual threat and thereby relieving his anxiety is itself an expression of sexuality—in this case, a quasi-necrophilic violation of Berenice's body. A deliberate air of unreality surrounds the conclusion of the tale because the narrator refuses to admit the act fully into consciousness. He calls it a "confused dream," a "horror more horrible from being vague, and terror more terrible from ambiguity." But it is also "exciting," and the remarkably calm way in which Egaeus, in the midst of all the incriminating evidence, waits to be apprehended indicates that he expects and wishes to be punished. He grasps the paradox that an act supposedly carried out to obliterate a sexual temptation also represents his giving in to his darkest desires. Reason, the life of the mind, has turned into its opposite—brutal and irrational sexuality. And we remember a sentence, now filled with meaning, from the opening paragraph of the tale which perfectly expresses the Freudian truth about repression that lies at the heart of the story: "the agonies which *are* have their origin in the ecstasies which *might have been.*"[34]

Poe, in his typically disingenuous fashion, was content to defend his supposedly bad taste in writing "Berenice" only on the grounds that readers like "the ludicrous heightened into the grotesque; the fearful coloured into the horrible; the witty exaggerated into the burlesque; the singular wrought out into the strange and mystical." This is, as Professor Arthur Hobson Quinn says, "not a satisfactory defense"; but hardly, as Quinn argues, because Poe's "lapse" in the tale "is only one more proof that . . . the horrible passes usually out of the realm of art."[35] Rather, "Berenice" is worth defending on the grounds that in Poe's hands the art of romance passes out of the realm of horror and into the realm of truth.

6. The Ultimate Romance

The Narrative of Arthur Gordon Pym can be considered a romance to end all romances, for it portrays the American romancer as an intrepid voyager into strange seas of thought from which he can hardly hope to return at all—or, if he does so, only long enough to tell his tale and then, like Pym, die that "sudden and distressing death" which suggests how maimed and undermined his experience has left him. Poe's longest tale is an American *Pilgrim's Progress* which leads not to eternal salvation but

---

34. "Poe dealt deliberately with the psychological themes of obsession and madness in 'Ligeia' and 'Berenice,'" says Roy P. Basler. Each "shows a similar preoccupation with the *idée fixe* or obsession in an extreme form of monomania which seems intended by Poe to be the psychological key to its plot." Poe treats of "the power of frustrate love to create an erotic symbolism and mythology in compensation for sensual disappointment" ("The Interpretation of 'Ligeia,'" p. 51).

35. *The Literature of the American People*, p. 302.

to eternal terror. Unlike Cooper's version of the archetypal American fable, in which the young hero's introduction to the wilderness is an initiation into life, Poe's version equates the exploration of the wilderness with the stalking of the darkest aspects of the self and suggests how fatal the American experience may ultimately prove to be. In characteristic American fashion Whitman would optimistically cry out for a "passage to more than India!"—to "primal thought" and "realms of budding bibles." But Pym's "primal thought" is a horror, and the only holy scripture he finds in Tsalal is an inscription of ominous ambiguity that predicts destruction.

Poe's interest in the theory of romance receives its most concise, and possibly clearest, expression in the introductory and concluding notes provided by him for the tale. If the original intent of all this ancillary material represents, as Leslie Fiedler suggests, "an involved attempt on Poe's part to convince himself that his primary purpose in publishing the tale was to perpetrate a hoax on the reader,"[36] it certainly ends up as more than an expression of authorial pusillanimity. What Poe really seems to be trying to say is that the public, in reading a romance, must willingly run the risk of being deceived: assurances of absolute truth to reality can be given only for writing that does not pretend to expose startling and unexpected aspects of experience. The reader's attention is drawn to the fact that he is beginning a *narrative*, not the "adventures" of A. Gordon Pym. This, in short, is art, not life: the romance is stylized, frequently fantastic, not committed to a *vraisemblable* rendition of experience. And yet the romance can compel belief, in the deepest sense, where the most realistic depiction of life would fail. Had the tale been offered as truth, Pym tells us in his introduction, it would have been considered "an impudent and ingenious fiction." But presented as a "ruse," and despite—we should say because of—its having been published "under the garb of fiction" with an "air of fable," the narrative was received as truth. Indeed, "Mr. Poe" himself, it is suggested in the concluding note, does not believe "in the entire truth of the latter portions of the narration." But the dedicated reader of romance has greater faith: he knows that the narrative finally portrays a truth that transcends the veracity of detail.

---

36. *Love and Death in the American Novel*, p. 372.

Looked at in another way, the notes to Poe's *Narrative* can be considered an attempt to establish credentials of identity. It is as if, by initiating this "argument" between Poe and Pym, the author were trying to suggest the questions fundamental to so many American romances: *When you write about the experiences of the American hero, whom are you writing about?* and *What does it mean to write a narrative of the self?* The question *Who are you?* leads naturally to the question *What are you?* as the announcement of identity immediately suggests the exploration of that identity. As Harry Levin has noted, the similarity between Arthur Gordon Pym (from Edgarton) and Edgar Allan Poe certainly implies that Poe's fictional hero is in some sense a description of himself.[37] In that period of American writing so aptly named by Emerson the age of the first person singular, all of our authors seem to be responding to the spirit of Hetty Hutter's question to Leatherstocking: "What's *your* name?" " My name is Arthur Gordon Pym," announces Poe's hero at the outset of his narrative, anticipating the first page of *Walden*, the beginning of "Song of Myself," and of course Melville's "Call me Ishmael."

Pym, however, is hardly introspective in the manner of a Thoreau or a Melville. He can say truly with Whitman, "I am the man, I suffered, I was there," but it never seems to occur to him to think seriously that his sufferings help define his nature or the permanent condition of mankind.[38] Poe, as we have seen, did not believe any man capable of writing that terrible little book entitled "My Heart Laid Bare," and his hero is very far from being interested in laying his vitals open to public or private inspection. I am the man to whom things happen, Pym might offer in innocent self-definition. And if these things demonstrate that human nature is radically duplex and experience ambiguous, Pym himself is not particularly eager to draw that conclusion.[39] He turns away from the dark inferences which Poe forces on the reader, determined to look on the

---

37. Cf. *The Power of Blackness*, p. 110.

38. Cf. *ibid.*, p. 108, and W. H. Auden's "Introduction" to *Edgar Allan Poe: Selected Prose and Poetry* (New York, 1950), p. vii.

39. *Pym*, says D. E. S. Maxwell, "advances the characters—in particular, Pym—through a series of situations the point of which is to emphasise their discontinuity, or, more accurately, that the only consistency in human behaviour is its compulsive liability to evil and to the irrational; and in the personality that it is fissile" (*American Fiction: The Intellectual Background* [London, 1963], p. 94). Maxwell offers an interesting general discussion of *Pym* and Poe's romanticism.

bright side of life—until that brightness itself becomes the crowning horror of ambiguity.

Pym's initiation into experiences that should teach him a lesson about the deceptiveness of appearances and his own capacity for doubleness begins at the very outset of the tale in an episode that epitomizes the whole narrative. Awakened from sleep by his friend Augustus Barnard, with whom he has been spending the night after both had gotten slightly tipsy at a drinking party, Pym is amazed to hear Augustus proposing a midnight sail. He is disposed to think his friend drunk, but Augustus "proceeded to talk very coolly . . . saying he knew that I supposed him intoxicated, but that he was never more sober in his life." Thoroughly convinced by his friend's lucidity and air of certainty, Pym agrees to the sail, but they are scarcely out to sea before he begins to understand that things are not what they seem. "In spite of his assumed nonchalance, he [Augustus] was greatly agitated," and soon the horrible truth dawns on Poe's hero: "He was drunk—beastly drunk—he could no longer either stand, speak, or see. His eyes were perfectly glazed; and as I let him go in the extremity of my despair, he rolled like a mere log into the bilge-water." The older and more experienced Augustus, Pym's guide and protector, proves utterly unreliable, and Pym notes—in a sentence that beautifully defines our own relation to so many of Poe's narrators—that he had been taken in by his friend's "highly-concentrated state of intoxication; a state which, like madness, frequently enables the victim to imitate the outward demeanor of one in perfect possession of his senses."

Augustus, of course, had no intention of consciously deceiving his friend, and is himself as much a victim as Pym of the deception that brings both close to death. But the episode is an ominous adumbration of that suggestion of universal trickery and delusion that increasingly pervades Poe's *Narrative*.[40] Indeed, the first chapter ends on a note of willful fraud, as Pym explains how he and Augustus succeeded in returning home after their desperate experience without creating any suspicion. "Schoolboys," Pym concludes innocently, "can accomplish wonders in the way of deception." If Poe is here trying to undercut the serious implications of his theme by allowing Pym to reduce a suggestion of radical human duplicity to the level of a classroom prank, the device is not

---

40. Cf. Patrick F. Quinn, "Poe's Imaginary Voyage," *Hudson Review*, IV (1952), 564–565, and Davidson, *Poe: A Critical Study*, p. 164.

convincing. In the next chapter Pym describes matter-of-factly the "scheme of deception" whereby he was enabled, through practicing "intense hypocrisy . . . an hypocrisy pervading every word and action of my life for so long a period of time," to bring off his plan of escaping to a life of adventure. But he cannot finally overlook the ominous implications of his actions: "I have since frequently examined my conduct on this occasion with sentiments of displeasure as well as of surprise"— surprise, apparently, at his own capacity for deceit, and displeasure at discovering that capacity within himself.

If the episode aboard the Ariel with Augustus is meant as a warning to Pym, it is largely lost, for he has the happy ability to protect himself by shrugging off memories of the unpleasant. The experience introduces him to the utmost extremes of emotion, from a "thrill of the greatest excitement and pleasure" and "a kind of ecstasy" to the "extremity" of terror: "Never while I live shall I forget the intense agony of terror I experienced. . . . My hair stood erect on my head—I felt the blood congealing in my veins—my heart ceased utterly to beat." And Pym tells us that when he and Augustus later discussed the adventure, it was "never without a shudder." But within a week Pym longs ardently for the "wild adventures" of a navigator's life, explaining that "this short period proved amply long enough to erase from my memory the shadows, and bring out in vivid light all the pleasurably exciting points of color, all the picturesqueness, of the late perilous accident."

Pym can still incorporate the dark hints of human ambivalence into the over-all light of a civilized eighteenth-century taste for the "picturesque." When he speaks here of that "melancholy" and "enthusiastic temperament and somewhat gloomy, although glowing imagination" that enable him to revel in "visions . . . of shipwreck and famine; of death or captivity among barbarian hordes; of a lifetime dragged out in sorrow and tears, upon some gray and desolate rock, in an ocean unapproachable and unknown," his "visions or desires" are little more than the expression of a taste for a varied canvas. "For the bright side of the painting I had a limited sympathy," he explains. It is painful experience rendered safe by aesthetic distance that Pym longs for (the kind of "tragedy" enjoyed by Tom Sawyer when he returns from Jackson's Island to view his own funeral). Like the narrator's friend Ellison in "The Domain of Arnheim," who "refuted the dogma, that in man's very nature lies some hidden principle, the antagonist of bliss," and yet incorporated in his Paradise of Arnheim a chasm with "an air of funereal gloom" and "an exquisite sense of the strange" to gratify safely that very "hidden principle," Pym both believes and refuses to believe seriously in his capacity and stated desire for "suffering and despair." Later on, when the romance world into which Poe introduces him becomes not a picture to contemplate but a life to live, Pym demonstrates his own paradoxes more convincingly. Hanging from a cliff in Tsalal, he finds it impossible to follow his better judgment and keep from looking into the abyss, whereupon his terror at the danger is converted into "*a longing to fall; a desire, a yearning, a passion utterly uncontrollable.*"

Increasingly, Pym becomes a credible representative of human ambivalence and self-deception. Dying of hunger on the hulk of the wrecked brig Grampus along with Augustus, Peters, and Parker, Pym is so shocked and horrified at Parker's suggestion that they draw lots and descend to cannibalism that he immediately attempts to throw Parker overboard, having already decided resolutely "to suffer death in any shape or under any circumstances rather than resort to such a course." Before long, however, he sits down with Peters and Augustus to engage in the "exquisite horror" of a "fearful repast" upon the body of Parker:

> Having in some measure appeased the raging thirst which consumed us by the blood of the victim, and having by common consent taken off the hands, feet, and head, throwing them, together with the entrails, into the sea, we devoured the rest of the body, piecemeal, during the four ever memorable days of the seventeenth, eighteenth, nineteenth, and twentieth of the month.

This experience of his own capacity for savagery and violence (at the moment of drawing lots, Pym tells us, "all the fierceness of the tiger possessed my bosom, and I felt towards my poor fellow-creature, Parker, the most intense, the most diabolical hatred"), which Pym assures us "no after events have been able to efface in the slightest degree" from his memory and "whose stern recollection will embitter every future moment" of his existence, has presumably permanently darkened and deepened his knowledge of universal human nature. Like Conrad's Marlow with his awareness of Kurtz, we expect Pym to be incapable henceforth of self-righteously distinguishing between civilized and primitive humanity. But Pym's memory is short. After his adventures on Tsalal, he declares the natives there "to be the most wicked, hypocritical, vindictive, bloodthirsty, and altogether fiendish race of men upon the face of the globe"![41]

Like the narrator of "The Fall of the House of Usher," Pym has a deep need to believe that his own essential nature is characterized by sweet reasonableness and that the universe, as the handiwork of a rational creator, is ultimately explicable. Introduced by Poe into a world where sinister ambiguities lurk everywhere, Pym tries desperately to bring everything within the purview of civilized reason. Trapped in the hold of the Grampus, for example, he is overjoyed to discover the presence of his trusty dog (ominously named Tiger). "Most people love their dogs," Pym gushes securely, "but for Tiger I had an affection far more ardent than common; and never, certainly, did any creature more truly deserve it." Yet before long the cherished and dependable Newfoundland has turned into a true beast of the jungle, whose "eyeballs flashing fiercely through the gloom . . . with an expression of the most deadly animosity" convert into terrible reality Pym's earlier dream of being attacked by "a fierce lion of the tropics" with "horrible teeth" and "a roar like the thunder of the firmament." Luckily saved from this experience of animal ferocity, Pym has also to protect himself from the perhaps more serious danger of being forced to conclude that his beloved pet has a primitive nature unfathomed by its master. "His strange conduct," Pym insists, "had been brought on, no doubt, by the deleterious quality of the air of the hold, and had no connection with canine madness."

Other fundamentally inexplicable oddities surround Pym. The "ferocious-looking" line-manager Dirk Peters, whose animal appearance is rendered more terrible by thin lips fixed permanently in an ear-to-ear smile that suggests only "the merriment . . . of a demon," turns out to be Pym's savior. Such a human paradox, Pym admits, goes "so far beyond the limits of human credulity" that he can only trust confidently "in time and progressing science" to explain this and other improbabilities.

---

41. Edwin Fussell remarks that "so far as deception, treachery, and pointless butchery are concerned, the white man is in every respect" equal to the savage in *Pym* (*Frontier: American Literature and the American West*, pp. 154–155). And D. E. S. Maxwell notes: "Pym expresses horror and disgust at some of the actions in the novel. The appropriate conventional judgments on cruelty and wrongdoing are thus given place. But the real interest is not that these actions are reprehensible but that they happen and that their occurrence is unpredictable: it is the 'sympathetic' characters, not the villainous mutineers, who eat human flesh" (*American Fiction: The Intellectual Background*, p. 94).

A far more ghastly paradox, in which delight is turned to horror and hope to despair, is presented to Pym and his fellow survivors by the arrival of an apparent savior ship that turns out to be a ship of death. What seems to be a friendly sailor, cheerfully and encouragingly nodding "and smiling constantly, so as to display a set of the most brilliantly white teeth," is discovered to be a rotting corpse, its smile a nightmare horror of missing lips. On the cadaver's back, "from which a portion of the shirt had been torn, leaving it bare, there sat a huge seagull, busily gorging itself with the horrible flesh, its bill and talons deep buried, and its white plumage spattered all over with blood." The bird, which flies over the Grampus with a "horrid morsel," seemingly inviting Parker to enjoy his first cannibal meal, becomes in the *Narrative* a symbol of deep ambiguity in nature. But to Pym the whole experience is only a "hideous uncertainty," which he attempts frantically and vainly to reduce to comprehensibility. Refusing to accept the awful suggestion of some diabolic visitation, he searches for a logical possibility that will allay his anxiety:

> From the saffron-like hue of such of the corpses as were not entirely decayed, we concluded that the whole of her company had perished by the yellow fever, or some other virulent disease of the same fearful kind. If such were the case (and I know not what else to imagine), death, to judge from the positions of the bodies, must have come upon them in a manner awfully sudden and overwhelming, in a way totally distinct from that which generally characterizes even the most deadly pestilences with which mankind are acquainted.

From such palpable contradictions Pym moves on to grasp at the notion "that poison, accidentally introduced into some of their sea-stores . . . or that the eating some unknown venomous species of fish, or other marine animal, or oceanic bird," might have brought about the tragedy. But his reason is ultimately faced with a blank wall. Pym admits that his conjecturing is "utterly useless . . . where all is involved, and will no doubt remain for ever involved, in the most appalling and unfathomable mystery."

As a central emblem of that appalling mystery inherent in all things which persistently and increasingly denies Pym's rational expectations, Poe employs the ambiguous white-black symbolism that Melville was to inflate to leviathan proportions. Unlike his insatiable fellow romancer, however, who even contemplated moving on to a kraken, Poe—at least until we reach that oversize abominable snowman at the end of the

Narrative—contents himself with a penguin.[42] Once again, the author foreshadows for us in the opening chapter an element of his tale that is to receive extended treatment later on. Thrown from the Ariel by its collision with a whaling ship, the Penguin, Pym is rescued from certain death in a manner whose gross improbability can only be justified by Poe's need to introduce symbolic implications. Impaled by a stray timber-bolt to the "smooth and shining bottom" of the very ship that has run him down, Pym is at once cruelly wounded and saved. The Penguin, with its "coppered and copper-fastened" hull, is thus an ambiguous benefactor, and looks forward directly to Poe's description of the royal penguin, with its "broad stripes of a gold color, which pass along from the head to the breast."

Like the ship which shares its name and duplexity of meaning, the penguin is a symbol of radical ambiguousness in nature, a compound of "the purest white imaginable" and the "most brilliant black." Poe elaborately draws out the perplexing implications of the penguin in the course of a long, detailed description of South Sea "rookeries"—those shared nests "constructed with great uniformity upon a plan concerted between . . . two species" of sea birds. The albatross, we are told, "is one of the largest and fiercest of the South Sea birds . . . of the gull species," yet "between this bird and the penguin the most singular friendship exists." As if to imply a sinister master plan in nature, a plan rendered more ominous by suggestions of universal deception (the words "gull" and "rookery" are themselves hints), Poe describes how "with one accord, and actuated apparently by one mind," the birds build and live together peaceably in their common homes, in which however some "precaution is rendered necessary by the thievish propensities prevalent." He clearly means for the reader to puzzle over the implications of this curious friendship between the "savior" penguin—whose "resemblance to a human figure is very striking, and would be apt to deceive the spectator at a casual glance"—and the ravening albatross.

Pym himself is content to sum things up with Augustan sententiousness and complacency: "In short, survey it as we will, nothing can be more astonishing than the spirit of reflection evinced by these feathered beings, and nothing surely can be better calculated to elicit reflection in every well-regulated human intellect." Poe's irony was never more

---

42. Poe's penguin, to be sure, is king-size! Melville's remark was made to Hawthorne after the completion of *Moby-Dick:* "Leviathan is not the biggest fish;—I have heard of Krakens."

thickly applied. The "reflection" elicited by the description of the rookery is much darker than what appears in Pym's well-regulated intellect: man is saved by the penguin only to be eaten by the gull. As a final turn of the screw, Pym informs us when he gets to Tsalal that he and his companions were astonished to see "black albatross . . . in a state of entire domestication, going to sea periodically for food, but always returning to the village as a home." In the realm of ultimate paradox, where all color values are reversed, ambiguity itself comes home to roost.

As he travels further and further into the world of romance, Pym tries hard, and without much success, to hold tight to all the familiar methods of measurement and control—the metaphors of his reason. He is determined to keep track of time, but his watch repeatedly runs down, and he ultimately ceases to be able to tell day from night or to keep an accurate record of dates and positions. He fervently believes that any vessel is safe, even in a storm, "*provided there be a proper stowage*," but the Grampus is clumsily stowed and he is capsized. (Poe's metaphoric undertone here suggests that it is precisely the *inner* life that is dangerous and finally betrays.) "A bright spot to the southward," Pym assures us in a discussion of the weather, "is the sure forerunner of . . . change, and vessels are thus enabled to take proper precautions." But that "luminous glare" (a kind of Miltonic darkness visible) which lures Pym on to the conclusion of his voyage is the sure sign only of a permanent change to eternal horror— the forerunner of that climax of terror which awaits the adventurer in his embrace with the gigantic "shrouded human figure" at the end.

And there are no precautions to be taken. The irrational steadily and inexorably pushes in on Pym. Although he tries to think of his dreadful experiences "rather as a frightful dream from which we had been happily awakened, than as events which had taken place in sober and naked reality," his worst dreams consistently blend with real events.[43] Indeed, he is simply discovering that his own desert places have a terrific reality that cannot be denied, as when, impersonating the ghost of the dead sailor Rogers, Pym is "so impressed with a sense of vague awe" at his own appearance that he is "seized with a violent tremor" and can "scarcely summon resolution to go on."

Ultimately Pym's ontogenic voyage to primitive lands and beyond

---

43. An interesting treatment of *Pym* as dream fantasy is Walter E. Bezanson, "The Troubled Sleep of Arthur Gordon Pym," in *Essays in Literary History Presented to J. Milton French*, edited by Rudolf Kirk and C. F. Main (New Brunswick, N. J., 1960), pp. 149–175.

suggests a phylogenic voyage to the past of mankind, a journey to the beginning of consciousness and to that core of fear at the heart of the interior self. From the restraints of the modern world Pym journeys back to absolute freedom and seemingly to non-being, as omnipotent primitive fantasies finally overwhelm his frail reason.[44] It is hard to keep one's allegoric imagination from running away with Poe's *Narrative:* as Pym flees from his hysterical mother to an all-encompassing whiteness, he almost seems to represent an archetypal son growing into a doomed producer of spermatozoa destined to be devoured by the ovum, his tale a fable of expulsion from the safe (or is it threatening?) dark womb into a bright but threatening (or is it really safe?) world.[45] Looked at in another way, Pym's voyage, as some commentators have argued, seems a political allegory representing a journey into a white South, where black men die of fear and the great white father is an ogre even to whites.[46]

But *The Narrative of Arthur Gordon Pym* finally defies circumscription of meaning, demonstrating how in Poe's hands the romance of New World adventure could become an illimitable allegory of self-exploration[47]—a symbolic journey that ends only because it is truncated and that issues, not in the expected self-knowledge, but in an apocalypse of cosmic mystery.

---

44. "If Pym's quest is for selfhood, for first principles and primal being, it is also a moving backward through the natural order as it presently exists and into the world's original condition, as primal first cause. . . . The quest for self-knowledge [leads] backward through natural forms and downward through historical and archaeological time" (Davidson, *Poe: A Critical Study*, pp. 178–179).

45. On the ending of *Pym*, Walter E. Bezanson writes: "Home to mother through a warm cosmic milk bath, one has to say, savoring the apocalyptic comedy to its full. Or, if one prefers older conventions, welcomed into his dream of oblivion by the White Goddess" ("The Troubled Sleep of Arthur Gordon Pym," p. 173). Cf. Leslie Fiedler, *Love and Death in the American Novel*, p. 381.

46. On the anti-Negro aspect of the ending, see Harry Levin, *The Power of Blackness*, pp. 120–123, and Sidney Kaplan, "An Introduction to *Pym*," in *Poe: A Collection of Critical Essays*, p. 161. Cf. Fiedler, pp. 380–382.

47. We thought "we were going to see the world; and yet it is the heart of man, that heart tormented and obscure, which lies at the center of it all. *The Narrative* . . . is one of the great books of the human heart," says Gaston Bachelard. (Quoted in Patrick F. Quinn, "Poe's Imaginary Voyage," p. 576.)

III

HAWTHORNE

1. *In Search of the Buried Life*

It is no exaggeration to say that without Hawthorne there could be no firm theory of American romance. For that theory rests most securely upon the gently ironic (at once serious and apologetic) prefaces in which Hawthorne tried both to explain and to argue for his own kind of writing—and, as it turns out, for a genre that subsumes much important nineteenth-century American fiction.[1]

The romance, Hawthorne insisted repeatedly, is radically different from the novel in not concerning itself with the possible, probable, or ordinary course of experience. It is not an imitation of nature, as nature generally appears, but an exposure of the "truth of the human heart." And this truth, as Poe argued, too terrible, too elusive, too strange to be captured by the ordinary methods of truth-telling, requires a kind of "*Kabbala*" for its portrayal. Poe's interest in those "psychal fancies" that belong to the realm "where the confines of the waking world blend with those of the world of dreams" is precisely analogous to Hawthorne's consistently expressed concern with that "neutral territory, somewhere between the real world and fairy-land, where the Actual and the Imaginary" meet and cross-fertilize one another, actual experience providing material for fantasy and fantasy exposing the hidden truth lurking in actual experience. It is the realm in which "fancy-pictures," creatures of the brain, and other "strange things" play "phantasmagorical antics" in "a sort of poetic or fairy precinct," where truth otherwise unavailable

---

1. See Jesse Bier, "Hawthorne on the Romance: His Prefaces Related and Examined," *Modern Philology*, LIII (1955), 17–24.

to daylight reason is represented obliquely in a kind of symbolic magic-lantern show.

The romancer's precinct is thus frequently that of daydream and nightmare, fantasy and revery, where things only "look like truth"—that is, are only partially connected to the world as we know it publicly—because they shadow forth that world as it would look if it were acting out its own inner meaning. Things in the romancer's world "have a propriety of their own," since everything there is "essentially a day-dream, and yet a fact"—both fanciful and meaningful. And the romancer is necessarily committed to a fictional world that is stylized and exaggerated, a world where human actions and events are heightened for the sake of "improved effects," namely, the representation of interior or ulterior significance. Like every man in his dreams, Hawthorne is an allegorist, dealing, not in the fixed meanings of a Spenser or a Bunyan, but in the myriad references of a modern symbolic author. Vis-à-vis the actual world, Hawthorne's art may sometimes seem false, but it is *always* true.

It is worth recalling that Hawthorne entitled or subtitled all of his four major fictions *romances*, and that his attempts to describe this special fictional entity center not only in discussions about a particular kind of treatment but also in a persistent association of the romance with certain themes. Chief among these (this is surely what Melville was referring to when he identified the "wondrous effects" of Hawthorne's romance art with the idea of "Puritanic gloom"—a "Calvinistic sense of Innate Depravity and Original Sin") is the notion of the continuing force of past experience, especially guilty or sinful experience, in the life of the present. "Romance and poetry," Hawthorne suggests in the preface to *The Marble Faun*, "like ivy, lichens, and wall-flowers, need ruin to make them grow." Romance battens on past or submerged suffering because to the present reason such experience seems as fabulous as romance. The task of re-evoking the reality of past pain, "the attempt to connect a by-gone time with the very Present that is flitting away from us," is one with the romancer's task of trying to convince us that his art has validity. In all of Hawthorne's romances, the problems of art and the problem of past suffering or guilt are commingled themes. The protagonists of Hawthorne's romances are all, in some sense, artists; and they are all concerned with *la recherche des peines perdues* and the possibility—or desirability—of making a fresh start. It is as if Hawthorne were saying that every man, when he attempts to confront his secret self, duplicates the experience of the romancer or, rather, composes the romance of his own being.[2]

Romance art for Hawthorne is not just one way of looking *at* experience; it is a metaphor for a particular kind of experience. The question of romance versus novel turns into and illuminates a moral question: the meaning and value of the inner life. Thus Henry James's celebrated comment—"The fine thing in Hawthorne is that he cared for the deeper psychology, and that, in his way, he tried to become familiar with it"— can be taken as an expression of Hawthorne's truly Jamesian concern with form if we only, as Hawthorne invites us to do, substitute "art" for "psychology." The American romancer's concern with the deeper art is synonymous with his search for the buried life; and he is of necessity an evoker of ghosts and a resurrector of dead bodies. Emerson's continual cry for release from the dead hand of the past could only elicit an ambivalent response from his fellow Concordian, who fervently shared the desire to be freed of the burden of memory, yet firmly believed that even a young country—or a young man—has a history it cannot shake. "Emerson, as a sort of spiritual sun-worshiper," James remarks, "could have attached but a moderate value to Hawthorne's catlike faculty of seeing in the dark." At a time when many literary watchmen were jubilantly reporting that "the morning cometh," it was Hawthorne's melancholy duty to add, "and also the night," offering his sombre romancer's depth as spiritual ballast for what so confirmed a novelist as Howells would call the "smiling aspects" of American life.[3] In an age when (as Perry Miller has remarked[4]) art, at least in New England, was in many ways

2. "Romance is a way of knowing and feeling, of realizing, the human situation," writes Roy Harvey Pearce ("Hawthorne and the Twilight of Romance," *Yale Review*, XXXVII [1948], 491).

3. I do not mean to imply in any way that Howells disapproved of Hawthorne's method or of the romance generally as a serious form. Indeed, Louis J. Budd has demonstrated clearly that Howells had a lasting love for Hawthorne's work and insisted on differentiating between "romantic" and "romanticistic" writing. "The romance," Howells wrote, "—which is not at all the romantic novel—has just as good right to be as the realistic novel, because it is just as true in its kind" ("W. D. Howells' Defense of the Romance," *PMLA*, LXVII [1952], 36).

4. Cf. *The Transcendentalists: An Anthology*, edited by Perry Miller (Cambridge, Mass., 1950), p. 9.

forced to take over the function of religion, it seems almost that Hawthorne felt constrained in his own dark scriptures to remind his countrymen that they had a soul.

2. *The Dark Blossom of Romance*

LIKE the introductory note to *The Narrative of Arthur Gordon Pym*, the "Custom-House" sketch which precedes *The Scarlet Letter* is partly a familiar romancer's device—an attempt to justify the fantastic materials that follow, and to relate them to normal experience, by establishing their provenience in the real world. The sketch, Hawthorne insists, "has a certain propriety, of a kind always recognized in literature, as explaining how a large portion of the following pages came into my possession, and as offering proofs of the authenticity of a narrative therein contained." As Leslie Fiedler remarks, however, Hawthorne's introduction is really an "apology" for the moonshiny romance art that he practiced.[5] But one should add that the sketch is also an apology in the more positive, traditional sense. It is Hawthorne's attempt to explain the real sources and value of his kind of writing: romance grows out of dark meditations on guilt, sin, suffering—passionate experience of all kinds—and its value lies precisely in its ability to bring out of the shadows and make available for use those ordinarily shunned emotions that deepen and humanize us.

Fiedler notes shrewdly that Hawthorne, like his heroine Hester, also embroiders a scarlet letter—that his art involves (shamefully, as Fiedler sees Hawthorne's relation to his work) the same "adornment of guilt by craft." A more sympathetic view, however, may help us understand why Hawthorne covertly but clearly parallels his own case with that of his protagonist. Without "guilt" there can be no "craft," but the avenue to insight about the human condition ultimately opened up by the artist's work finally justifies both that work and the normally forbidden or avoided experiences that provoked it. All the major characters in *The Scarlet Letter*, including Hawthorne himself, aspire to the condition of the romancer—a position of spiritual depth and understanding earned through sympathy with or experience of pain. The price of attaining such a bad

---

5. For Fiedler's discussion, see *Love and Death in the American Novel* (New York, 1960), pp. 485 ff.

eminence is worldly danger: "decapitation" for Hawthorne when he is removed as Surveyor of the Customs and thus permitted to return to writing, or pariahdom for Hester, the hated and feared dark lady as sinner-artist. *The Scarlet Letter*, in short, can be read as an allegory of art.[6]

Hawthorne's meditation on his Puritan ancestors in "The Custom-House" is rich with implications that link it to the tale proper and to the question of artistic inspiration.[7] "Sable-cloaked" and "conspicuous in the martyrdom of the witches," whose "blood may fairly be said to have left a stain upon" them all, they are perfect emblematic parallels to Hester Prynne, with her scarlet letter set against a dress of "most sombre hue." They were sinners like Hester—Hawthorne clearly implies that their sins were at least as bad as hers—and bequeathed to their descendant, by virtue of their participation in the crimson crime of passionate persecution, a capacity for insight into the darkest human emotions. Hawthorne takes their "shame" upon himself; and his work is indeed "sufficient retribution" for their sins, both a recompense for and a result of their actions, precisely as Hester's expiatory needlework owes its very existence to "the passion of her life." "Let them scorn me as they will," Hawthorne says of his ancestors' probable attitude toward his profession, "strong traits of their nature have intertwined themselves with mine."

Since his power as a romancer is based on the awful past of his forebears, Hawthorne is constrained to accept the "doom" of seeing Salem, the town where his race enacted their painful history, as "the inevitable centre of the universe." This "home-feeling with the past" that enables him to be an artist—this "sensuous sympathy of dust for dust"—he considers to be a hard destiny reserved only for the artist. "Few of my coun-

---

6. "To relate the pattern of Hawthorne's life to the attitudes and actions of the characters in the novel is to discover that they represent different sides of his own personality. Through them he explores the necessity of Art as a way of expiating his feeling of guilt towards his Past. . . . *The Scarlet Letter*, seen in terms of the function of Art, appears to be the pivotal writing of Hawthorne's career," says John E. Hart ("*The Scarlet Letter*: One Hundred Years After," *New England Quarterly*, XXIII [1950], 381, 383). See also Rudolph Von Abele, *The Death of the Artist* (The Hague, 1955), p. 52, and Roy R. Male, *Hawthorne's Tragic Vision* (New York, 1964), pp. 102 ff.

7. Parallels between Hawthorne's own plight and that of his characters are discussed in Frank McShane, "The House of the Dead: Hawthorne's Custom House and *The Scarlet Letter*," *New England Quarterly*, XXXV (1962), 93–101. Cf. Charles Feidelson, Jr., *Symbolism and American Literature* (Chicago, 1953), p. 10.

trymen can know what it is; nor . . . need they consider it desirable to know." He alone must live with and make art out of his race's guilt, although he hopes that his children "shall strike their roots into unaccustomed earth"; for his counterpart-protagonist Hester Prynne, "there was a more real life . . . in New England, than in that unknown region where Pearl had found a home." Hawthorne can never really leave Salem, just as Hester can never quit the Boston of her tale, because the strength of the romance artist is based on his reviving and coming to terms with past pain.

That it is Hawthorne's function to reanimate and, if possible, cast a magic spell around the past is made abundantly clear throughout the introductory sketch. As the new Surveyor of the Custom-House, it was to be supposed that Hawthorne, a Democrat, would want to dispose of the Whig influence embodied in the aged officers formerly in control by bringing "every one of those white heads under the axe of the guillotine." But the new chief of revenues, as a romancer, was an arch-conservative. He bent his efforts toward drawing out the tragic histories of his fellow officials. Some of his human material, however, was utterly intractable. One Old Inspector—whose "three wives, all long since dead," and "twenty children, most of whom, at every age of childhood or maturity, had likewise returned to dust," should have provided "sorrow enough to imbue the sunniest disposition, through and through, with a sable tinge"—turned out to possess "no power of thought, no depth of feeling, no troublesome sensibilities." His remarkable memory for the past is limited to recalling "the ghosts of bygone meals," which rose before him "not in anger or retribution, but as if grateful for his former appreciation":

> A tenderloin of beef, a hind-quarter of veal, a spare-rib of pork, a particular chicken, or a remarkably praiseworthy turkey, which had perhaps adorned his board in the days of the elder Adams, would be remembered; while all the subsequent experience of our race, and all the events that brightened or darkened his individual career, had gone over him with as little permanent effect as the passing breeze.

Hawthorne discovers that "the chief tragic event" of the Old Inspector's life was a certain tough goose that defied the carving-knife. Another important functionary is "a man of business; prompt, acute, clear-minded," with a head so perfectly adapted to his profession that Hawthorne calls him "the Custom-House in himself." The very reverse of the romancer, with his "magic moonshine" cast over the permanent darkness of past sorrow, this man's "merest touch" makes "the incomprehensible as clear as daylight," and he would regard "a stain on his conscience" as little more than a removable "ink-blot on the fair page of a book of record."

Only one of the inmates of the Custom-House, the Collector, "our gallant old General," truly stirs Hawthorne's romance imagination. Rich in memories of heroic suffering, the old General seems to Hawthorne's fancy still capable, "under some excitement which should go deeply into his consciousness,—roused by a trumpet-peal, loud enough to awaken all of his energies that were not dead, but only slumbering," of coming impressively to life. And in an extended simile (looking forward to the sentence already quoted from *The Marble Faun*—"Romance and poetry, ivy, lichens, and wall-flowers, need ruin to make them grow") that likens the noble old warrior to the blasted Fort Ticonderoga, Hawthorne makes important metaphoric connections among romance, blossoms, and human ruin. The "sounds and circumstances [of the Custom-House] seemed but indistinctly to impress" the Collector "and hardly to make their way into his inner sphere of contemplation," and he "lived a more real life within his thoughts, than amid the unappropriate environment of the Collector's office." If, accordingly, in his inwardness and devotion to the past he seems the type of the romancer,[8] in his very being he almost appears to be an emblem of romance itself:

> To observe and define his character . . . was as difficult a task as to trace out and build up anew, in imagination, an old fortress, like Ticonderoga, from a view of its gray and broken ruins. . . . Many characteristics—and those, too, which contribute not the least forcibly to impart resemblance in a sketch—must have vanished, or been obscured.

Moreover, nature does not "adorn the human ruin with blossoms of new beauty, that have their roots and proper nutriment only in the chinks and crevices of decay, as she sows wall-flowers over the ruined fortress of Ticonderoga." The floral ornaments to be seen on the Collector are no more than metaphoric: "the bloody laurel on his brow" and the "grass

---

8. McShane (p. 100) stresses the importance of the contrasting portraits of the gourmand and the old General, who "represents the human element—that understanding of the human heart that Hawthorne wished to have."

and alien weeds" of solitude and neglect. By implication, the only true "flower" that blooms out of human ruin is that provided by the imagination of the artist. Romance is the dark blossom that flourishes on the tomb of human experience.

In the second story of the Custom-House, Hawthorne discovered that "the past was not dead" when he came across a document—"the corpse of dead activity"—that needed only his magic touch to bring it back to life. His characters "retained all the rigidity of dead corpses" as long as he was enslaved to the drudgery of the Surveyorship, but once he was released, Hawthorne could force his "rag of scarlet cloth" to open into the exotic blossom of *The Scarlet Letter*. If that plant is not the "sweet moral blossom" that the author ironically presents to the reader in the first chapter of his tale, it is because the whole narrative, as Hawthorne tells us in the same chapter, issues from the "inauspicious portal" of the prison—"the black flower of civilized society." Moving from the prison to the cemetery (sin and death providing the necessary frame for Hawthorne's art), the romance may be seen metaphorically as springing from a "black flower" and growing into another dark ornament, that heraldic device on Hester's tomb which indeed "might serve for a motto and brief description," not only of Hawthorne's "concluded legend," but of his romance art in general, "so sombre is it, and relieved only by one ever-glowing point of light gloomier than the shadow:—'ON A FIELD, SABLE, THE LETTER A, GULES.'"

Set against a background of darkness, the art of the romancer is that even darker growth that springs from and illuminates the shadows. As Roger Chillingworth explains knowingly, the "germ of evil" brings forth a "dark necessity": that "typical illusion," or symbolic fantasy, which is the romance itself. "Let the black flower blossom as it may!" Yet none of the characters in the tale are really "sinful," as Chillingworth himself admits. It is not Hawthorne's purpose in *The Scarlet Letter* to assign blame, but rather to illustrate the process by which past pain and secret suffering flower into moral truth. For individual figures, that process is always analogous to the growth of consciousness in the romance artist.

In a remarkable insight underlying much of his work and clearly anticipating Freud's notions, not only of the sources of art in general, but more particularly of those dreams and fantasies which are the type of romance, Hawthorne suggests that there is a connection between "sin" (by which he means sexual knowledge and passion) and artistic understanding and power. In our sexual past or present, Hawthorne seems to say, lies our artistic—indeed, our human—future. Of this proposition *The Scarlet Letter* is a continual illustration, as if the tale had been designed to symbolize the theory that lies behind it, both form *and* theme thus being "the romance."

Hester Prynne is clearly the type of the artist; and if her art is limited to needlework it is only because (as Hawthorne somewhat incredibly insists) "it was the art—then, as now, almost the only one within a woman's grasp." The main embodiment, of course, of Hester's "rich, voluptuous, Oriental characteristic,—a taste for the gorgeously beautiful," is that very scarlet letter, "so artistically done, and with so much fertility and gorgeous luxuriance of fancy," that becomes Hawthorne's "mystic symbol"—Hester's art of the needle turned art of the romance. Not only do Hawthorne's adjectives suggest that Hester's "voluptuousness" has issued in art; we are told explicitly that her needlework was "a mode of expressing, and therefore soothing, the passion of her life." The letter itself, the talisman of art, "transfigured the wearer. . . . It had the effect of a spell, taking her out of the ordinary relations with humanity, and inclosing her in a sphere by herself." Thrown away in that moment in the forest when Hester attempts the impossible—to cast off the doom of being an artist and return to simple womanhood—the "mystic token" is described in terms suggestive of romance art itself: "some ill-fated wanderer might pick it up, and thenceforth be haunted by strange phantoms of guilt." By the end of Hester's life, the letter comes to be regarded with that "awe" and "reverence" ultimately due to the truth and power of art.

As a sinner Hester is set off from the rest of the world precisely as is the artist, and Hawthorne describes her in terms he often used for describing himself, confessionally or fictitiously:

> In all her intercourse with society . . . there was nothing that made her feel as if she belonged to it. Every gesture, every word, and even the silence of those with whom she came in contact, implied, and often expressed, that she was banished, and as much alone as if she inhabited another sphere, or communicated with the common nature by other organs and senses than the rest of human kind. She stood apart from mortal interests, yet close beside them.

The scarlet letter, symbol and embodiment of both her sin and her art, "endowed her with a new sense . . . . a sympathetic knowledge of the hidden sin in other hearts." The secret truth about venerable ministers and righteous magistrates, chaste matrons and virginal maidens, is known to Hester. And Hawthorne, leaning heavily on the archetypal associations of the dark lady's sexuality with intellect and ultimately with art, makes it clear that her sexual experiences have increased those speculative powers that are necessary for the true artist. To be sure, Hawthorne hints first at a theory of sublimation, insisting that it was *because* the normal expression of passion had for so long been denied her that she turned from feeling to thought, assuming "a freedom of speculation . . . which our forefathers, had they known of it, would have held to be a deadlier crime than that stigmatized by the scarlet letter." But Hester's two "crimes"—intellectual freedom and sexual experience—are necessarily stigmatized by the same symbol, as any New England forefather would have known, since Adam fell simultaneously into both sexual awareness and that burdensome knowledge which brought literature, as well as death, into the world.

Hawthorne finally makes manifest the vital connection between the initial release of Hester's sexuality and the subsequent flourishing of her artistic power and understanding. "The scarlet letter was her passport into regions where other women dared not tread." Hester's "lawless passion" has turned her into a kind of white Indian, and she becomes in Hawthorne's mind a focus for all those associations of knowledge with sexual power which we have already observed in Cooper's mythic red men and dark ladies:

> Her intellect and heart had their home, as it were, in desert places, where she roamed as freely as the wild Indian in his woods. For years past she had looked from this estranged point of view at human institutions, and whatever priests or legislators had established; criticizing all with hardly more reverence than the Indian would feel for the clerical band, the judicial robe, the pillory, the gallows, the fireside, or the church. The tendency of her fate and fortunes had been to set her free.

Like the Promethean archetype of the artist, Hester uses her freedom to become the benefactor of mankind, through her offer of artistic skill and the sympathy and understanding of her "warm and rich" nature. Throughout, Hawthorne makes it plain that her "well-spring of human tenderness" is fed by the subterranean river of barely submerged sexual passion. Or, to return to our original figure, "her sin, her ignominy, were the roots which she had struck into the soil," and the valuable—if dark—fruit of that buried "evil" is *The Scarlet Letter*.

As a corollary to Hester's position, we should note that by metaphoric implication and symbolic suggestion Pearl—the object of great price purchased by her mother's sexuality—comes to stand for that romance art which has the truth of secret human passion as its basis. Plucked by her mother, as Pearl herself insists, from the wild-rose bush growing in front of the prison, the "little creature" is described by Hawthorne as "a lovely and immortal flower" which had sprung "out of the rank luxuriance of a guilty passion." Nevertheless—and Hawthorne here exposes his own ambivalent attitude toward the curious romance art he practices—she is also "an imp of evil, emblem and product of sin." As she grows, her mother watches her carefully, "ever dreading to detect some dark and wild peculiarity, that should correspond with the guiltiness to which she owed her being." But the romance rarely reflects directly the obscure emotions to which it owes its being; these are perhaps manifested only as that "spell of infinite variety" and "trait of passion, a certain depth of hue," characteristic of the art. Pearl is indeed *The Scarlet Letter* "endowed with life."

As Hawthorne protracts his description of the child, he seems to be commenting, to some extent consciously, on his own difficult art, observed from the viewpoint of that world of novelistic verisimilitude whose rules of decorum he was painfully aware of violating:

> Her nature appeared to possess depth . . . as well as variety; but . . . it lacked reference and adaptation to the world into which she was born. The child could not be made amenable to rules. In giving her existence, a great law had been broken; and the result was a being, whose elements were perhaps beautiful and brilliant, but all in disorder; or with an order peculiar to themselves, amidst which the point of variety and arrangement was difficult or impossible to be discovered.

The point of suggesting that Hawthorne is here, at some level of awareness, talking about the art of romance is not to prove how cleverly he went about composing an aesthetic allegory under the guise of doing something else, but rather to instance once more how in writing *The Scarlet Letter* he was preoccupied generally with the very nature of his chosen fictional genre. That some such barely conscious process is operative throughout Hawthorne's treatment of Pearl seems clear enough (although to demonstrate this thoroughly it would be necessary to quote almost everything he says about the child). Speaking of Pearl in another context, Daniel Hoffman calls attention to one passage in particular:

> The spell of life went forth from her ever creative spirit, and communicated itself to a thousand objects, as a torch kindles a flame wherever it may be applied. The unlikeliest materials, a stick, a bunch of rags, a flower, were the puppets of Pearl's witchcraft, and, without undergoing any outward change, became spiritually adapted to whatever drama occupied the stage of her inner world

and observes that Hawthorne here writes of her in precisely the terms he uses to describe the romance imagination in "The Custom-House."[9] If Pearl has never seemed a convincing reality to readers and critics of Hawthorne's tale, it may simply be because she is essentially a complex symbolic representation of the sources and attributes of the romance itself[10]—an embodiment of that bond of sex and creativity linking the artist Hester and her lover, the would-be romancer Dimmesdale.

For the minister, too, has many of the characteristics of the kind of artist typified by Hester—his major limitation being a fear of exposing, even symbolically, that truth of the human heart which is the romancer's ultimate theme. Could he so expose his inner being, the minister would prove himself an exceptionally successful romancer. In Chapter XI ("The Interior of a Heart"), the first which is devoted entirely to Dimmesdale, Hawthorne compares him to his fellow divines—men of intellect and learning, "of a sturdier texture of mind than his, and endowed with a far greater share of shrewd, hard, iron or granite understanding"—and to saintly fathers of great spiritual purity. What they lack, and what Dimmesdale has in tragic abundance, is artistic eloquence—"the Tongue of Flame," "not the power of speech in foreign and unknown languages, but that of addressing the whole human brotherhood in the heart's native language," the ability "to express the highest truths through the humblest medium of familiar words and images." This gift was "won . . . in great part, by his sorrows," for it was his burden of guilt "that

9. *Form and Fable in American Fiction* (New York, 1965), p. 180. Cf. Richard Chase, *The American Novel and Its Tradition* (New York, 1957), p. 78.

10. John E. Hart calls Pearl "the living symbol of both sin and art" ("*The Scarlet Letter:* One Hundred Years After," p. 392). Rudolph Von Abele sees Pearl "as a symbol of Hawthorne's own art-works, or rather as embodying his theory of art" (*The Death of the Artist*, p. 53).

gave him sympathies so intimate with the sinful brotherhood of mankind
... that his heart vibrated in unison with theirs, and received their pain
into itself, and sent its own throb of pain through a thousand other
hearts, in gushes of sad, persuasive eloquence."

As with Hester, Dimmesdale's artistic power is based on sexual experience. And robed in the "black garments of the priesthood," turning
his "pale face heavenward," he seems the living embodiment of that
dark blossom of romance truth about the "pollution" in his secret soul
that is struggling to express itself through his religious eloquence. (Much
later, when Dimmesdale is finally about to unburden himself, Hawthorne's
controlling metaphor returns in full force. On the way to writing his
Election Sermon the minister is tempted to drop into the bosom of a virgin
"fair and pure as a lily that had bloomed in Paradise .... a germ of evil
that would be sure to blossom darkly soon, and bear black fruit betimes.")

Alone in his chamber, sitting in "utter darkness" or with the light
of a "glimmering lamp," Dimmesdale keeps secret vigils in which,
"viewing his own face in a looking-glass," he "typified the constant
introspection wherewith he tortured, but could not purify, himself."
His glimpses into his own heart are still vague and obscure. Purification
will come only when he manages to bring to clarity that vision which
will embody the truth of his inner being. Dimmesdale is thus seen by
Hawthorne as a romancer struggling to transform furtive emotions into
glimpses of imaginative truth.[11] He is, we should notice, precisely in the
position of the author in "The Custom-House," whose imagination had
become "a tarnished mirror" which either "would not reflect, or only
with miserable dimness," the "tribe of unrealities" that embody his
art because he had sold his soul for Uncle Sam's gold. Freed from the
Custom-House, Hawthorne would once again be able to sit in his "deserted parlour, lighted only by the glimmering coal-fire and the moon,"
and call up from within the "haunted verge" of the looking-glass those
"strange things" that romance converts into truth.

The minister does in fact manage to scare up, both in the chamber
and in the mirror, ghostlike images of the romance meaning that is

---

11. "That Hawthorne had the artist in mind when he created Dimmesdale there
is little doubt, especially if we recognize the parallel between the minister's situation
and Hawthorne's own as he outlines it in 'The Custom House,'" observes Charles
R. O'Donnell ("Hawthorne and Dimmesdale: The Quest for the Realm of Quiet,"
Nineteenth-Century Fiction, XIV [1960], 328–329).

eluding him. He sees "diabolic shapes" that grin and mock; then "his white-bearded father, with a saint-like frown, and his mother, turning her face away"; and finally "Hester Prynne, leading along little Pearl, in her scarlet garb, and pointing her forefinger, first, at the scarlet letter on her bosom, and then at the clergyman's own breast." Hester seems clearly to be offering herself as a paradigm for the minister's creative efforts, but at this point he can believe only in "the anguish in his inmost soul," not in the truth of his visions.

On just such a night and in such a mood, "walking in the shadow of a dream, as it were, and perhaps actually under the influence of a species of somnambulism," Dimmesdale does indeed act out—in effect, composes—just the kind of symbolic fantasy that goes by the name of romance. Forcing himself to mount the scaffold of his mistress's ignominy, he imagines the townspeople horror-stricken the next morning to discover him "half frozen to death, overwhelmed with shame, and standing where Hester Prynne had stood!" Before long Hester and Pearl arrive to help the minister perform his symbolic charade, which is lit by the eerie glow of a meteor that gives a singular "moral interpretation" to the scene through "the awfulness that is always imparted to familiar objects by an unaccustomed light." (The light, that is, of romance, for Hawthorne is again reminding us of "The Custom-House," where the "unusual" moonlight of romance is described as spiritualizing the familiar by investing it "with a quality of strangeness and remoteness.") In this "light that is to reveal all secrets" the minister is also driven by his "long, intense, and secret pain" to paint an allegory of his secret on the firmament itself, turning the whole cosmos, with the fantastic imagination of the romancer, into "no more than a fitting page for his soul's history and fate." Soon the sinister Roger Chillingworth arrives to offer the minister a devil's definition of the work of the romance artist—"we dream in our waking moments, and walk in our sleep"—whereupon Dimmesdale seems to awake from his "ugly dream."

The culmination of Dimmesdale's apprenticeship in converting submerged sexual energy into imaginative expression is his composition and performance of his Election Sermon and the concomitant "Revelation of the Scarlet Letter."[12] And it is, of course, Hester who incites simultane-

---

12. The view I take of Dimmesdale here has been anticipated at many points by Frederick C. Crews in his brilliant chapter on *The Scarlet Letter* in *The Sins of the Fathers: Hawthorne's Psychological Themes* (New York, 1966), pp. 136–153.

ously his passion and his artistic impulse. "Begin all anew!" she exclaims
headily, exhorting him to exchange guilt over the sexual past for present
satisfaction and creative energy. "Preach! Write! Act! Do any thing,
save to lie down and die!" And to implement Dimmesdale's improved
career as lover and artist, Hester releases her dark, luxuriant, abundant
hair, whereupon "her sex, her youth, and the whole richness of her
beauty, came back from what men call the irrevocable past." Dimmesdale
returns to the village from his forest interview with Hester visibly excited,
as Hawthorne tells us, with his hitherto repressed and still forbidden sexuality straining toward consciousness in odd ways. He thinks he is going
mad as his erotic energy first displaces itself into an evil urge "to do some
strange, wild, wicked thing or other, with a sense that it would be at once
involuntary and intentional; in spite of himself, yet growing out of a profounder self than that which opposed the impulse."

Barely managing to suppress his impulse to whisper obscenities and
blasphemies, the minister is aware that some internal change is taking
place: "he had yielded himself with deliberate choice, as he had never
done before, to what he knew was deadly sin. And the infectious poison
of that sin had been thus rapidly diffused throughout his moral system."
He now feels a true "sympathy and fellowship with wicked mortals and
the world of perverted spirits" and is thus fully prepared for the role of
artist. Reaching his study, he sees the unfinished Election Sermon on his
desk and thinks with scorn and pity (and some slight envy: dark knowledge is a burden) of that relatively innocent self who had aspired to inspiration before: "Another man had returned out of the forest; a wiser
one; with a knowledge of hidden mysteries which the simplicity of the
former never could have reached." Now in full contact with his primitive
self, Dimmesdale is ready to convert sexual guilt into imaginative power.[13]
He eats "with ravenous appetite" the food he requests from a servant.
Then:

> Flinging the already written pages of the Election Sermon into the fire,
> he forthwith began another, which he wrote with such an impulsive flow
> of thought and emotion, that he fancied himself inspired; and only won-
> dered that Heaven should see fit to transmit the grand and solemn music
> of its oracles through so foul an organ-pipe as he.

---

13. Concerning the composition of the Election Sermon, Ernest Sandeen writes:
"Clergyman and lover work together in a fruitful, ecstatic harmony" ("*The Scarlet
Letter* as a Love Story," *PMLA*, LXXVII [1962], 430).

But "leaving that mystery to solve itself, or go unsolved for ever, he drove his task onward, with earnest haste and ecstasy," finding in the morning in front of his "bedazzled eyes" a "vast, immeasurable tract of written space."

Hawthorne's attitude toward Dimmesdale's "inspiration" is noticeably dual, and we should not overlook his ironies. The "grand and solemn music" that is being transmitted through the foul organ-pipe of the minister's emotion is (no matter what Dimmesdale may delude himself into thinking) clearly not a heavenly oracle but the still, sad music of humanity. Guilty passion turns him into a romancer, not a religious prophet. The truth of Dimmesdale's achievement is exposed by the response of the artist Hester—at once his most appreciative audience, his best critic, and his only muse—to his performance. The power of romance art lies more in connotation than in denotation, and it is Dimmesdale's soul music, not his religious libretto, that signifies for Hester. His words are "indistinguishable," since the meaning resides in the plaintive undertone of his song:

> A loud or low expression of anguish,—the whisper, or the shriek, as it might be conceived, of suffering humanity, that touched a sensibility in every bosom! At times this deep strain of pathos was all that could be heard, and scarcely heard. . . . The complaint of a human heart, sorrow-laden, perchance guilty, telling its secret. . . . It was this profound and continual undertone that gave the clergyman his most appropriate power.

Romance art, we must remember, is oblique art, the true meaning often contradicting what apparently is being said. The prophetic message contained in Dimmesdale's sermon differed, we are told, from that of the Old Testament prophets because "whereas the Jewish seers had denounced judgments and ruin on their country, it was his mission to foretell a high and glorious destiny for the newly gathered people of the Lord." The minister's listeners can explain the "sad undertone of pathos" discernible in the sermon only by assuming that it signaled his approaching holy death. But Hester (and the reader) knows the truth: Dimmesdale's romance/sermon is really a song of human woe. Why, then, does the sermon's religious message seem to contradict its inner meaning? Herein lies Hawthorne's most telling irony. Dimmesdale's Election Sermon is not complete until he has performed the coda: the revelation of the scarlet letter and his final speech. What he actually—and incredibly—does in his last utterance is to apply the sermon's prophetic message of a high and glorious destiny for the people of New England to himself. Dimmesdale concludes his Election Sermon by claiming that he is one of the Elect! All of his "afflictions" (the "burning torture" on his breast, the "dark and terrible" old Chillingworth, his "death of triumphant ignominy") are signs of salvation: "Had either of these agonies been wanting, I had been lost for ever!" To say the least, Dimmesdale's reading of providential signs is curious: he is surely saved because he appears thoroughly damned. Why—we certainly are expected to ask—may not his suffering be the type of what, being indeed damned, he will undergo throughout eternity? Dimmesdale himself, in his moment of truth with Hester in the forest, had already said, "The judgment of God is on me. . . . I am irrevocably doomed"; and Hawthorne has echoed this judgment by calling the minister, when he returns to the village, a "lost and desperate man."[14]

The fantastic pride evinced by Dimmesdale's Election Sermon is the final sign of his utter damnation. Thus the *real* meaning of the minister's prophetic claims does not contradict at all the underlying tone of pathos. The romance truth conveyed through Dimmesdale's performance is the inevitable one: sin, suffering, and ineluctable human tragedy. And the

---

14. The question of Dimmesdale's salvation or damnation is hotly disputed. For a vigorous defense of the authenticity of Dimmesdale's regeneration, see Darrel Abel, "Hawthorne's Dimmesdale: Fugitive from Wrath," *Nineteenth-Century Fiction*, XI (1956), 81–105; also, Hugh N. Maclean, "Hawthorne's *Scarlet Letter:* 'The Dark Problem of This Life,' " *American Literature*, XXVII (1955), 12–24. Roy R. Male sees Dimmesdale's final performance as a kind of apotheosis (*Hawthorne's Tragic Vision*, pp. 115–117). Hyatt H. Waggoner speaks of Dimmesdale's "final act of courageous honesty" but points out that the possibility of his being saved is ambiguous (*Hawthorne: A Critical Study*, revised edition [Cambridge, Mass., 1963], pp. 149–150). Ernest Sandeen argues forcefully against Dimmesdale: the image "of Dimmesdale as the idealized Puritan Everyman who vindicates the whole theocratic idea is obviously intended to strike the reader as ironic. For the reader knows, as the people cannot, that the creative energy which produced the sermon and sustained Dimmesdale in the pulpit had its source in the lovers' meeting in the forest. To put it bluntly, the inspiration which breathed through the preacher's apologia for the Puritan system is simply, from the Puritan point of view, 'outlawed passion' " ("*The Scarlet Letter* as a Love Story," p. 432). Edward H. Davidson also argues persuasively for Dimmesdale's damnation, both as a Puritan and as a nineteenth-century romantic, in "Dimmesdale's Fall," *New England Quarterly*, XXXVI (1963), 358–370. See, too, William H. Nolte, "Hawthorne's Dimmesdale: A Small Man Gone Wrong," *New England Quarterly*, XXXVIII (1965), 168–186; and cf. Crews, *The Sins of the Fathers*, pp. 149 ff.

"mystery" of why heaven should use the energy of dark passion to express religious truth has been solved—it does not. The truth of romance is a human one, and it is dark indeed.

Dimmesdale ends up a potent romancer in spite of himself. He is defended after his death by admirers who claim that his confession and the "revelation" of the scarlet letter were meant only as a parable: "After exhausting life in his efforts for mankind's spiritual good, he had made the manner of his death a parable, in order to impress on his admirers the mighty and mournful lesson, that, in the view of Infinite Purity, we are sinners all alike." As Daniel Hoffman remarks, "there are ironies within the ironies of Hawthorne's style."[15] For Hawthorne, with infinite slyness, himself immediately disputes the view that would turn into *mere* parable clear proof of guilt, whereas the whole burden of his art goes to demonstrate that parables *are true!* The minister's friends speak more wisely than they know. Dimmesdale finally is inspired to reveal the secret truth about himself in the very fashion of Hawthorne's art—through the symbolic gestures of romance.

We are left with the most curious of Hawthorne's major characters in *The Scarlet Letter*, the diabolical Roger Chillingworth, whose role we might say is that of the romancer as necromancer. Like Hester and Dimmesdale he too harbors a hidden guilt and anguish, but unlike them he is unable to invest his secret passion in a symbolic art capable of relieving himself and others. Instead, he uses his dark knowledge and pain to foment further suffering. Chillingworth represents the sinister side of romance, Hawthorne's awareness (expressed elsewhere through his alter ego Oberon in "The Devil in Manuscript" and in "Ethan Brand") that the insight of the artist can be dangerous, truly satanic in its ability to darken counsel permanently and drive men to despair and destruction. But ultimately, as with Oberon and Brand, Chillingworth's machinations bring about mainly his own downfall. Diabolism in art, Hawthorne seems to say, is self-defeating.

Chillingworth's close connection to the art of romance is established metaphorically by Hawthorne's constant association of the old man with herbs, roots, plants, blossoms—all manner of somewhat exotic vegetable life. The most telling description of Chillingworth is furnished by Hester Prynne, who sees with the true romancer's eye the emblematic meaning

---

15. *Form and Fable in American Fiction*, p. 177.

of his existence. She watches him grubbing up his simples and roots and "wondered what sort of herbs they were, which the old man was so sedulous to gather."

> Would not the earth, quickened to an evil purpose by the sympathy of his eye, greet him with poisonous shrubs, of species hitherto unknown, that would start up under his fingers? Or might it suffice him, that every wholesome growth should be converted into something deleterious and malignant at his touch? . . . Would he not suddenly sink into the earth, leaving a barren and blasted spot, where, in due course of time, would be seen deadly nightshade, dogwood, henbane, and whatever else of vegetable wickedness the climate could produce, all flourishing with hideous luxuriance?

As the most sinister practitioner of the art of symbolic expression, Chillingworth both inspires and collects the flowers of evil, and the secret of his own dark nature will ultimately be converted into a hideous example of "vegetable wickedness."

As with Hester and Dimmesdale, the underlying impetus for the metaphoric flowering of Chillingworth's expressive powers is shown to be passion—in this case, a twisted sexuality. Hawthorne hints, obscurely but unmistakably, at Chillingworth's involvement in backstairs carnality by associating him with Doctor Forman and the Overbury murder case.[16] Furthermore, there is a suggestion that Chillingworth's intense interest in converting "weeds . . . into drugs of potency" has something to do with sexual inadequacy. Hawthorne makes it sufficiently clear that this "bookworm of great libraries,—a man already in decay," formed the first link in this chain of mutual guilt and sin by taking to wife a lusty young bride, "glowing with girlish beauty," whom he could never hope to satisfy. "Mine was the first wrong," he admits to Hester, "when I betrayed thy budding youth into a false and unnatural relation with my decay." Hester herself "deemed it her crime most to be repented of, that she had ever endured, and reciprocated, the lukewarm grasp of his hand, and had suffered the smile of her lips and eyes to mingle and melt into his own." As if his language were not a clear enough indication of Hester's sexual disgust at Chillingworth's inadequacy, Hawthorne unequivocally points the moral:

---

16. See Alfred S. Reid, *The Yellow Ruff and The Scarlet Letter: A Source of Hawthorne's Novel* (Gainesville, Fla., 1955).

> Let men tremble to win the hand of woman, unless they win along with it the utmost passion of her heart! Else it may be their miserable fortune, as it was Roger Chillingworth's, when some mightier touch than their own may have awakened all her sensibilities, to be reproached even for the calm content . . . which they will have imposed upon her as the warm reality.

Hawthorne's reticence here is remarkable, for of course it was the old man's miserable fortune, because of his sexual failure, not simply to be "reproached," but to be humiliatingly cuckolded.

The Scarlet Letter grows out of Hester Prynne's search for sexual fulfillment and expression, and—odd as it may seem—Roger Chillingworth's career can be explained in similar fashion. "Were it only for the art's sake, I must search this matter to the bottom!" he exclaims as he sets out to satisfy the "lurid fire" of sexual loathing and hatred for his supplanter smoldering in his soul by helping to bring to birth on Dimmesdale's breast the dark blossom of anguish. Chillingworth's quest for weeds convertible into "drugs of potency" is a perfect emblem of his role as a perverted romancer who, "by devoting himself . . . to the constant analysis of a heart full of torture, and deriving his enjoyment thence, and adding fuel to those fiery tortures which he analyzed and gloated over," gluts his hidden sexual urges—in effect compensating for his impotence—on the black flower of "mortality and corruption." Chillingworth's passionate hatred, Hawthorne explains in a most revealing passage at the end of the book, and the passionate love of a Dimmesdale or a Hester Prynne, come to "the same thing at bottom." Each, in the world of *The Scarlet Letter*, turns the sufferer into a kind of artist—in the case of Chillingworth, the artist as spiritual bloodsucker (he is indeed a "Leech"), converting all his passion and knowledge into aggression and destructive power. Like Ethan Brand, Chillingworth is competent finally to produce only an abortive romance—his own wretched secret self lying "like an uprooted weed . . . wilting in the sun."

3. *Redemption Through Art*

As Daniel Hoffman notes, the sprawling *House of the Seven Gables* manifestly lacks the taut economy of *The Scarlet Letter*. But Hoffman's allegation that Hawthorne's second major romance is without a "single controlling symbol like the letter" to unify its dispersed materials must certainly be disputed.[17] As with all of Hawthorne's books, the central symbol is signalled by the title, and its meaning is vitally connected with the implications of Hawthorne's art itself. *The House of the Seven Gables* can be read, with much less difficulty than is posed by *The Scarlet Letter*, as a fable explaining the nature and function of romance.[18]

Fortunately, in *The House of the Seven Gables* the central meaning of the controlling symbol is made admirably clear by the author. On the first page we are told that there was something human about the house, and before long Hawthorne makes his meaning explicit:

> So much of mankind's varied experience had passed there—so much had been suffered, and something, too, enjoyed—that the very timbers were oozy, as with the moisture of a heart. It was itself like a great human heart, with a life of its own, and full of rich and sombre reminiscences.

Later Hawthorne will confirm and expand the meaning of his symbol: as Phoebe prepares to leave temporarily the "heavy-hearted old mansion," she finds that every object in the place "responded to her consciousness, as if a moist human heart were in it." The house comes to stand for that "dungeon"—the individual heart—wherein the emotions of each of its inhabitants are imprisoned. And Hawthorne himself metaphorically poses the central problem of the book in a revealing passage near the end when, with Jaffrey Pyncheon lying dead at its core, the house is serenaded by an Italian organ-grinder: "The gloomy and desolate old house, deserted of life, and with awful Death sitting sternly in its solitude, was the emblem of many a human heart, which, nevertheless, is compelled to hear the trill and echo of the world's gaiety around it."

More important than this slightly fatuous meaning deceptively read out of the episode by the author himself is its true contextual significance.

---

17. *Form and Fable in American Fiction*, p. 187. The centrality of the house as well as the general unity of symbol and theme in the book are discussed by Maurice Beebe in "The Fall of the House of Pyncheon," *Nineteenth-Century Fiction*, XI (1956), 1–17.

18. In "Who Killed Judge Pyncheon? The Role of the Imagination in *The House of the Seven Gables*," *PMLA*, LXXI (1956), pp. 355–356, Alfred H. Marks argues that this is "the work in which [Hawthorne] is most serious in his devotion to the powers of beauty and the imagination . . . . the imagination is both subject matter and process: Hawthorne calls upon the reader to recognize the validity of imaginative truth by means of the imagination itself."

The Italian musician, who knows the "heart's language" and is elsewhere in the narrative elaborately presented as a type of the artist, is here trying with "pertinacity" to get the house to respond, to open up. "Will he succeed at last? Will that stubborn door be suddenly flung open?" The organ-grinder will of course not succeed in forcing the house to yield up the secret of its "inner heart," but his attempt—it will be successfully completed by another artist, Holgrave—symbolizes the major task of the romancer. Hawthorne is surely inviting us to recall his observation, in the preface to the tale, that it is the romancer's job to present the "truth of the human heart" and that this purpose is hopefully achieved in *The House of the Seven Gables* through an "attempt to connect a by-gone time with the very Present that is flitting away from us." The past of the house, the buried life, and the secrets of the heart are all caught up in one comprehensive metaphor that defines the function of the romancer.

The representative of Hawthorne's own art in the book is Holgrave, the daguerreotypist—his very profession an emblem of that method of viewing reality at "one remove farther from the actual, and nearer to the imaginative," which for Hawthorne characterized romance—who presumably inherited from his Maule ancestors that power of imaginative insight into human nature, uneasily called "witchcraft" by the author, which is the dangerous gift of the artist. Like Hawthorne, who in Chapter 18 conjures up in the looking-glass ("which, you are aware, is always a kind of window or door-way into the spiritual world") a ghostly dumb show symbolic of the house's history which is a stylistic and thematic epitome of his book, the Maule posterity have a special relation to the magic glass:

> By what appears to have been a sort of mesmeric process—they could make its inner region all alive with the departed Pyncheons; not as they had shown themselves to the world, nor in their better and happier hours, but as doing over again some deed of sin, or in the crisis of life's bitterest sorrow.

Just such a "looking-glass" is Holgrave's own romance, the "legend" of Alice Pyncheon, which brings alive the sins and sorrows of the Pyncheons and almost mesmerizes poor Phoebe. (There is a "magnetic element" in Holgrave's nature that frightens Phoebe from the start, and the final elucidation of the house's mystery is obtained by Holgrave "from one of those mesmerical seers"—doubtless either himself or Hawthorne—"who, now-

a-days, so strangely perplex the aspect of human affairs, and put every-
body's natural vision to the blush, by the marvels which they see with
their eyes shut.")

Like the romancer, the Maules control the symbolic world of dream
and fantasy. ("The Pyncheons . . . , haughtily as they bore themselves in
the noonday streets of their native town, were no better than bond-ser-
vants to these plebeian Maules, on entering the topsyturvy common-
wealth of sleep.") The grandson of Matthew Maule "was fabled . . . to
have a strange power of getting into people's dreams, and regulating
matters there according to his own fancy, pretty much like the stage-
manager of a theatre." This ability to conjure up and control the secrets
of consciousness—in effect, insight into the human heart—is what licenses Holgrave to explore the darkest aspects of the house and empowers
him finally to transform Phoebe into a mature, sexually aware woman.
She may accuse him—after hearing him assert that it was not his impulse
"to help or hinder; but to look on, to analyze, to explain matters to myself, and to comprehend the drama" of the house—of talking "as if this old
house were a theatre" and of looking "at Hepzibah's and Clifford's mis-
fortunes, and those of generations before them, as a tragedy . . . played
exclusively for your amusement." But the romancer is necessarily committed to such a view, since his understanding of human nature is predicated on, and can only be expressed through, the refracting power of art.
Hawthorne was, however, keenly aware of the danger—principally that
of becoming a dilettante of symbolic gestures—lurking for the romance
artist in his commitment to non-realistic modes of viewing and expressing
human truth, and Phoebe's remark embodies his anxiety over such a danger. In another sense, Holgrave's tendency to aesthetic coldness might be
considered the expression of an instinct of self-defense. The artist, reluctant
to bear the dark knowledge that his art teaches, sometimes feels driven to
treat that art as no more than an amusement. Indeed, for the sensitive
Holgrave, the unattractive alternative to detachment seems to be a personal
involvement in human suffering that leads to revulsion. "I dwell in it for
a while," he says of the house, "that I may know the better how to hate it."

But there is also a possibility—the one which in fact opens up for
Holgrave, as for Hester Prynne—that his painful knowledge of the human
heart will carry him beyond smugness or misanthropy to the theory and
practice of redemptive sympathy. And if Holgrave devotes himself to the
art of romance only, as it would seem, to give it up at the end, his reluctant

pursuit of his profession may be viewed as a reflection of Hawthorne's
own dual attitude toward his art: his devotion to it and his desire to be
released from its shadows. The intensity of this wish would enable him,
by the time he came to write *The Marble Faun*, apparently to forget his
previous productions and to insist that his own "dear native land" happily
contained "no shadow, no antiquity, no mystery, no picturesque and
gloomy wrong, nor anything but a common-place prosperity, in broad
and simple daylight."

In the context of *The House of the Seven Gables* such an opinion is
worthy only of the sunshiny hypocrisy of a Jaffrey Pyncheon, who, in his
fear of romance truth and with his "hard, stern, relentless look," is directly
opposed to the compassionate Holgrave, with his "deep, thoughtful, all-
observant eyes," and to another artist figure, Clifford.[19] Like the other
Pyncheon patriarchs, the Puritan Colonel and Gervayse, Jaffrey wants
possession of the house so that he can exploit it to increase his worldly
power: for him, the "secret" of the human heart is only another way to
wealth. As for the true secret of his inner being, the "evil and unsightly
thing" lurking at his core, he is devoted to keeping it "hidden from
mankind,—forgotten by himself, or buried so deeply under a sculptured
and ornamented pile of ostentatious deeds that his daily life could take no
note of it." In a metaphoric tour de force which amounts to a defense of
his art, Hawthorne implicitly invites us to compare with the romance
sensibility (whose commitment to truth, however dark, expresses itself in
the shaping and exploring of a *House of the Seven Gables*) the "art" of
Jaffrey Pyncheon—a glittering palace of daylight fakery:

> Men of strong minds, great force of character, and a hard texture of
> the sensibilities, are very capable of falling into mistakes of this kind. They
> are ordinarily men to whom forms are of paramount importance. Their
> field of action lies among the external phenomena of life. They possess
> vast ability in grasping, and arranging, and appropriating to themselves,
> the big, heavy, solid unrealities, such as gold, landed estate, offices of trust
> and emolument, and public honors. With these materials, and with deeds
> of goodly aspect, done in the public eye, an individual of this class builds

19. Rudolph Von Abele suggests "that Hawthorne is promulgating, in the Maule
and Pyncheon family lines, images of the artist and the anti-artist in himself" (*The
Death of the Artist*, p. 63). Alfred H. Marks contrasts Clifford's imaginative and spiritual nature with Jaffrey's coarse materiality.

up, as it were, a tall and stately edifice, which, in the view of other people, and ultimately in his own view, is no other than the man's character, or the man himself. Behold, therefore, a palace! Its splendid halls and suites of spacious apartments are floored with a mosaic-work of costly marbles; its windows, the whole height of each room, admit the sunshine through the most transparent of plate-glass; its high cornices are gilded, and its ceilings gorgeously painted; and a lofty dome—through which, from the central pavement, you may gaze up to the sky, as with no obstructing medium between—surmounts the whole. With what fairer and nobler emblem could any man desire to shadow forth his character?

Despite its apparent splendor and solidity, however, this sunbathed reality is a fraud. "In some low and obscure nook" lies "a corpse, half-decayed, and still decaying, and diffusing its death-scent all through the palace!" The inhabitant of the edifice is himself inured to the stench, and his admirers are fooled by his cleverness and their own willingness to be duped: "they smell only the rich odors which the master sedulously scatters through the palace, and the incense which they bring, and delight to burn before him!" But the romancer knows the truth of the human heart: "Now and then, perchance, comes in a seer, before whose sadly gifted eye the whole structure melts into thin air, leaving only the hidden nook . . . and the decaying corpse within."

Unlike the romancer, who builds his life on the sad but secure knowledge of human guilt and pain reflected in the magic looking-glass of his art, Jaffrey Pyncheon, "a hard, cold man . . . seldom or never looking inward, and resolutely taking his idea of himself from what purports to be his image, as reflected in the mirror of public opinion, can scarcely arrive at true self-knowledge"—not even, the author suggests, at the final hour. As the governor-to-be lies inanimate in the house, Hawthorne exhorts him repeatedly to return to life, saying—with bitter irony—"ambition is a talisman more powerful than witchcraft." But Jaffrey is, has been, and will always remain spiritually dead, as he is now physically so; his devotion to worldly ambition purchases him only eternal damnation. For it is the "witchcraft" of a Holgrave that is the true talisman. Romance, with all it implies, is shown in the meaning embedded at the heart of Hawthorne's tale to contain mankind's only real hope for re-entering Paradise.

This notion, along with Hawthorne's familiar metaphors for his art, is developed by Holgrave just after he has almost bewitched Phoebe by reading her his manuscript on Alice Pyncheon. As the moon begins "to shine out, broad and oval, in its middle pathway," everything, Hawthorne tells us, is "transfigured by a charm of romance," and Holgrave is inspired to propound his theory to that gentle Pyncheon descendant who, though "by nature as hostile to mystery, as the sunshine to a dark corner," is destined to redeem her race through her ultimate acceptance of the deepest mysteries of the heart:

> "After all, what a good world we live in! How good, and beautiful! How young it is, too, with nothing really rotten or age-worn in it! This old house, for example, which sometimes has positively oppressed my breath with its smell of decaying timber! And this garden, where the black mould always clings to my spade, as if I were a sexton delving in a graveyard! Could I keep the feeling that now possesses me, the garden would every day be virgin soil, with the earth's first freshness in the flavor of its beans and squashes; and the house!—it would be like a bower in Eden, blossoming with the earliest roses that God ever made. Moonlight, and the sentiment in man's heart, responsive to it, is the greatest of renovators and reformers."

Despite the schoolgirl gushiness of his exclamatory periods (he is, after all, a novice at literature), Holgrave's effusion has a vital relation to the book at large. His discovery that he really does not hate the house, when he sees it in the proper light, reflects Hawthorne's belief that romance has the power to transform the odor of decay and the sight of death into usable human truth. Tragedy, refracted through imagination, can redeem the fall of man into knowledge of good and evil by helping us to accept our "nastiness"—passion, cruelty, vice. Paradise will be regained only when art teaches us to accept our inner darkness as the quality that peculiarly defines the state of being human. It is as if Hawthorne were agreeing with the Calvinists that we are depraved, and yet insisting—with the artists and psychoanalysts—that we are not therefore culpable and worthy only of guilt and punishment.[20] The sadness attendant on our learning the secrets of sinful humanity (Paradise lost), as Holgrave goes on to explain to Phoebe, is the necessary prelude to adult rapture (Paradise regained).

> "I hardly think I understand you," said Phoebe.
> "No wonder," replied Holgrave, smiling; "for I have told you a secret

---

20. "Moral and religious concerns," writes Hyatt H. Waggoner, "are almost always central in Hawthorne's work, but Hawthorne's interest in them is primarily subjective and psychological . . . existential" (*Nathaniel Hawthorne* [Minneapolis, 1962], p. 17).

which I hardly began to know, before I found myself giving it utterance. Remember it, however; and when the truth becomes clear to you, then think of this moonlight scene!''

Phoebe will shortly have a chance to test on her own pulses the validity of Holgrave's moonlight paradoxes when she is actually led by him into the heart of darkness—awareness of sex and death.

This new awareness can flower literally only over the dead body of Judge Jaffrey Pyncheon, the hypocritical representative of societal law, who has, as it were, banished the truth of the human heart from the House of the Seven Gables. Jaffrey's hostility toward the spirit of romance is emblematized in his attitude toward Clifford, "for whose character he had at once a contempt and a repugnance."[21] Clifford is clearly a type of the artist (in this case turned pitiful and self-indulgent because of the harshness of reality)—almost a caricature of Hawthorne himself. He has extremely delicate sensibilities, is in danger of falling into cold aestheticism, wants to live in the south of France or Italy, believes in mesmerism, is fond of blowing bubbles (Hawthorne calls them "brilliant fantasies," and in "The Custom-House" he referred to his own romance as a "soap-bubble"), and sees visions in Maule's well. Clifford, the living embodiment of human emotion (when Phoebe first heard his voice it seemed "less like articulate words than an unshaped sound, such as would be the utterance of feeling and sympathy, rather than of the intellect"), is a "thunder-smitten Adam," driven from the once Edenic garden of the house and imprisoned by the flaming sword of Judge Pyncheon's legal authority. Jaffrey not only hates Clifford but fears him, because Clifford is capable of discerning and exposing the brutal, aggressive nature hidden beneath Jaffrey's cloak of legality. For Jaffrey the truth of the human heart (his own) is ugly and must be suppressed; for Clifford it is painful, even terrible, but ultimately redemptive.

The sexual mentality of the two men is clearly contrasted by Hawthorne in their sharply different reactions to Phoebe's burgeoning womanhood. Watching her bud open into a blossom makes Clifford feel consciously lonely and melancholy, but he is able to accept his own reaction to her deepening sexuality and turn his response to emotional use:

> His sentiment for Phoebe . . . was not less chaste than if she had been his daughter. . . . [But] he took unfailing note of every charm that

---

21. "Clifford's artistic spirit is something the grasping spirit of the Pyncheons has placed in bondage," says Alfred H. Marks ("Who Killed Judge Pyncheon?" p. 367).

appertained to her sex, and saw the ripeness of her lips, and the virginal developement of her bosom. All her little, womanly ways, budding out of her like blossoms on a young fruit-tree, had their effect on him, and sometimes caused his very heart to tingle with the keenest thrills of pleasure.

Hawthorne obviously approves of the openness of Clifford's response and of his ability to convert "the fragrance of an earthly rosebud" into "visions of all the living and breathing beauty, amid which he should have had his home." Clifford—the artist as surrogate father—demonstrates the compatibility of love with authority when that authority is used, not to repress, but to make available and to direct the fullest human consciousness.

In the world of Jaffrey Pyncheon, however, sexuality is under a dark ban. Because it is seen as sinful, involving lechery, violation, and concomitant guilt, it must be repressed from public view—only to return as unabashed cruelty, first to others and finally to oneself (the gurgling, blood-in-the-throat death of the Pyncheon patriarchs), demonstrating that the price of self-deception is ultimate self-defeat. For Phoebe, the Judge is a kind of Electral ogre, the surrogate as ravishing father, whose inability to convert sexuality into tenderness serves to intimidate the developing woman. Meeting this "young rosebud of a girl" behind the counter of Hepzibah's cent-shop, Jaffrey offers to bestow "on his young relative a kiss of acknowledged kindred and natural affection," but for Phoebe "the man, the sex, somehow or other, was entirely too prominent," and she draws back from this "dark-browed, grisly bearded, white-neckclothed, and unctuously benevolent Judge." By "benevolence" Hawthorne clearly means to imply lust, since he tells us that the Judge's benevolence was "much like a serpent, which, as a preliminary to fascination, is said to fill the air with his peculiar odor." Thus surprised in the act of exhibiting his aggressive sexuality, Jaffrey's reaction is defensive —a hypocritical admonition that at once warns her off sex and cloaks his own exposed lust behind a mask of quasi-parental approval of her rejection:

"I like that, Cousin Phoebe!" cried he, with an emphatic nod of approbation.—"I like it much, my little cousin! You are a good child, and know how to take care of yourself. A young girl—especially if she be a very pretty one—can never be too chary of her lips."

Denied an outlet for his sexuality, Jaffrey ends up retreating to repressive authority. Unlike the artist Clifford, whose easy and unthreatening acceptance of his own and Phoebe's sexuality inspires the girl to expose her womanhood and, as it were, makes secret emotions available for public use, the anti-artist Jaffrey serves to drive such emotions underground, whence they will reappear in a more sinister form.

Hawthorne makes it clear that behind the limitless evil-doing and malevolence of the old Puritan Pyncheon and his contemporary avatar lies a fund of hidden sexual cruelty.[22] But Phoebe, who belongs to "the trim, orderly, and limit-loving class," in order to avoid being "tumbled headlong into chaos" and "to keep the universe in its old place, was fain to smother, in some degree, her own intuitions as to Judge Pyncheon's character" and to discount Hepzibah's clear assertion of Jaffrey's infinite wickedness. Equipped only with her fragile "natural sunshine," Phoebe does not yet dare to exchange the apparent security of Jaffrey Pyncheon's law for the dark, and possibly dangerous, truths of the human heart. It will be the function of the "lawless mystic" Holgrave, girded with a "law of his own"—the romancer's imaginative insight—to lead Phoebe safely and lovingly into the inner sanctum of the house's secret. As Hawthorne suggests, Holgrave will play the Sybil to Phoebe's Aeneas, guiding her on the perilous journey to that Hades of the heart wherein reside all wisdom and power.

In *The House of the Seven Gables*, as in *The Marble Faun*, the one episode that can truly be called a love scene takes place in the presence of a corpse. Since a Poesque taste for necrophilia is totally alien to the spirit of Hawthorne's writing, we are forced to seek the meaning of this persistent motif otherwise than in the notion of a gratuitous dabbling with gothic horror. One thing at least is clear in *The House of the Seven Gables*: the death of the anti-romancer Jaffrey Pyncheon is the general signal for the release of all sorts of vital human energies. Art flourishes, love is consummated, and the protagonists are freed from the incubus of guilty subjection to a dark history; the bans on art, sex, and an understanding of the past are lifted all at once. Perhaps less clear at first glance is why Holgrave's leading Phoebe to knowledge of the corpse at the center of the house should be treated so momentously, and why that knowledge should be so intimately

---

22. Roy R. Male has commented on Jaffrey's "sexual brutality" (*Hawthorne's Tragic Vision*, p. 73).

connected with their first real *pleasure* in each other. But the two questions can be answered together. Phoebe's introduction into an active awareness of death represents her introduction to knowledge of human evil—corruptibility—in others and at least potentially within herself, and the emotional and psychological depth obtained thereby will purchase her adult sexuality. It is this terrible job of deepening Phoebe's nature that is entrusted to the artist, Holgrave.

> [To him] it . . . seemed almost wicked to bring the awful secret . . . to her knowledge. It was like dragging a hideous shape of death into the cleanly and cheerful space before a household fire, where it would present all the uglier aspect, amid the decorousness of everything about it. Yet it could not be concealed from her; she must needs know it.

To mitigate the shock, Holgrave uses his art to present the corpse of Jaffrey to Phoebe at one remove, in a photographic image. But there is no mitigating the dark truth that our capacity for bearing tragedy and terror also measures our capacity for experiencing ecstasy—except as Holgrave had tried to prepare Phoebe in his moonlight theorizing. "In some cases," he had explained, "the two states come almost simultaneously, and mingle the sadness and the rapture in one mysterious emotion." Now, as he draws her into the secrets of love and death, he offers the "firm, but gentle and warm pressure" of his hand, "imparting a welcome which caused her heart to leap and thrill with an indefinable shiver of enjoyment."

"We must love one another or die," W. H. Auden has said notably with subdued irony, since we must die in any case. But the anxiety and terror engendered by the fact of death can be assuaged, and indeed compensated for, through sexual expression. Hawthorne accepts the full weight of the Miltonic truth that sex and death come into the world together, but he departs from Milton in proposing other than a purely religious solution to the problem. Our woe can be transformed into something like bliss, and the knowledge that kills can become the knowledge that cures, if only we can manage to cast off the nightmare of inherited guilt over our "corrupt" natures and achieve self-transcendence through sexual love. Symbolically joined in such a union of mutual acceptance and understanding, Phoebe and Holgrave are "conscious of nothing sad nor old. They transfigured the earth, and made it Eden again, and themselves the two first dwellers in it." Paradise is regained when the romance "truth of the human heart" is made available for Phoebe, and thus in some measure for society at large.

With the destruction of the "defunct nightmare" (Jaffrey), art itself is enabled to emerge from the shadows. "Alice's Posies" (the "one object" which Hawthorne hoped "would take root in the imaginative observer's memory"!)—palpable emblems of romance with their "crimson-spotted flowers," Italian origin, and affinity for the water from Maule's well— "were flaunting in rich beauty and full bloom, to-day, and seemed, as it were, a mystic expression that something within the house was consummated." Here again is the familiar association of successful romance art and sexual affirmation. But we should notice that the conclusion of Hawthorne's tale, besides celebrating the triumph of sexual love, also suggests that the Maule-Pyncheon marriage, with its simultaneous revelation and liquidation of the corpse of the past, will hopefully obviate much of the need for romance. The darkness has been dispersed, and compromise, in art as in life, is the order of the day. Now that his "lawlessness" has added a note of romance depth to Phoebe Pyncheon's law-abiding world view, Holgrave seems relieved to be able to renounce his witchcraft: "I have a presentiment, that, hereafter, it will be my lot to set out trees, to make fences—perhaps, even, in due time, to build a house for another generation—in a word, to conform myself to laws, and the peaceful practice of society."[23]

If Holgrave's promise to Phoebe is a covert expression of Hawthorne's own desire to be released from the burden of being a romancer, it may help to explain why he went on to write his next book. From a romance that ends by seemingly denying the future necessity for the form, Hawthorne moved on to a book that questions the aesthetic and moral premises of his own admittedly fantastic art.

4. *Fire or Ice*

BY choosing as the narrator of *The Blithedale Romance* a "small poet," deprecatingly self-defined as "a devoted epicure" of his own emotions, who can scarcely believe either in the existence of those very emotions or in the truth of the fantasies lavishly manufactured by his perfervid imagina-

---

23. On Holgrave's "conversion" away from art see Rudolph Von Abele, *The Death of the Artist*, pp. 67–68.

tion, Hawthorne succeeded in producing an ironic romance: one which consistently undercuts the familiar Hawthornian notion that romance art has the power to reveal terrible truths about the human heart. It is typical of the self-conscious American romancer, from Hawthorne to James, that he should pause at some point in his career to dispute the very basis of his art. (Melville's *The Confidence-Man* is a parallel example.) And the hard question of deciding just what *Blithedale* is really about can perhaps most simply be answered with the suggestion that it is largely concerned with the difficulty its "author" has in discovering and conveying the truth of his experience.[24]

"Real life," Miles Coverdale asserts, "never arranges itself exactly like a romance." More pointedly, Coverdale can never quite believe that the postures of romance art bear a truly vital relation to real life. He complains that "the presence of Zenobia caused our heroic enterprise to show like an illusion, a masquerade, a pastoral, a counterfeit Arcadia," whereas the reader is likelier to feel that it is precisely the participation of this splendidly tragic dark lady that at once makes the masquerade possible and fills it with human meaning. It is she, as Coverdale recognizes, who lends the most theatrical scenes in the world of Blithedale the "atmosphere of strange enchantment" which endows romance characters with a "propriety of their own" necessary for credibility. As Hawthorne tells us in his preface to the book:

> This atmosphere is what the American romancer needs. In its absence, the beings of imagination are compelled to show themselves in the same category as actually living mortals; a necessity that generally renders the paint and pasteboard of their composition but too painfully discernible.

Odd as it may seem in view of Hawthorne's own plea, it is in fact the almost unrelievedly ironic presence of Coverdale himself that invests the extraordinary happenings in the book with an air of illusion and counterfeit. Coverdale's characteristic attitude toward the heroic, tragic, and epic modes is defined by his perpetually bantering manner. (Taking leave of Blithedale he explains with mock gravity, "I thought of going

---

24. Terence Martin, *Nathaniel Hawthorne* (New York, 1965), pp. 145–159, contains a good discussion of *The Blithedale Romance* focusing largely on Coverdale. Frederick C. Crews, "A New Reading of *The Blithedale Romance*," *American Literature*, XXIX (1957), 147–170, stresses the importance, for the book as a whole, of Coverdale's desire to produce a romance.

across the Rocky Mountains, or to Europe, or up the Nile—of offering myself a volunteer on the Exploring Expedition"; and his obvious feeling about such activities is clarified at the end of the book: "If Kossuth ... would pitch the battle-field of Hungarian rights within an easy ride of my abode, and choose a mild, sunny morning, after breakfast, for the conflict, Miles Coverdale would gladly be his man.") He seems particularly to enjoy picquing the ever-serious Hollingsworth by implicitly mocking the claims of the Blithedale participants, including himself, to permanent enshrinement as the archetypes of great art:

> "In a century or two, we shall every one of us be mythical personages, or exceedingly picturesque and poetical ones, at all events. . . . What legends of Zenobia's beauty, and Priscilla's slender and shadowy grace, and those mysterious qualities which make her seem diaphanous with spiritual light! In due course of ages, we must all figure heroically in an Epic Poem; and we will ourselves—at least, I will—bend unseen over the future poet, and lend him inspiration, while he writes it."

The visionary blacksmith accuses Coverdale of mouthing nonsense, whereupon the latter retorts: "I wish you would see fit to comprehend ... that the profoundest wisdom must be mingled with nine-tenths of nonsense; else it is not worth the breath that utters it"—at once describing his usual habit of mind and offering an eiron's theory of romance. (Of Zenobia's legend, "The Silvery Veil," Coverdale remarks: "from beginning to end it was undeniable nonsense, but not necessarily the worse for that."[25])

As both man and artist, Coverdale's nature is patently divided.[26] On the one hand, by his own confession "having a decided tendency towards the actual," he makes us feel that his largest commitment is to the normal world of social existence. Stricken down upon his arrival at Blithedale by that fever which, he will insist later, ultimately caused him to die to "old conventionalisms," to be divested "of a thousand follies, fripperies, prejudices, habits," and to be reborn into that knot of dreamers who inhabited "the freer region that lay beyond," he thinks longingly of the conventional city life he has left behind:

---

25. "What Coverdale believes he cannot trust himself always to feel; and what he feels he does not believe" (Waggoner, *Hawthorne: A Critical Study*, p. 205).
26. Cf. Crews, "A New Reading of *The Blithedale Romance*."

> . . . My morning lounge at the reading-room or picture-gallery; my
> noontide walk along the cheery pavement, with the suggestive succession
> of human faces, and the brisk throb of human life, in which I shared; my
> dinner at the Albion, where I had a hundred dishes at command . . . my
> evening at the billiard-club, the concert, the theatre, or at somebody's
> party.

Coverdale's description of his usual routine reads like a catalog of the
ordinary resources of the novelist and suggests how much at home he
feels in that realm of comfortable reality which is the furthest thing from
the romancer's haunted imagination.

But Coverdale has his Hamlet side. Afflicted by bad dreams pregnant
with dark meanings, he frequently views the world, even when awake,
with that surrealistic eyesight which is the mark of the romance artist.
Zenobia with her exotic flowers, for example, continually strikes him as
preternatural, and he vexes Hollingsworth by spinning out his fantasy:
"Zenobia is an enchantress! . . . She is a sister of the Veiled Lady! That
flower in her hair is a talisman. If you were to snatch it away, she would
vanish, or be transformed into something else!" Hollingsworth, as usual,
pronounces the poet a fool, but Coverdale's vision accurately defines
Zenobia's inner meaning and prophesies her end. Again, when Coverdale
first sees Priscilla she inspires in him a "fantasy . . . that she was some
desolate kind of a creature, doomed to wander about in snow-storms
. . . she would not remain long enough to melt the icicles out of her hair";
and however absurd this may seem as a description of the presumably
warmhearted and lovable young maiden, it really does suggest the essential frigidity of her perpetually chaste and unsexual nature.

Coverdale's vividly metaphoric imagination also captures the repressed
passion that is the secret of Hollingsworth's nature: in a startling figure
that clearly looks forward to Henry James, he speaks of Hollingsworth's
glaring at his Blithedale companions "from the thick shrubbery of his
meditations, like a tiger out of a jungle."[27] And Coverdale has a repeated
fantasy in which the philanthropist's "features grew more sternly prominent than the reality, duskier in their depth and shadow, and more lurid
in their light; the frown, that had merely flitted across his brow, seemed
to have contorted it with an adamantine wrinkle." Similarly, when the

---

27. Indeed, James quotes this passage in his *Hawthorne*, reprinted in *The Shock
of Recognition*, edited by Edmund Wilson (New York, 1955), p. 530.

impressionable young poet first meets the sinister Professor Westervelt, his descriptive imagery runs all to diabolism, and he has a fantasy about Westervelt's "spectral character" that effectively hints at the wizard's strange powers. Throughout the book Coverdale alternates between being an urbane and sarcastic wit, whose banter makes light of all mysteries, and a moody romance artist with an apt eye for the hidden and sinister.

Two episodes in particular, both apparently digressive, seem designed to suggest the alternative possibilities open to Coverdale as an artist and his attitude toward them. In "A Village Hall" we find him in a Massachusetts lyceum waiting for the start of a mesmeric demonstration (which turns out to be Professor Westervelt's final attempt to get possession of Priscilla's soul). Coverdale drifts near a "knot of people who might be considered as representing the mysticism, or, rather, the mystic sensuality," of the age and is fascinated by their conversation:

> I heard, from a pale man in blue spectacles, some stranger stories than ever were written in a romance; told, too, with a simple, unimaginative steadfastness, which was terribly efficacious in compelling the auditor to receive them into the category of established facts. He cited instances of the miraculous power of one human being over the will and passions of another; insomuch that settled grief was but a shadow, beneath the influence of a man possessing this potency, and the strong love of years melted away like a vapor. At the bidding of one of these wizards, the maiden, with her lover's kiss still burning on her lips, would turn from him with icy indifference; the newly made widow would dig up her buried heart out of her young husband's grave, before the sods had taken root upon it; a mother, with her babe's milk in her bosom, would thrust away her child. Human character was but soft wax in his hands; and guilt, or virtue, only the forms into which he should see fit to mould it. The religious sentiment was a flame which he could blow up with his breath, or a spark that he could utterly extinguish.

Despite his manifest approval for the storyteller's method, Coverdale is horrified and disgusted by what he hears—which we might say represents Hawthorne's sly attempt to justify his art while disclaiming affection for his subjects. In any case, the story nuclei outlined here read like entries from Hawthorne's literary notebook, for the theme of dark possibilities in human relations is a staple of his fiction (Aylmer and Georgiana, Ethan Brand and Esther, Chillingworth and Dimmesdale, the Maule men and the Pyncheon women). More to the point, the stories told by the pale man in blue spectacles seem all to make up one parable: the terrible power, for good or ill (but mainly for ill), residing in the gifted hands of the romance artist. The intensity of Coverdale's unwillingness to acknowledge the reality of this sinister power is a measure of his emotional pusillanimity, in art as in life: to express himself passionately in either realm would be to run the risk of assuming responsibility for stirring others to the depths. So upset does he become at the pale man's suggestion of the existence of dark psychic "phenomena" that he launches a veritable harangue, bitterly attacking the symbolic stock in trade of the romancer—the subjective spectres of past pain and guilt that crowd the pages of Hawthorne's fictions:

> These goblins, if they exist at all, are but the shadows of past mortality, outcasts, mere refuse-stuff, adjudged unworthy of the eternal world, and, on the most favorable supposition, dwindling gradually into nothingness. The less we have to say to them, the better; lest we share their fate!

Coverdale prefers to be known, or forgotten, as the author of "pretty verses" (his fate is to be entombed in Dr. Griswold's anthology), rather than court the danger of dabbling in eternal darkness as a committed romancer.

By his own admission, that danger really does exist for him. The diabolical Westervelt, the mesmerist who tries to exhibit his power over Priscilla (ultimately, by clear implication, attempting to violate her "virgin reserve" and thus to convert her, as he has Zenobia, into an experienced woman), exercises a strange fascination over Coverdale, who admits that "a part of my own nature showed itself responsive to him." And this suggestion is drawn out in the following chapter when the satanic fiddler in the Blithedale masquerade shouts apropos of Coverdale: "He is always ready to dance to the devil's tune!" That dance—in which Coverdale as "a mad poet hunted by chimaeras" (that is, a romancer) would be forced "to approach, and pay his duty" to "Queen Zenobia"— is unquestionably sexual. When Coverdale turns away in repugnance from mesmerism and other such "phenomena," he is really refusing to involve himself in those dark experiences involving human will and passion on which Hawthornian romance is always predicated.

Coverdale's dilemma as an artist is obliquely, but truly, portrayed in another way when he is moved to give us his impressions of a saloon in which he is waiting for old Moodie (the father, as it turns out, of both

Priscilla and Zenobia). The narrator's attention is rather more than casually drawn to the paintings on the walls of the drinking establishment. Significantly, there are two kinds. First, we have realistic representations meant to satisfy or provoke the appetite, "among them an oil-painting of a beef-steak, with such an admirable show of juicy tenderness, that the beholder sighed to think it merely visionary, and incapable of ever being put upon a gridiron." Art is seen here as a true reproduction of nature, so satisfying in its fidelity that the audience can only wish that the art were life itself. Meditating on these images of sirloin, deer, salmon, duck, cheese, and sardines, Coverdale theorizes:

> All these things were so perfectly imitated, that you seemed to have the genuine article before you, and yet with an indescribable, ideal charm; it took away the grossness from what was fleshiest and fattest, and thus helped the life of man, even in its earthliest relations, to appear rich and noble, as well as warm, cheerful, and substantial.

These pictures have been wrought "with the accuracy of a daguerreo-type," yet they go life one better by refining out of existence whatever is unpleasant or uncomfortable. (Coverdale thus seems to hint at a notion of "realistic" art that is particularly satisfying to him: it can be defined not only by what it sees, but by what it overlooks.[28]) More in line with the fact that this gallery is actually a saloon, Coverdale goes on to describe pictures of

> gallant revellers, those of the old time, Flemish, apparently, with dou-blets and slashed sleeves, drinking their wine out of fantastic, long-stemmed glasses; quaffing joyously, quaffing forever, with inaudible laughter and song; while the champagne bubbled immortally against their mustaches, or the purple tide of Burgundy ran inexhaustibly down their throats.

These representations are rendered somewhat less "realistic" by their distance in time and perhaps by the treatment, but for Coverdale they belong essentially to the same category of art. All these paintings present a gay, sunshiny, eternally happy view of existence.

As we should expect, however, there is another side to the canvas:

> In an obscure corner of the saloon, there was a little picture—excellently done, moreover—of a ragged, bloated, New England toper, stretched out on a bench, in the heavy, apoplectic sleep of drunkenness. The death-in-

---

28. "Coverdale's artistic ideal is a marriage of actual life with an ennobled taste" (Crews, "A New Reading of *The Blithedale Romance*," p. 155).

life was too well portrayed. You smelt the fumy liquor that had brought on this syncope. Your only comfort lay in the forced reflection, that, real as he looked, the poor caitiff was but imaginary, a bit of painted canvass, whom no delirium tremens, nor so much as a retributive headache, awaited, on the morrow.

Coverdale is too fair a critic to deny that this picture has its points; indeed, he seems almost willing to admit that on some level the portrayal can lay claim to being called "real." But this image of life does not please him, and far from sighing "to think it merely visionary," he is relieved to consider it "imaginary"—only "a bit of painted canvass," fortunately relegated to obscurity in the dimmer recesses of the room. Thus although he knows perfectly well that all art is really only "show," he likes to think that art which approaches life lightheartedly is closer to truth than art which takes a dark view (and therefore can be dismissed as merely art).

For Coverdale, art, like alcohol, should contain and engender pleasure, not pain; and an illuminating set of analogies between these two illusion-producers obviously underlies all of Hawthorne's aesthetic theorizing in this chapter. Thus Coverdale describes the talented young bartender as if he were talking about just the sort of joy-dispensing artist that he himself would like to be:

> It was a spectacle to behold, how, with a tumbler in each hand, he tossed the contents from one to the other. Never conveying it awry, nor spilling the least drop, he compelled the frothy liquor, as it seemed to me, to spout forth from one glass and descend into the other, in a great parabolic curve, as well-defined and calculable as a planet's orbit. He had a good forehead, with a particularly large development just above the eyebrows; fine intellectual gifts, no doubt, which he had educated to this profitable end; being famous for nothing but gin-cocktails, and commanding a fair salary by his one accomplishment.

Who, Coverdale seems to be asking, would not devote his life to the art of the cocktail-shaker if he could thereby both earn a good living and provide mankind with "about a quarter-of-an-hour" of "renewed youth and vigor, the brisk, cheerful sense of things present and to come"?

That our narrator is thinking of banishing the darkness from his own imagination is further suggested by the final object that engages his attention, a kind of miniature aquarium. The fishes that go "gleaming about, now turning up the sheen of a golden side, and now vanishing into the shadows of the water," suggest to him "the fanciful thoughts that coquet with a poet in his dream," and it strikes him as a "delightful idea" that some "freakish inebriate" should pour his liquor into the water. "Who would not be a fish, if he could inhale jollity with the essential element of his existence!" What a joy to be an artist, Coverdale implies, if all a poet's imaginings were happily tipsy. But he knows—and the painting of the "caitiff" has disclosed—that inebriation (read "art") is a dangerous gift. Seeing the "abundant clusters" of deep purple Blithedale grapes, Coverdale may rhapsodize over the wine which "might be pressed out of them, possessing a passionate zest, and endowed with a new kind of intoxicating quality, attended with such bacchanalian ecstasies as the tamer grapes of Madeira, France, and the Rhine, are inadequate to produce," insisting that he "longed to quaff a great goblet of it, at that moment!"; but he contents himself with "devouring the grapes." Just as he limits his drinking to a safe glass of sherry, Coverdale is usually careful to water his metaphors ("the sun shone dimly out, as if the golden wine of its beams were mingled half-and-half with water"; "each breath [of air] was like a sip of ethereal wine, tempered . . . with a crystal lump of ice"), choosing the temperate over the tempestuous in both his potations and his poetry.

Ultimately, the notion of a necessary choice in art and life is embodied in *The Blithedale Romance* in the opposed personalities of Priscilla and Zenobia. Spiritually they are sisters, as Hawthorne makes them so literally: the Janus faces of human possibility turned alternately toward every man. Every major male character in the book is obliged in some sense to make a choice between the two women. The girls' father must decide which one, the daughter of his pride or the daughter of his shame, he loves best, thereby discovering whether his real self is old Moodie or Fauntleroy. Westervelt, after trying his wizardry on both women, is constrained to learn the limitations of his mesmeric power; and Hollingsworth is presumably led to explore the truth of his emotional being in deciding which of the two he will marry.

For Coverdale, the choice lies between sexual truth and sentimental deception—between the terrible opportunity to develop into a poet of tragic depth and the comfortable decision to lapse into "minor minstrelsy" and fatuous ease. Like the narrators of Poe's "Ligeia" and "The Raven," Coverdale must in fact choose between a Ligeia and a Rowena, between dusky passion and marmoreal virtue. For the sisters of *Blithedale* are unmistakable incarnations of the familiar archetypal dark and fair ladies. Priscilla, putatively but not convincingly brown-haired and brown-eyed, is remembered as a wan face and a silvery veil. She is Hawthorne's virginal snow-maiden, who, despite her supposed "gift of second-sight and prophecy," is notable for her lack of insight and her bland disregard for past pain. Priscilla is the enemy of knowledge (she is particularly annoyed when Coverdale sees in her a resemblance to Margaret Fuller!) and is shown in "Zenobia's Legend" as demanding of the worldly and cynical Theodore pure love and commitment *before* agreeing to allay his anxiety about her sexual attractiveness. (Theodore, having refused her offer of "life-long household fireside joy," is condemned to "waste life in a feverish quest"—banished for his nastiness, as it were, from the hearth to the witches' kitchen.)

Priscilla's habitual impulse toward concealment has led Daniel Hoffman to remark "that she has no character at all, only a presumptive innocence";[29] but Hawthorne has actually made her character quite definite. She is the exponent of emotional thrift and sexual parsimony—nicely symbolized, as Coverdale seems to recognize, by those silk purses on which she is perpetually working, whose "peculiar excellence . . . lay in the almost impossibility that any uninitiated person should discover the aperture."[30] We see her repeatedly in postures of withholding or denying. ("I could have embroidered it and made it much prettier, if I pleased," she remarks to Coverdale of the nightcap she has made him; and he finds it particularly "bewitching" when she becomes imperious and, with "a little gesture of dismissal," tells him to "go on before.") Her nature is beautifully described when Coverdale observes that "with all her delicacy of nerves, there was a singular self-possession in Priscilla, and her sensibilities seemed to lie sheltered from ordinary commotion." Imperturbable and unreachable, this self-contained fair maiden reinforces in Coverdale that habit of emotional sterility which finds expression in his brittle, superficial persiflage—the certain mark of his artistic impotence.

Coverdale himself clearly sees the absolute opposition between Priscilla and Zenobia in imaginative terms when, at the base of Eliot's Pulpit, he envisions Hollingsworth as "a Puritan magistrate, holding inquest of

---

29. *Form and Fable in American Fiction*, p. 215.
30. Cf. Rudolph Von Abele, *The Death of the Artist*, p. 80.

life and death in a case of witchcraft," Zenobia being "the sorceress herself, not aged, wrinkled, and decrepit, but fair enough to tempt Satan with a force reciprocal to his own," and Priscilla "the pale victim, whose soul and body had been wasted by her spells." Zenobia's satanic "force" is obviously her sexual knowledge and attractiveness, which threaten to draw away from the pale virgin all interest and power. The familiar association of the dark lady's sexual force with artistry—or "witchcraft"— is further suggested in Zenobia's complementary fantasy, "The Silvery Veil." Once again, the two ladies are presented as deadliest enemies; and this time, since the fable is Zenobia's own creation, she is successful in removing Priscilla from the scene and presumably in ensuring her violation (by delivering the Veiled Lady over to the bearded magician at the conclusion of the legend). But Zenobia's power over Priscilla is shown in this chapter to be real as well as fanciful (art and life being interchangeable and mutually enriching for the dark lady). When she has finished telling her tale, she protracts its effect into actuality by flinging a piece of gauze over Priscilla and thereby nearly frightening her to death. Thus, in doubly "destroying" Priscilla by means of her legend, Zenobia demonstrates her superiority as both an artist and a woman, the interdependent attributes associated with her archetypal role.

Priscilla demonstrates that an apparently artless person can embody the spirit of concealment. Zenobia, in contrast, with her flamboyantly dramatic habits and histrionic postures (Coverdale calls her a "work of art"), tends to suggest that in art, as in wine, there lies emotional truth. In the first moments of her initial meeting with Coverdale, she willingly adopts the role of Eve, inspiring the narrator to postlapsarian Adamic feelings and fantasies that give us a deep insight into his submerged nature. When Zenobia promises "playfully" that she will assume the "garb of Eden" when the weather warms up, "something in her manner" causes Coverdale to conjure up a vivid image of her "fine, perfectly developed figure, in Eve's earliest garment." Thereafter, the presence of this "magnificent woman" is always the signal for the release of unabashedly sexual dreams and speculations in the narrator. With a surprising frankness, Hawthorne allows a habit of sexual innuendo to grow up between Zenobia and Coverdale which clearly suggests passionate possibilities in the life of this seemingly effete minor poet. Zenobia, with her "hot-house flower—an outlandish flower—a flower of the tropics, such as appeared to have sprung passionately out of a soil, the very weeds of which would be fervid and spicy"—that exotic bloom which here, as so frequently in Hawthorne's writings, is the unmistakable talisman of both sexual knowledge and the spirit of romance—holds out to Coverdale a key to the deepest secrets of art and life which he seems more than half willing to grasp. Feigning perplexity at his intense fascination, she asks a crucial question manifestly designed to draw Coverdale to her:

> "What are you seeking to discover in me?"
> "The mystery of your life," answered I, surprised into the truth by the unexpectedness of her attack. "And you will never tell me."
> She bent her head towards me, and let me look into her eyes, as if challenging me to drop a plummet-line down into the depths of her consciousness.
> "I see nothing now," said I, closing my own eyes, "unless it be the face of a sprite, laughing at me from the bottom of a deep well."

There is none so blind, Hawthorne seems to imply, as he who will not see. Truly Prufrockian in his ambivalence, Coverdale retreats in fear from the truth of desire that is trying to break through his timidity. Zenobia's "womanliness incarnated," he had admitted earlier in this chapter, "compelled me sometimes to close my eyes." Now he complains that the "riddle" of Zenobia's sexuality makes him "nervous": "I most ungratefully began to wish that she would let me alone." Rendered anxious throughout the book by her power to stir thoughts and feelings that he seems always to have avoided, Coverdale continually makes "a positive effort to bear up against the effect which Zenobia sought to impose."[31] Eager as he sometimes seems to pass through those "gates of mystery" from behind which Zenobia appears to beckon, Coverdale is nevertheless afraid of the dark knowledge that such experience will bring. "I reasoned against her, in my secret mind," he confesses, "and strove so to keep my footing." Zenobia, ultimately becoming aware of Coverdale's timorousness, rejects the offer he finally makes of companionship and counsel: "No, no, Mr. Coverdale; if I choose a counselor . . . it must be either an angel or a madman; and I rather apprehend that the latter would be likeliest of the two to speak the fitting word. It needs a wild steersman when we voyage through Chaos!"

---

31. "Obviously infatuated with her [Zenobia], he is not the man to submit to such a feeling," writes Philip Rahv; ". . . the whole point of Coverdale's behavior is to avoid involvement" ("The Dark Lady of Salem," *Partisan Review*, VIII [1941], 376–377). Rahv's article contains a now classic discussion of Hawthorne's simultaneous fascination for and horror of dark ladies and what they represent.

Just as the guide on Zenobia's voyage of passion must be a kind of madman, the poetic chronicler of her deeds should himself be a true sufferer, and Coverdale is as unfit for the one post as for the other. "By all means, write this ballad," she urges him at the end:

> "and put your soul's ache into it, and turn your sympathy to good account, as other poets do, and as poets must, unless they choose to give us glittering icicles instead of lines of fire. As for the moral, it shall be distilled into the final stanza, in a drop of bitter honey."

This challenge concisely summarizes Coverdale's problem as an artist and predicts the outcome of his writing career. The sympathy, necessarily based on personal experience, that is needed for the production of tragic art he is finally shown to be incapable of. His characteristic mode is that of ironic banter—ice, not fire—and the "moral" conveyed by the final stanza of his "ballad" is a perfect piece of bittersweet humbug. Coverdale's stunningly fatuous confession on the last page ("I—I myself—was in love—with—PRISCILLA!") demonstrates just how purblind he really is, for his "one secret"—his safe and sane predilection for the fair lady— has been painfully obvious all along; and, noticing the ultimate twist of Hawthorne's irony, one can hardly refrain from remarking that Coverdale's "confession" only underlines the open secret of his obvious inability to love anybody.

The larger moral of *The Blithedale Romance* would in fact appear to be that if a man is a sentimental fraud, he cannot hope to produce art that reveals the truth of the human heart. In Coverdale's hands, romance proves to be a deception, as much a masquerade as the abortive Blithedale experiment itself. Is it, however, the fault only of the artist, or perhaps also of the art? Hawthorne's uncertainty over the answer to this question doubtless contributed to the fact that he waited "seven or eight years"— "so many, at all events, that I cannot precisely remember the epoch"— before attempting another romance.

5. *Saints and Assassins*

HAWTHORNE's last complete exercise in his chosen form, *The Marble Faun*, leaves no doubt about the durability of his original belief that dark truths exist and that the romance artist has the power to portray them. If anything, the book represents a deepening almost to religious pro- portions of Hawthorne's faith in his art. His only apparent doubt is whether it is necessary that *all* men—and women—become permanently aware of those burdensome truths, which, once recognized, cannot be argued away. Here we are not in the hands of a bantering Coverdale, whose authorial timidity protects us from the tragic view. In *The Marble Faun*, the dusky Miriam and the darkling Donatello are ineluctable features of Hawthorne's fictional world, not to be dispelled by narrative irony. All that Hawthorne can do—and he attempts it with a kind of desperation—is to practice a sort of artistic and spiritual isolationism, banishing sin and guilt to prison and penitence in Europe, while allowing his untransformed Americans to return to the sunshine of their "dear native land." But the device is patently unsuccessful. Romance darkness (as Poe might have said, and as Hawthorne convinces us only too well) is not of Italy, but of the soul.[32]

Hawthorne's constant preoccupation with the function of the artist, so intimately connected with the whole notion of romance, engrossed him to such a degree by the time of *The Marble Faun* that it at last became the actual subject of his book.[33] All four of the protagonists are, literally or metaphorically, artists; and the tale is essentially devoted to describing the relationship between individual experience and its reflection in art, which is seen as both the key to and an expression of character. The romancer's belief in the living force of true art—that is, art based on profound human experience—is embodied by Hawthorne in the very person of his eponymous hero. Donatello, who bears a sculptor's name, is shown in the course of the action to be the creator of his new self. He transforms himself (and *Transformation* was the title given the book by Hawthorne's English publishers) from a statue, the innocent marble faun, into a sinful adult man by a conscious act of will—demonstrating, as it were, that all that is needed to make art truly alive is the touch of suffering humanity.

Just as Donatello becomes the human emblem of a truth about art, so artistic objects are used to emblematize the human meaning of his

---

32. Roy Harvey Pearce argues ("Hawthorne and the Twilight of Romance," p. 487) that *The Marble Faun* marks the failure of "romance as Hawthorne knew it . . . to give shape and meaning to the life which it was to comprehend."

33. In "Art Allegory in *The Marble Faun*," *PMLA*, LXXVII (1962), 254–267, Paul Brodtkorb, Jr., presents an interesting discussion in which he sees the book as an allegory about the relative value of different aesthetic/moral positions. "The characters have become spokesmen for various elements of Hawthorne's self-divisive view of his total world" and "operate as counters on the plane of aesthetic theory."

transformation. Walking through the Capitoline Museum in the opening scene of the book, Miriam, Hilda, and Kenyon are struck by Donatello's resemblance to the Faun of Praxiteles. But while they are discussing this fancied similarity, Donatello shows a decided propensity for circling around the statue of the Dying Gladiator (the first object described by Hawthorne when the four friends entered the museum). Thus, briefly but tellingly, Hawthorne suggests Donatello's fate as a living piece of sculpture—from a young and simple prelapsarian faun to a tragic warrior who discovers his own mortality in the act of bringing death to another. The inverse case of Hilda (an example of obstinate non-transformation) is also prefigured in Hawthorne's presentation of a statue showing "the Human Soul, with its choice of Innocence or Evil close at hand, in the pretty figure of a child, clasping a dove to her bosom, but assaulted by a snake." No other sculpture is described to foretell a change in Hilda's symbolic posture; and she does indeed begin and end as a child, desperately clutching her dove in the face of omnipresent evil.

The central scheme of *The Marble Faun* is concisely outlined in three significantly consecutive chapters near the start of the book ("Miriam's Studio," "The Virgin's Shrine," and "Beatrice") in which Hawthorne neatly presents the opposed figures of the dark and fair ladies as artists and then allows them to interact and expose their inner meanings over the touchstone portrait of Beatrice Cenci. Miriam—unmistakably the archetypal brunette with her sable locks, dark eyes, vaguely Jewish ancestry, and neurotically passionate nature—is the romance artist par excellence. Entering her studio, Donatello naively asks, "Why do you make it so shadowy?" thereby eliciting from Miriam a capsule theory of Hawthornian romance:

> "We artists purposely exclude sunshine, and all but a partial light . . . because we think it necessary to put ourselves at odds with Nature, before trying to imitate her. That strikes you very strangely, does it not? But we make very pretty pictures, sometimes, with our artfully arranged lights and shadows."

Miriam's art, like Hawthorne's, is purposely stylized—artificial and frequently fantastic, a chiaroscuro dreamworld—but rich in symbolic implications. In the "mysterious dusk" of her studio, "one of those delightful spots that hardly seem to belong to the actual world, but rather to be the outward type of a poet's haunted imagination," Donatello sees "glimpses, sketches, and half-developed hints" of her secret soul in pictures filled with "warmth and passionateness." One in particular is an especially apt representation of both Miriam's nature and the role she will play in Donatello's life: "In the obscurest part of the room, Donatello was half-startled at perceiving, duskily, a woman with long dark hair, who threw up her arms with a wild gesture of tragic despair, and appeared to beckon him into the darkness along with her." Miriam, noting the faun's fearful response to the portrait (he is, as it seems, with his "sinister freaks of fancy," peculiarly subject to the suggestive powers of romance art), immediately tries to dispel it by insisting that the picture is art, not life, and therefore not to be taken seriously. Its heroine, she argues, "is a lady of exceedingly pliable disposition; now a heroine of romance, and now a rustic maid," and therefore "all for show." (Miriam has in fact described herself. Her full name, Miriam Schaefer, suggests precisely such an ability to play both tragic and pastoral roles, and she does indeed masquerade as a *contadina* toward the end of the book.) But it is a familiar dictum for the reader of Hawthorne that in the self-consciously theatrical posturings of his romance heroes and heroines there is more than "show." Self-dramatization always implies both artifice *and* truth.

In two other sketches described in "Miriam's Studio," the artist has cast herself in Old Testament roles—Jael killing Sisera, and Judith with the head of Holofernes—her treatment of which gives a new twist to the old tales. A quirk of her imagination, we are told, turned her Jael into a "vulgar murderess," while her paradoxical version of the Judith story undercuts the moral earnestness of that heroine by permitting the decapitated Holofernes "a diabolical grin of triumphant malice," which somehow implicates Judith herself more than was originally intended. In each case, Hawthorne tells us (looking forward to the Cenci portrait), "there was the idea of woman, acting the part of a revengeful mischief towards man." Having provoked man with her beauty, woman punishes him for being attracted, only to learn that her own hand has been "crimsoned by the stain" of mutual guilt. Miriam "failed not to bring out the moral, that woman must strike through her own heart to reach a human life, whatever were the motive that impelled her"—the inextricable links that join the passions binding her to a dark view of her own nature.

Apologizing for the sketches, Miriam cries out: "Ah! I did not mean you to see those drawings. They are ugly phantoms that stole out of my mind; not things that I created, but things that haunt me." Donatello's "look of trouble, fear, and disgust" shows, however, that despite Miriam's disclaimer of conscious responsibility for her productions (and the fact that they are obsessive and inevitable only increases their importance as spontaneous revelations of her inner being), he is aware of having caught an important glimpse of that necessary nexus of violence, sexuality, and artistic power associated with the femme fatale of romance. And his presumed anxiety and disgust notwithstanding, Donatello's desire will initiate him into that secret of Miriam's potent to render him a metaphoric artist, a literal lover, and her companion in the ranks of death. "My secret is not a pearl," Miriam says portentously to Kenyon in a remark that unites her capacity as art-critic (she is commenting on his statue of a diver) with her role as sexual prize and worldly danger, "yet a man might drown himself in plunging after it!" And she adds to herself: "my dark-red carbuncle—red as blood—is too rich a gem to put into a stranger's casket!" Not the timorous Kenyon, but the impetuous and passionate Donatello, is the soul mate who will be deemed worthy of receiving the dark lady's ambiguous gift.

Kenyon, of course, despite his sporadic attraction to the force of darkness, is inseparably allied to the "fair-haired Saxon" virgin, Hilda. F. O. Matthiessen has remarked that Hawthorne let himself "be caught off guard in his creation of these lovers, who are the perfect bleached protagonists of the genteel tradition."[34] Whatever truth this suggests about Hawthorne's presumed weakness for the stereotypes of nineteenth-century sentimental fiction, the comment overlooks the fact that *The Marble Faun* without Hilda would be radically incomplete. Her immaculate presence in the book attests, not to Hawthorne's lack of judgment as a writer, but rather to his nearly obsessive attachment to that dialectical scheme of opposed notions which we have been examining all along. Hilda is the final avatar of Hawthorne's archetypal fair lady, this time appearing as artist and muse in the debate over the relationship between experience and aesthetics.

---

34. *American Renaissance: Art and Expression in the Age of Emerson and Whitman* (New York, 1941), p. 360. Hawthorne's blonde maidens, writes Waggoner, reflect "the mid-century idealization of woman" and are "wholly inconsistent with his own persistent and consistent idea of mankind's brotherhood in guilt" (*Nathaniel Hawthorne*, pp. 44–45). Hawthorne's changing, largely darkening, attitude toward the fair lady is well presented by Virginia Ogden Birdsall, "Hawthorne's Fair-Haired Maidens: The Fading Light," *PMLA*, LXXV (1960), 250–256.

The most significant thing about Hilda's artistry is that, in sharp distinction to Miriam's powerful and terrible originality, she is a copyist. Hawthorne informs us that in her schooldays she had done some original work, but even in this her diametric opposition to Miriam is clear, since her sketches were of "scenes delicately imagined, lacking, perhaps, the reality which comes only from a close acquaintance with life," drawings that "seemed to be looking at humanity with angel's eyes." The author then insists that "with years and experience, she might be expected to attain a darker and more forcible touch," but we have every reason to disbelieve such a possibility exists. For it is precisely the tenebrous and the violent in human experience that Hilda fears and avoids; and at the close of the action she is represented as straining hopefully to see "sunlight on the mountain-tops."

Hilda's abandonment, upon her arrival in Italy, of the "impulse of original design," and her devotion to copying, Hawthorne ascribes to the girl's "sensitive faculty of appreciation" and to her repugnance at the idea of putting herself forward in the face of the "mighty old masters" (as if self-expression were a kind of sin). "Reverencing these wonderful men so deeply, she was too grateful for all they bestowed upon her—too loyal—too humble, in their awful presence—to think of enrolling herself in their society." Although Hawthorne is here praising Hilda's humility, he might with deeper justification have complimented her instinctive shrewdness in choosing a métier which excuses her from putting herself forward in a far more important sense. Original art, as in Miriam's case, demands an exposure of the secret self that Hilda is not prepared to make. And it is also predicated on an openness to experience, a willingness to gaze steadily at all possibilities of existence, that is alien to Hilda's virginal nature. Examining a cartoon which presumably represents Guido's "original sketch for the picture of the Archangel Michael, setting his foot upon the demon," Hilda reverently describes "the Archangel, who turns away his eyes in painful disgust" from the vindictive scowl of the demon, whereupon Miriam laughs to scorn the "daintiness" of Guido's Michael: "He never could have looked the Demon in the face!" Hilda is predictably shocked at Miriam's irreverence, but the full measure of Hilda's devotion to Guido's Archangel—in her opinion, "the most beautiful and the divinest figure that mortal painter ever drew"—becomes clear only later in the book, when she prays to him in her trouble. For Guido's Michael, in his desire to oppose evil but not to gaze on it, is the perfect emblem of Hilda's own nature. Oppressed by a general sense of Miriam's crime, she tries to dispel her anxiety not by understanding the mystery, and possibly sympathizing with the motive, but simply by shedding the whole business. She determinedly enters the confessional not as a Catholic but as a Protestant, her desire being not for "confession" —which would imply an admission of personal guilt—but only to unload her burden.

Just as she flees from what is sordid in experience, so her copying of works of art is usually selective. "It was not Hilda's general practice," Hawthorne remarks significantly, "to attempt reproducing the whole of a great picture, but to select some high, noble, and delicate portion of it, in which the spirit and essence of the picture culminated"; she concentrates on the Virgin, an angel, or a saint. Unlike Miriam, whose art beckons mankind into the lonely dark, Hilda is the apostle of light and uplifting popular culture:

> From the dark, chill corner of a gallery—from some curtained chapel in a church, where the light came seldom and aslant—from the prince's carefully guarded cabinet, where not one eye in thousands was permitted to behold it—she brought the wondrous picture into daylight, and gave all its magic splendour for the enjoyment of the world.

Hilda's function as an artist is to disseminate licit pleasure and that "white wisdom" which Kenyon begs for at the end of the book.

The major picture, however, whose magic splendor Hilda is responsible for bringing into the light embodies a wisdom which is disturbingly ambiguous and serves further to sharpen the opposition between Hawthorne's two heroines. This painting—Hilda's copy of the presumed portrait of Beatrice Cenci by Guido Reni—and its subject in fact underlie Hawthorne's total scheme in *The Marble Faun*, for Beatrice and the art she inspires comprise the book's chief center of reference. Miriam is insistently, if vaguely, identified with Beatrice Cenci, and her history by clear implication repeats that of her supposed ancestress. Tortured by the taint of real or imagined incest, Miriam brings about the death of the man presumably responsible for her initiation into evil and thereby introduces her friends, through participation or knowledge, into the world of sin—just as Beatrice not only both suffers and commits crime, but also passes along an awareness of it to mankind by herself becoming a subject for art. Hilda, too, is likened to Beatrice—but in this case to a Beatrice "whose character and history," as Henry A. Murray notes, "had been assimilated to the most moving theme of the . . . [nineteenth-century] mythology of the heart, that of *abused female innocence*."[35] An unspecified Italian artist, Hawthorne tells us, in a sketch "supposed to have been suggested by the portrait of Beatrice Cenci," "represented Hilda as gazing, with sad and earnest horrour, at a blood-spot which she seemed just then to have discovered on her white robe" and named his creation "Innocence, dying of a Blood-stain!" Furthermore, Beatrice's story becomes a *locus classicus* for that need for sympathetic understanding which both the women in Hawthorne's tale will ultimately feel and which the self-righteous virtue of a Hilda would deny to the suffering guilt of a Miriam. (Sending Hilda off on an errand to the Palazzo Cenci, Miriam recommends that Hilda, if she meets Beatrice's ghost, should try to "win her confidence": "Poor thing! she would be all the better for pouring her heart out freely, and would be glad to do it, if she were sure of sympathy. It irks my brain and heart to think of her, all shut up within herself. . . . For she was still a woman, Hilda, still a sister, be her sin or sorrow what they might.")

But the most important function of the Cenci archetype lies in the portrait itself, which serves as a paradigm of Hawthorne's own romance art—an art that reveals the secret soul of (in this case) woman to the perceptive eye. "Everywhere," Miriam explains, "we see oil-paintings, crayon-sketches, cameos, engravings, lithographs, pretending to be Beatrice, and representing the poor girl with blubbered eyes, a leer of coquetry, a merry look, as if she were dancing, a piteous look, as if she were beaten, and twenty other modes of fantastic mistake." Only in Hilda's copy do we have "Guido's very Beatrice"; whence Miriam asks her friend to "interpret what the feeling is, that gives this picture such a mysterious force." Hilda's response is predictably high-minded: "She is a fallen angel, fallen, and yet sinless." Yet this is so transparently evasive that under cross-examination from Miriam she revises her interpretation to "terrible guilt, an inexpiable crime," and concludes on a strongly defensive moral note: "Her doom is just." If Beatrice *is* a sinner, Hilda is content to see her "forever vanish away into nothingness!" Miriam, as we should expect, has little doubt of Beatrice's "evil" nature. Her

---

35. Herman Melville, *Pierre: Or, The Ambiguities*, edited by Henry A. Murray (New York, 1949), p. 503.

major uncertainty concerns Beatrice's *attitude* toward her "sin": "If she viewed it as a sin, it may have been because her nature was too feeble for the fate imposed upon her. . . . I would give my life to know whether she thought herself innocent, or the one great criminal since time began!" Somewhat chary of his own subject, Hawthorne purposely leaves it unclear whether his characters are talking about incest or murder, but the terms of the discussion and Miriam's almost hysterical interest in it make perfectly clear the inference that the picture owes its "mysterious force" to female sexuality (ambiguously, and therefore fascinatingly, portrayed in Beatrice's angelic face with eyes that "met those of the spectator, but evidently with a strange, ineffectual effort to escape"). Miriam's profound need to understand and justify her own nature gives her an insight into the picture, which the magical work of art seems to reward with a moment of eerie communion. After Miriam has delivered her opinion, Hilda is "startled to observe that her friend's expression had become almost exactly that of the portrait; as if her passionate wish and struggle to penetrate poor Beatrice's mystery had been successful."

This gesture, which seems simultaneously to confirm Miriam's interpretation and to reveal her own hidden self, elicits a notable reaction from Hilda: " 'Oh, for Heaven's sake, Miriam, do not look so!' she cried. 'What an actress you are! And I never guessed it before! Ah; now you are yourself again,' she added, kissing her. 'Leave Beatrice to me, in future.' " Disturbed by the double revelation of an unsuspected side to both Miriam and Beatrice, Hilda insists—in effect, denying the very premises of Hawthorne's art—that the impression was theatrical and therefore false. She assumes that Miriam's true self (which for Hilda is necessarily a pure one, and thus rewardable with a virginal embrace) returns with the disappearance of artifice. And as she demands a familiar version of womanhood in her friend, Hilda also wants the right to continue thinking of Beatrice in conventionally proper terms as a sentimental portrait of abused female innocence. But neither the suggestion of ambiguity in woman's nature nor the strange power of the picture (with which that suggestion is allied) can be so easily suppressed. Miriam's final remark about the picture to her friend, archly calculated to undermine Hilda's certainties, points unmistakably in the direction of a disturbing problem that touches the fair maiden herself: "It is strange, dear Hilda, how an innocent, delicate, white soul, like yours, has been able to seize the subtle mystery of this portrait; as you surely must, in order to reproduce it so perfectly." Hilda's ability to reproduce the portrait of Beatrice seems to imply an unsuspected consonance of souls, some hidden sharing of natures. And in fact Miriam's remark looks forward directly to another episode of magic communion between the portrait and an observer, this time Hilda. Sitting in her room after the momentous crime that stirs her psychic depths has been committed by Miriam and Donatello, Hilda happens to glance in a looking-glass that reflects both her own face and the Cenci portrait (the familiar Hawthornian mirror suggesting a moment of particular romance intensity). "She fancied—nor was it without horrour—that Beatrice's expression . . . had been depicted in her own face," and she concludes miserably: "Am I, too, stained with guilt?"

Hawthorne immediately assures us that it was "not so, thank Heaven!" —not necessarily, as regards Beatrice; and certainly not as regards Hilda— and he offers a "theory" which may explain the "unutterable grief and mysterious shadow of guilt" that seem to touch both girls and make them sisters under the skin. "It was the intimate consciousness of her [Beatrice's] father's sin that threw its shadow over her, and frightened her into a remote and inaccessible region, where no sympathy could come. It was the knowledge of Miriam's guilt that lent the same expression to Hilda's face." Whether he fully intended it or not, Hawthorne has allowed this moment of strange resemblance and his own subsequent theory to reveal something important about his sunshiny heroine. For as the Cenci father's "sin" and thus his daughter's "intimate consciousness" are sexual, so too (by analogy and by the clear implication of Hawthorne's plot) are Miriam's "guilt" and Hilda's new "knowledge." The discovery that has darkened Hilda's life is that of actual or potential female sexuality— undeniable not only in Beatrice and in Miriam, but even, all too horribly and inexplicably, in her own pure virginal self. Thus has the uncanny power of the Cenci portrait made itself felt in the white bosom of the unsuspecting copyist.[36]

In fact, contrary to the now standard critical complaint that his snow

---

36. Cf. Crews, *The Sins of the Fathers*, p. 217. "It is all very mysterious," writes Frederic I. Carpenter, "but Hawthorne seems in his roundabout way to be suggesting that Hilda is connected with the sin of the Cenci" ("Puritans Preferred Blondes: The Heroines of Melville and Hawthorne," *New England Quarterly*, IX [1936], 268).

maiden is no more than a cardboard representation of unspotted virtue,[37] Hawthorne succeeds in sketching in Hilda the credible portrait of a woman in desperate flight from her own sexuality. "What a discovery is here!" thinks Kenyon toward the end of the book when he stumbles on an antique Venus. "I seek for Hilda, and find a marble woman! Is the omen good or ill?" Good or ill, the omen is exact and indicative (as art objects tend to be in Hawthorne), predicting that a woman who suffers such intense anxiety and near-pathological fear at the approach of people or ideas suggesting carnality will make a chilly bride as well as a cold companion. "He cannot be my friend," Hilda says of Kenyon to Miriam, "because—because—I have fancied that he sought to be something more." The unwillingness, implied in the stutter, even to speak of certain matters is a mark of Hilda's extreme dissociation of sensibility. "With so much tenderness as Hilda had in her nature," Hawthorne admits in apparent perplexity at his own creation, "it was strange that she so reluctantly admitted the idea of love."

Hilda's reluctance, however, is not strange at all but proof of a rigorous consistency in her nature. "Tenderness" and "love"—delicately pure sentiment and carnal passion—are necessarily distinct categories for a woman who seems to equate defloration with death. Indeed, Hilda must logically prefer death to what she conceives of as the sinful alternative, since in a state of non-being she would at least be removed from further danger or temptation.[38] Hilda herself all but admits that she views life as a wicked trial through which she must work her way as carefully as possible back to immaculate non-existence: "I am a poor, lonely girl,

37. Feidelson speaks of "the simple morality of Hilda, a purely allegorical creature equipped with white robe, tower, lamp, and doves" (*Symbolism and American Literature*, p. 15).

38. With remarkable sureness of touch, Hawthorne in fact allows Hilda, as she wanders through Saint Peter's burdened to the point of hysteria by her unwelcome knowledge of Miriam's sin, to project her favorite fantasy (of permanent separation from her corruptible flesh) onto a convenient work of art: "Next to the shrine where she had knelt, there is another, adorned with a picture by Guercino, representing a maiden's body in the jaws of the sepulchre, and her lover weeping over it; while her beatified spirit looks down upon the scene, in the society of the Saviour, and a throng of Saints. Hilda wondered if it were not possible, by some miracle of faith, so to rise above her present despondency that she might look down upon what she was, just as Petronilla in the picture looked at her own corpse."

whom God has set here in an evil world, and given her only a white robe, and bid her wear it back to Him, as white as when she put it on." Miriam's response, the perspicacity of which Hawthorne must have shared, recognizes that such a view is strictly incompatible with human life: "As an angel, you are not amiss; but, as a human creature, and a woman among earthly men and women, you need a sin to soften you." Hilda's refusal to accept her own sexuality—in effect, to admit that her "pure" self harbors "impurity" and is therefore a mixed, or human, nature—turns her into a rigid dualist, an absolutist in morals and the sworn enemy of ambiguity. What appears to her "almost more shocking than pure evil," she affirms to her would-be lover, is any "dreadful mixture of good and evil." Kenyon's reply, "Alas for poor human nature, then!"—expressing a terrible truth of which he seems not entirely conscious (he delivers his remark "sadly, and yet half smiling")—might more pointedly read: Alas for poor human art, then. For Hilda's fear of any suggestion of moral complexity in human affairs is, as Hawthorne certainly was aware, a major obstacle, not only to sympathy among men, but also to the production or comprehension of serious art.[39]

In a curious chapter ("The Emptiness of Picture Galleries") whose full intent is obscured by the difficulty one has in separating the author's attitudes from Hilda's,[40] Hawthorne seems to suggest that the psychic shock dealt Hilda by the dark knowledge that (to borrow a phrase from *The House of the Seven Gables*) "life is made up of marble and mud"— her inability to accept what seems sordid as part of an idealizable human condition—turns her away from the great Italian masters. Tortured by the notion that the sacred and the profane should ever be mixed, Hilda recoils in disgust from those formerly "venerated painters" who have played her "the tremendous jest . . . of offering the features of some venal beauty to be enshrined in the holiest places"—that is, who have used their own mistresses as models for paintings of the Madonna. (Hilda is herself presented throughout *The Marble Faun* as the devoted vestal— indeed, almost a Protestant version—of the Virgin Mary, and there is a lurking implication here that she is particularly distressed at seeing her own fantasized ideal self represented by trollops.) That "the same il-

---

39. "Hawthorne shows that we must choose between artistic profundity and Hilda-ism; they are incompatible" (Crews, *The Sins of the Fathers*, p. 236).

40. Cf. Richard Harter Fogle, *Hawthorne's Fiction: The Light and the Dark*, revised edition (Norman, Okla., 1964), pp. 206–207.

lustrious and impious hands" that painted "impure pictures" of nude women should have also created "the august forms of Apostles and Saints, the Blessed Mother of the Redeemer, and her Son" seems to her unspeakable.

What a more sympathetic critic might consider the great glory of Italian religious art—its intuition of spiritual meaning in unspiritual matter and its large appetite for all of experience—Hilda considers a profanation. Wanting only to soar in "maiden elevation . . . above our vanities and passions, our moral dust and mud," she rejects art—as she rejects Miriam—when it threatens to prick her ethereal bubble. After glimpsing dark truth in the reflected resemblance of her face and the Cenci portrait, "Hilda nervously moved her chair, so that the images should be no longer visible." Now, standing in front of the profound masters of the Old World with uncomfortably deepened vision, she chooses instead to dream of "her native village, with its great, old elm-trees, and the neat, comfortable houses, scattered along the wide grassy margin of its street, and the white meeting-house, and her mother's very door"; and she yearns for "those days that never brought any strange event, that life of sober week-days, and a solemn Sabbath at the close!" Faced with the disturbingly complex world of Italian art and her own consequent inner turmoil, Hilda has eyes only for her memory of a simple and rigorous New England, whitewashed through girlish fantasy into eternal immaculateness.

All the things that Hilda fears and finally flees—sexual awareness, guilty memories, moral ambiguity, artistic depth—are conveniently, if perplexingly, summed up in the fantastic person of Miriam's model, who is unquestionably Hawthorne's most improbably complete symbol of the dark spirit of romance. "He looked as if he might just have stept out of a picture, and, in truth, was likely enough to find his way into a dozen pictures; being no other than one of those living models, dark, bushy bearded, wild of aspect and attire, whom artists convert into Saints or assassins, according as their pictorial purposes demand." By turns the Wandering Jew, Satan, an antique satyr, the unholy Memmius, a mad artist, or a reverend monk, the model is that ultimate portmanteau figure who combines Hawthorne's cognate interests in myth and psychology. In him the notion of a shadowy racial memory glides imperceptibly into Miriam's own "subterranean reminiscences," uniting to form the single idea of that dark interior world of primitive consciousness which inspires both nightmares and art.[41] No more, it is frequently suggested, than a creation of Miriam's own brooding imagination, the model is somehow responsible for her initiation into both unspeakable sexual knowledge and the secrets of her craft. Playing the part of Chillingworth to her Hester, or of Westervelt to her Zenobia, he also functions more or less as a Jaffrey Pyncheon to Donatello's Phoebe, for it is Donatello's participation, with Miriam, in the murder of the model that simultaneously introduces the faun to sex and death and prepares the way for his becoming the creator of his new self. (Hilda, conversely, may be seen as a Phoebe who refuses to cross the threshold into the house.)

As in *The House of the Seven Gables*, but with a much more lurid and suggestive touch, the single love scene in *The Marble Faun* is enacted over a "heap of mortality." Here, however, Hawthorne makes it much clearer than in the earlier book that the curious combination of horror and ecstasy which makes up the lovers' rapture is the very index of adult sexual passion: a moment of pleasure that flowers over corruption, a furtive joy with sin and guilt lurking at its base. This insight forms an important part of Hawthorne's theme, for the newly born adult consciousness is indeed (in James Joyce's deadly accurate word-play on *felix culpa*) a *foenix culprit*,[42] a sexual criminal born out of the ashes of various discarded pieties: the innocent old self, the supplanted father, the disobeyed God. Miriam's model, like Jaffrey Pyncheon, is a version of the real or imagined ravishing surrogate father, whose ritual murder—like the acting out of an Oedipal fantasy—supposedly releases the adult sexual potential of the young couple. But Hawthorne's treatment of this archetypal scheme is considerably more sombre in *The Marble Faun* than in *The House of the Seven Gables*, for the death of Jaffrey Pyncheon (who has the good grace to die of his own accord, thus mooting the question of murder) is seen unmitigatedly as the end of a rascal and purely fortunate in its results: Phoebe receives depth, and Holgrave relief, without guilt. In the later book, however, Hawthorne seems to be grappling with a profounder truth: that the fall into adult consciousness, however fortunate

---

41. In "Suggestions for Interpreting *The Marble Faun*," *American Literature*, XIII (1941), 224–239, Dorothy Waples suggests that the archetypal specter may be both "a product of an individual's imagination" and "a summary of racial experience" (pp. 230–231).

42. Cf. R. W. B. Lewis, *The American Adam: Innocence, Tragedy, and Tradition in the Nineteenth Century* (Chicago, 1955), p. 11.

it may be in terms of deepening one's humanity, is still and always a fall, requiring that one live henceforth in the painful realm where pleasure and unpleasure, good and evil, are inextricably mixed. Donatello's moment of triumph on the Tarpeian Rock is followed by many moments of tortured doubt, for the seeming devil incarnate, whose death appeared so justified, returns surrounded by an "odour of sanctity" and is buried as the sacred Father Antonio, his supposed "crimes" perhaps as much a figment of Miriam's febrile imagination as the Electral father's "nastiness" is a creation of the hysterical daughter's fantasies.

Thus by moving into Miriam's world Donatello has entered the only too human realm of moral ambiguity, where all are both innocent and culpable. It is the realm of tragic art, where Othello and Ophelia are neither as black nor as white as each would seem at first glance. Miriam's Shadow, the ultimately inscrutable embodiment of romance truth, teaches the same lesson—as man, as myth, as model—which is contained in the portrait of Beatrice Cenci, a lesson too terrible for Hilda to bear: we are all just such figures as "artists convert into Saints or assassins, according as their pictorial purposes demand."

IV

MELVILLE

1. *"Marianna's Face"*

To speak of Melville as a romancer is, initially at least, to require a recapitulation of all those themes and concerns with which we have dealt in treating our previous authors. As with Cooper, Melville's abiding interest in the wilderness life, in primitivism, in hunting and being hunted, in the splendors and terrors of the physical world, in discussing the large questions of race, sex, time, and eternity—all these interests, and more, culminate in a grand American epic of man, society, and nature. Like Poe (whose influence, notably that of *Arthur Gordon Pym*, is widely diffused throughout Melville's writings[1]) Melville was obsessively concerned with the paradoxes of human reason and passion, and with all those baffling ambiguities that make experience a maze of inscrutable alternatives and unsoundable depths. Like Hawthorne—though here one especially hesitates to delimit the similarities—Melville was born to brood on the sources of sin, guilt, and pain, and to chronicle mankind's dubiously fortunate fall into experience. "The discovery we have made that we exist," Emerson wrote in an unwontedly gloomy mood, "is called the Fall of Man." Melville, like Hawthorne, took as his province the exploration of that very discovery, involving himself in an endless (some would say fruitless) debate over the implications of consciousness and of its reflection in art.

---

1. For extensive parallels between *Pym* and Melville's work, especially *Moby-Dick*, see Patrick F. Quinn, "Poe's Imaginary Voyage," *Hudson Review*, IV (1952), 579–585. To the evidence adduced by Quinn one other detail might be added: Melville's mention of "the nests in the geometrical towns of the associate penguin and pelican" in Chapter XV of *The Confidence-Man*.

This self-conscious concern with the premises of art is another all-important link connecting Melville with Poe and Hawthorne. Like them, he found it increasingly difficult to separate the notion of truth-seeking from his own problems as a writer searching for his ideal form. A manifest concern in Melville's writing, beginning as a noticeable current in *Mardi* and *Moby-Dick* and swelling to major proportions in *Pierre* and *The Confidence-Man*, is the romancer's need to define, within his own fictions, both his role as a creator and the relationship of experience to his productions. One curious but revealing example of this concern is "The Piazza," a sketch Melville wrote in 1856 to serve as a kind of frame for his *Piazza Tales* (at least three of which, it is worth noting—"Bartleby," "The Lightning-Rod Man," and "The Bell-Tower"—have intense personal reference, the first and last clearly being allegories of the artist's life). The sketch, which presumably originates in the author's decision to add a piazza, or porch, to his farmhouse, is actually a consideration of the imaginative possibilities available to Melville and of his attitude toward them. "The Piazza" is a kind of prolegomenon to all future romances, a vantage point from which Melville and the reader can survey both the tales that follow and the surrounding world. It serves, in Melville's own figure, as a bench from which he can view the picture gallery of art and life.[2]

From his piazza the author spies, on "a wizard afternoon in autumn . . . a mad poet's afternoon," a far-off place which (reminiscent of Hawthornian definitions of romance) was "so situated as to be only visible, and then but vaguely, under certain witching conditions of light and shadow" and which seems to him "one spot of radiance, where all else was shade." Determined to reach this "haunted ring," he sets off, with many a reference to Spenser, on an "inland voyage to fairy-land"—and Melville adds, slyly insisting on both the reality of his narrative and the superior force of fantasy: "A true voyage; but, take it all in all, interesting as if invented." Reaching the "fairy-mountain house," he finds that "the fairy queen sitting at her fairy window" is an extremely doleful girl named Marianna who is threatened by dark shadows of indefinable evil and oppressed by solitude and painful thoughts. Shocked by her sinister description of what he fervently believed to be so pleasant a realm, the narrator tries to argue his way to clarity:

2. " 'The Piazza' concerns vision, perspective, illusion, and reality," notes Richard Harter Fogle in *Melville's Shorter Tales* (Norman, Okla., 1960), p. 85.

"Yours are strange fancies, Marianna."

"They but reflect the things."

"Then I should have said, 'These are strange things,' rather than, 'Yours are strange fancies.' "

"As you will;" and took up her sewing.

Is darkness the fault of the imagination or of the material upon which it builds? In this oddly pregnant interchange Melville seems to put himself in the position of an artist, not yet certain of his own view, who has made a symbolic journey to the personified spirit of romance in order that she might define her meaning for him. Marianna, however, like a true sibyl, refuses to comment on the relative truth of the alternative possibilities, leaving the narrator to believe, apparently, that artistic gloom ("strange fancies") can be attributed to uncommon experience ("strange things"). Thus, by presumably convincing him that his world of romance illusion is a dreary place, Marianna frightens the narrator back to the supposed reality of his sunshiny piazza:

—Enough. Launching my yawl no more for fairy-land, I stick to the piazza. It is my box-royal; and this amphitheatre, my theatre of San Carlo. Yes, the scenery is magical—the illusion so complete. And Madam Meadow Lark, my prima donna, plays her grand engagement here; and, drinking in her sunrise note, which, Memnon-like, seems struck from the golden window, how far from me the weary face behind it.

It would seem that the author, by limiting himself to the daylight view from his piazza, has banished from his world the "weary face" of romance, proving, as it were, that the "strange things" of fairyland were no more than a bad dream. But we must not overlook the ominous rhetoric lurking in this passage which likens the joyous reality to a show. It is, in fact, this brilliant vista which is flatly called an illusion. And Melville finishes his debate, and his sketch, by admitting that reality lies in what he had tried to convince himself was only gloomy fantasy: "But, every night, when the curtain falls, truth comes in with darkness. No light shows from the mountain. To and fro I walk the piazza deck, haunted by Marianna's face, and many as real a story."

Any art is after all a kind of illusion, but the art of the night, Melville seems to suggest, reaches beyond illusion to truth. The conclusion of his sketch makes it clear that what he had written about Hawthorne six years before was equally—if not mainly—a description of himself: "spite of all the Indian-summer sunlight on the hither side of Hawthorne's soul, the other side—like the dark half of the physical sphere—is shrouded in a blackness, ten times black. . . . You may be witched by his sunlight— transported by the bright gildings in the skies he builds over you; but there is the blackness of darkness beyond." Musing on his porch with the seductive and soothing note of sunrise still ringing in his ear, Melville is none the less forced to opt for the night. All of the tales that follow "The Piazza" testify to the continuing force of Marianna's face and haunted fancies, and to Melville's unshakable belief in the reality of darkness.

2. *A Portrait of the Artist as Devil*

THE year 1856 was obviously a watershed for Melville as an artist, a time of deep reflection and reconsideration, intensified by his anxiety over his health and future. And it ended with the composition of a work which in a sense completed, as it publicly concluded, his career as a romancer.[3] Thus *The Confidence-Man* is a good book with which to begin a study of Melville, for like the revolving Drummond light employed as a metaphor for its chief character, it casts an illuminating beam forward and backward on Melville's achievement. Speaking of this book, Elizabeth Foster has noted that paradoxically "the indifference and hostility of the public did not turn Melville back to writing the South Sea idylls that the public demanded, but perhaps it is what pushed him into a symbolism, a kind of double-talk, that seems intended rather to darken than to illuminate meanings."[4] One might attempt to explain Melville's curious reaction to his waning popularity simply by instancing that characteristic perverseness which drove him repeatedly to combat incomprehension with incomprehensibility. But another possible explanation of why Melville's career followed the course it did may lie in the nature of romance itself. Beginning normally as entertainment, it gravitates inevitably toward mystery, inexorably turning into the kind of literature that illuminates meanings, when it does so at all, only by

---

3. In his edition of Melville's *Journal Up the Straits, October 11, 1856—May 5, 1857* (New York, 1935), p. xii, Raymond Weaver remarks that "the five years between the publication of *Moby-Dick* and his advent to the Holy Land were the most crucial in Melville's long life" (cited in Merton M. Sealts, Jr., "Herman Melville's 'I and My Chimney,'" in *The Recognition of Herman Melville*, edited by Herschel Parker [Ann Arbor, 1967], p. 238).

4. "Introduction" to *The Confidence-Man: His Masquerade*, edited by Elizabeth S. Foster (New York, 1954), p. xvii.

advancing steadily into the dark. Melville could plausibly have believed that an audience which followed him eagerly into South Sea adventure, and ultimately into the stalking of physical and metaphysical monsters, might show particular interest in an American voyage down our internal river in search of just about everything. What better way was there to combat the indifference of a public that had seemed originally to have a taste for romance than by offering it a culminating example of the genre, a masquerade in which "there was no lack of variety"? Melville's advertised wares included "natives of all sorts, and foreigners; men of business and men of pleasure; parlor men and backwoodsmen; farm-hunters and fame-hunters; heiress-hunters, gold-hunters, buffalo-hunters, bee-hunters, happiness-hunters, truth-hunters, and still keener hunters after all these hunters"—everything, in short, from Leatherstocking to the Devil!

Whether or not Melville's offer of a kind of literary vaudeville show was indeed an attempt to revive dwindling interest in his productions, *The Confidence-Man* represents a response to his public in a far more serious sense. It was a final attempt to explain his aims and premises to an audience which had apparently come to think he had none.[5] Undoubtedly the most curious concoction to be found in a genre notable for its curiosities, *The Confidence-Man* is a lecture with illustrations, as it were, on the theory and practice of romance. It is also a bizarre portrait of the artist as a gay Devil, the confidence-man supreme, who "lightly hums to himself an opera snatch" as he goes to and fro in the earth, eternally tempting man to follow him into a dangerous world of knowledge and speculation where truth and falsehood are beguilingly mixed. Melville's brilliant identification of his professional self with the archetypal figure of the great artificer/deceiver should have perplexed an American audience less than it did (and has!), since he only rendered explicit and writ large a notion everywhere suggested in the American romance—from Cooper's diabolically clever, untrustworthy Indians and dark ladies to James's mysteriously omniscient, duplicitous Bloomsbury antiquario: that the ambiguous gifts of art lie in the province of Satan.

The Devil's masquerade takes place appropriately on the first of April—for it is always April Fool's Day in the illusionistic realm of art—

---

5. Merton M. Sealts, Jr., argues that in much of the work of 1851–56 Melville "committed his deepest spiritual problems to subtle analysis in print" in symbolic disguise ("Herman Melville's 'I and My Chimney,'" p. 251).

when our host and guide, "essentially a fool, though effectively a knave," leads a "flock of fools" aboard a "ship of fools" for a make-believe voyage into fantasy. Our ship, the "Fidèle" (one must have faith, since art is patently a contrivance and moves only upon a willing suspension of disbelief[6]), "might at distance have been taken by strangers for some whitewashed fort on a floating isle"—a description that looks forward directly to James's definition of romance as a "commodious car of the imagination" which has been disconnected from experience as we usually know it, leaving us free to deal with "experience liberated, so to speak; experience disengaged, disembroiled, disencumbered."

The purest type of such a "ship," as we have seen in dealing with Poe and Hawthorne, is the dream, and this is precisely the status of Melville's book. "Some one talks in his sleep," the confidence-man observes in the last chapter, defining the condition of his characters, whereupon an old man shrewdly parries, "And you—*you* seem to be talking in a dream." Appearing on stage at the start of the book with studied ambiguity as a conspicuously white "lamb-like figure" (he will re-appear as a black sheep before stepping forth in full costume as a solidly white Devil), the artist/confidence-man, after some important business, is "gradually overtaken by slumber," putting himself in the attitude necessary for the production of the book that follows. Thereupon a chorus of voices neatly defines his role as a "spirit-rapper," a "kind of daylight Endymion," or a "Jacob dreaming at Luz";[7] and our romancer, "like some enchanted

---

6. "The Piazza" provides a valuable gloss on the meaning of the name of Melville's ship: "to reach fairy-land, it must be voyaged to, and with faith."

7. Once again, Melville himself seems to provide a key to his own intent in creating the sleepy mute, for in his poem "Art" the figure of the artist is represented anew by the dreaming Jacob and endowed with just those contradictory qualities suitable for a Christ whose image is fused with that of the Devil:

> In placid hours well-pleased we dream
> Of many a brave unbodied scheme.
> But form to lend, pulsed life create,
> What unlike things must meet and mate:
> A flame to melt—a wind to freeze;
> Sad patience—joyous energies;
> Humility—yet pride and scorn;
> Instinct and study; love and hate;
> Audacity—reverence. These must mate,
> And fuse with Jacob's mystic heart,
> To wrestle with the angel—Art.

man in his grave, happily oblivious of all gossip . . . tranquilly slept, while now the boat started on her voyage."

By employing a literary device stamped with the oldest possible credentials, Melville must have felt that he was fairly licensing himself to engage in the most absurd-seeming imaginative high jinks. ("The fact is," Hawthorne once wrote, "in writing a romance, a man is always, or ought to be, careering on the utmost verge of a precipitous absurdity, and the skill lies in coming as close as possible, without actually tumbling over.") To his readers' common complaint that he had gone off the deep end and left terra firma far behind, what could Melville respond except that that was precisely his point? "Speeds the daedal boat as a dream," he reminds us at the start of Chapter XVI. An ingenious and variegated invention, as his very accurate adjective indicates, the "Fidèle" and her voyage represent an excursion into pure romance, at once an example of the genre and an exploration of its principles—an object lesson in romancer-reader relations.[8]

That those relations had deteriorated since the beginning of Melville's career is made abundantly clear by the mordant self-portrait contained in the figure of the dubiously messianic "moon-calf" dressed "in cream-colors" who is about to dream our book for us. It is a pathetically humorous picture of the romancer (characterized by "abstraction and dreaminess") as an alienated ("from the shrugged shoulders, titters, whispers, wonderings of the crowd, it was plain that he was, in the extremest sense of the word, a stranger"), dispossessed ("he had neither trunk, valise, carpet-bag, nor parcel . . . he had long been without the solace of a bed"), unrespected ("no badge of authority about him, but rather something quite the contrary"), idiotic nobody ("taking him for some strange kind of simpleton . . . they made no scruple to jostle him aside"). Out of touch with his environment (he is deaf) and unable to communicate directly (he is also dumb), his only recourse lies in the printed word; but because he is "singularly innocent," his writing, like his personality, is considered "somehow inappropriate to the time and place." Our author, however, seemingly inured to neglect and indefatigably single-minded ("with the air of one neither courting nor shunning regard, but evenly pursuing the path of duty, lead it through solitudes or cities, he held on his way"),

---

8. On *The Confidence-Man* as a dream, cf. James E. Miller, Jr., "*The Confidence-Man: His Guises*," *PMLA*, LXXIV (1959), 102.

proceeds to hold up his own slate—next to a placard that defames the confidence-man as a "mysterious imposter"—and to offer his audience succinct examples of his "inappropriate" writings. These are all variations on the theme of Charity, beginning with "Charity thinketh no evil." But perhaps more significant than the mute's unexceptionable message is his manner of presentation, to which Melville draws our special attention. Leaving "the word charity, as originally traced . . . throughout uneffaced," he simply erases the right-hand portion and changes the application ("Charity suffereth. . . . endureth. . . . believeth. . . . never faileth").

The point of Melville's swipe at himself seems reasonably plain. Not shrewd enough to realize that the timeless message contained in all his writings has had little appeal for a nineteenth-century American audience, he has made the further mistake of increasing his readers' annoyance by re-using the same tired materials (the device of a sea voyage, for example) as a medium for his theme.[9] But perhaps he has finally learned his lesson. "Not wholly unaffected by his reception," the mute draws off to a "retired spot," presumably acquiescing in his fate. Or has he something up his sleeve? Melville's final comment on this scarcely redoubtable self-representation is freighted with complicated ironies: "Though hitherto, as has been seen, the man in cream-colors had by no means passed unobserved, yet by stealing into retirement, and there going asleep and continuing so, he seemed to have courted oblivion, a boon not often withheld from so humble an applicant as he." By seeking his final refuge in the obscurities of sleep, Melville suggests, the romancer will in all likelihood be granted precisely what he seems all along to have been flirting with—complete nullity. But something further may indeed follow of this masquerade: disappearing from the scene as the colorless and rejected avatar of Christ, our author will reappear in his own fantasy

9. "It is worth noting," says Thomas Philbrick, "that the relative unpopularity of Melville's later fiction, a phenomenon usually explained in terms of his ideological divergence from his audience and his refusal to repeat the formulas he had used in *Typee* and *Omoo* or in *Redburn* and *White-Jacket*, may also be a result of the fact that he was firmly established in the mind of the reading public as a *nautical* writer, a producer of the kind of fiction that was no longer in demand. Thus if Melville had attempted to return to the methods and concerns of *Typee* or *White-Jacket* in the late 1850's, it seems unlikely that he could have regained his earlier popularity" (*James Fenimore Cooper and the Development of American Sea Fiction* [Cambridge, Mass., 1961], p. 325, note 4).

as a gaudy reincarnation of Satan, hoping to win back by means of deviltry the popularity he has lost through his apparent innocent simplicity.[10]

That Melville, the committed romancer who praised Hawthorne so extravagantly for his unrelievedly dark view of human existence, should body himself forth as an attractively persuasive, fantastically clever, perfidious exponent of the opposite view—herein lies the essential diabolism and infinite trickiness of *The Confidence-Man*. It is a complex exercise in self-satire such as only the bitterest, most disappointed, and most brilliant romancer could ever have conceived. Melville's Devil-as-literary-critic-and-practitioner is a self-confident booster of artistic boosterism,[11] whose knowing decision to ride and swell the crest of American optimism makes him a successful salesman and the friend of everyone—except, of course, those unattractively serious curmudgeons who obstinately take a gloomy view of life.

The notion of the Fall of Man, insists the confidence-man (in a merciless parody of Milton's—later Hawthorne's—theory of ultimate spiritual gain through the experience of sin), was only a literary "panic contrived by artful alarmists," hypocritical scribbling bears who thrive upon "the simulation of things dark instead of bright; souls that thrive, less upon depression, than the fiction of depression; professors of the wicked art of manufacturing depressions; spurious Jeremiahs; sham Heraclituses," who "trump up their black panics in the naturally-quiet brightness, solely with a view to some sort of covert advantage." That advantage, we may understand, consists of their being able easily to peddle their lugubrious views in a depressed atmosphere of their own contriving. But, the confidence-man assures us, "there will be a reaction." Convinced by him that the rumor of a fall was only an unfortunate sham, the public will confidently invest in the Devil's optimism. And they will benefit from it permanently: having learned that the threat of darkness is always a fraud, they will be enabled henceforth to rest secure in the belief that brightness is here to stay.

That we may have reason, however, to doubt and fear such a diabolical

---

10. H. Bruce Franklin remarks that "Christ and Satan are the shape-shifting joker known as the Confidence Man" (*The Wake of the Gods: Melville's Mythology* [Stanford, 1963], p. 177). Cf. Leon F. Seltzer, "Camus's Absurd and the World of Melville's *Confidence-Man*," *PMLA*, LXXXII (1967), 19–20.

11. On Melville as a critic of boosterism and Babbittry, see Edward H. Rosenberry, *Melville and the Comic Spirit* (Cambridge, Mass., 1955), pp. 156 ff.

formulation and the fool's paradise it produces, is made sufficiently clear much later in the book when we are invited, in the conclusion to the story of China Aster, to inspect the epitaph composed by that unfortunate for himself at the end of his sad life:

HERE LIE

THE REMAINS OF

CHINA ASTER THE CANDLE-MAKER,

WHOSE CAREER

WAS AN EXAMPLE OF THE TRUTH OF SCRIPTURE, AS FOUND

IN THE

SOBER PHILOSOPHY

OF

SOLOMON THE WISE;

FOR HE WAS RUINED BY ALLOWING HIMSELF TO BE PERSUADED,

AGAINST HIS BETTER SENSE,

INTO THE FREE INDULGENCE OF CONFIDENCE,

AND

AN ARDENTLY BRIGHT VIEW OF LIFE,

TO THE EXCLUSION

OF

THAT COUNSEL WHICH COMES BY HEEDING

THE

OPPOSITE VIEW.

China Aster, who failed in his trade "of shedding some light through the darkness of a planet benighted," might be said to have succeeded in another way, and at a regrettably late date, in this exhibition of hidden talent in the non-sentimental school of graveyard writing. But the confidence-man has no reason to regret the nipping in the bud of this developing romancer. Predictably pained by the tale of China Aster, he finds it "a story I can no way approve." For the kind of sensibility ultimately displayed by the tragic candle-maker the confidence-man professes, despite all his benevolence, to feel something like hatred. Finding a college sophomore engaged in the perusal of Tacitus, the confidence-man inveighs fiercely against that author's "moral poison," claiming that "his subtlety is falsity," a gloomy libel against human nature. Further warming to his topic, he warns against Aeschylus, Thucydides, Juvenal, and Lucian and offers the young student a critical touchstone that the late China Aster would have viewed with alarm: "Whatever our lot, we should read serene and cheery books, fitted to inspire love and trust." Later on, as a final twist of Melville's irony, we learn that the canny sophomore had no need of the Devil's advice, for he admits to an acquaintance (the confidence-man in a different disguise, who is distressed to find out that he has been made a fool of) that he reads Tacitus for his gossip, not for his gloom, and thus was only humoring his would-be tutor by letting him fulminate.

Melville's suggestion here that the Devil's insidiously cheerful tastes in literature hardly need to be forced on a world which has already been corrupted to such a view is strengthened in the following chapter, when the confidence-man comes upon a "dried-up" fellow "reading a small sort of handbill of anonymous poetry, rather wordily entitled" (but here we abbreviate):

ODE

ON THE INTIMATIONS

OF

DISTRUST IN MAN . . .

Picking up a copy of this "moonstruck production of some wandering rhapsodist," the confidence-man intones the plaintive opening ("Alas for man, he hath small sense/Of genial trust and confidence") and then makes a pronouncement which shows that even the Devil is willing to give the Lake School its due as regards craft, though he is naturally constrained to regret its morality: "If it be so, alas for him, indeed. Runs off very smoothly, sir. Beautiful pathos. But do you think the sentiment just?" The wizened man's diabolical interlocutor is of course prepared, with his usual skill, to convince his sad-seeming acquaintance not to credit such melancholy trash, but there is no need. The little man turns out to be a curious kind of reader, for his inspection of the lamentational ode has made him "feel as it were trustful and genial"; and the confidence-man, spared his effort, is naturally "glad to hear it." Thus on a ship of fools does sober philosophy overreach itself!

As a practitioner of literary art, the confidence-man is a particularly tricky embodiment of Melville's ironic deviltry who, as it were, works both sides of the street in his attempt, ostensibly to foment, but ultimately to undermine belief in the truth of romance. In the person of the man with the weed, he tells his own tale of woe—the story of his married life with the fantastical Goneril—which not only demonstrates that his mourning is a sham, but also reduces the notion of romance to a lurid, if ridiculously funny, absurdity. It is hard to overlook, though some sober critics have done so, Melville's obvious intent of stylistic and thematic self-parody in this perfect bit of foolishness:[12]

> Goneril was young, in person lithe and straight, too straight, indeed, for a woman, a complexion naturally rosy, and which would have been charmingly so, but for a certain hardness and bakedness, like that of the glazed colors on stone-ware. Her hair was of a deep, rich chestnut, but worn in close, short curls all round her head. Her Indian figure was not without its impairing effect on her bust, while her mouth would have been pretty but for a trace of moustache. Upon the whole, aided by the resources of the toilet, her appearance at distance was such, that some might have thought her, if anything, rather beautiful, though of a style of beauty rather peculiar and cactus-like.

> It was happy for Goneril that her more striking peculiarities were less of the person than of temper and taste. One hardly knows how to reveal, that, while having a natural antipathy to such things as the breast of chicken, or custard, or peach, or grape, Goneril could yet in private make a satisfactory lunch on hard crackers and brawn of ham.

Melville goes on in this way for five pages without faltering, nor is the matter less funny than the manner. For just as the description of Goneril, with a shrewdly humorous mixing of archetypes, presents that heroine in the image of the dark lady as cigar-store Indian, so the secret truth about her revealed in the tale is a black-comic parody of the Melvillian romance theme (seriously embodied, for example, in *Billy Budd* in the person of Claggart) of natural depravity:

> In company she had a strange way of touching, as by accident, the arm or hand of comely young men, and seemed to reap a secret delight from it, but whether from the humane satisfaction of having given the evil-touch, as it is called, or whether it was something else in her, not equally wonderful, but quite as deplorable, remained an enigma.

Be the evil secret of this dark—one finally hesitates to say—lady moral or venereal, the upshot of this "touching case" (the pun is Melville's) is that the unfortunate husband effects a separation, taking with him his

---

12. Egbert Oliver, in an attempt to prove that Goneril was intended as a satiric portrait of Fanny Kemble, concedes that "Melville certainly caricatures—in fact, he stops just short of burlesque—in this study in temperament" ("Melville's Goneril and Fanny Kemble," *New England Quarterly*, XVIII [1945], 490).

little daughter (whom the mother had been torturing), whereupon Goneril sues for custody and support. In vain does the poor man build his case on his wife's "derangement," mental or otherwise. Goneril wins and, as an added fillip, prepares to have her husband committed as a lunatic.

> Upon which he fled, and was now an innocent outcast, wandering forlorn . . . with a weed on his hat for the loss of his Goneril; for he had lately seen by the papers that she was dead, and thought it but proper to comply with the prescribed form of mourning in such cases. For some days past he had been trying to get money enough to return to his child.

In short, the confidence-man's tale about Goneril's evil touch is but the prelude to his own soft touch, a patent piece of fakery contrived to win sympathy for his spurious grief and money for his undoubtedly equally spurious paternal project. As a romancer the confidence-man is accurately unmasked by Melville's true suffering Adam, the "invalid Titan in home-spun," who calls him a "profane fiddler on heart-strings." His creation is the type of sham art, the kind of bad literary currency which casts doubt on all coinage.[13]

But Melville's fun has only just begun. For we must remember that the man-with-the-weed's tale of woe is being told at third hand by a good merchant, who offers it to his audience as a serious example of the evil actually existing in the world. That audience, not unexpectedly, is none other than the confidence-man (now appearing as the man with the traveling-cap), who after listening to the story affirms that, although "it did in some degree affect him," he can only consider it a travesty—an exaggerated and imprudent attack on human nature and human life. Elizabeth Foster, in a comment that says much for her sense of justice but little for her sense of humor, remarks that "it is the lying Confidence Man, not the good country merchant or Melville, who tries to explain away this story of 'unmerited misery . . . brought about by unhindered arts of the wicked.' "[14] But of course the confidence-man (whose own

---

13. One should not overlook the truly sinister side of Melville's "joke" in this episode, for his description of Goneril (the name clearly refers more to sexual problems than to Shakespeare) unmistakably suggests that the confidence-man's "wife"—her putative child in the story notwithstanding—is in fact slyly described as a transvestite homosexual. The whole business casts a strange light, not so much on the confidence-man's actual tastes (since his tale is sheer fabrication), as on the weird quality of his imagination.

14. *The Confidence-Man*, p. 314.

insincere words Miss Foster is in fact quoting) is only trying to explain away a tale that he has himself created! If the merchant, or Melville, or we the readers, take it seriously, we have been gulled—not because it is foolish to believe in the romance truth of inscrutable evil, but because it is silly to put credence in a piece of manifest absurdity and wasteful to spend our sympathy in the wrong place. And yet if we go along in spirit with the confidence-man's attempt to impugn his own nonsense, we may also be fooled into allowing our faith in romance to be undermined speciously. Thus the Devil remains true to form throughout the whole episode, for by first creating a tale that lowers romance to the level of farce and then rejecting his own sham tragedy, he proves himself once again the eternal enemy of serious art.

A more straightforward illustration of the Devil's refusal to take romance seriously, either formally or thematically, occurs later in the book when, as the cosmopolitan, he tells another tale of derangement: the story of Charlemont, the gentleman-madman. At the close of the narration, asked by his auditor whether the curious tale is "true," the confidence-man replies perfidiously: "Of course not; it is a story which I told with the purpose of every story-teller—to amuse. Hence, if it seem strange to you, that strangeness is the romance; it is what contrasts it with real life; it is the invention, in brief, the fiction as opposed to the fact." Moreover, insinuates our plausible demon, the dark view of human character implied in Charlemont's "malady"—distrust—is a libel on mankind. "Would you, for one," the confidence-man (moving from art to life) asks his auditor, "turn the cold shoulder to a friend—a convivial one, say, whose pennilessness should be suddenly revealed to you?" Whereupon friend Charlie, verifying by example the truth of the cosmopolitan's tale, beats a hasty retreat! Apart from the humor of Melville's anecdote, the Charlemont business suggests that the Devil is as adept at begging questions as alms, for by facilely equating fiction with fakery and insisting that romance "strangeness" implies falsity to life, he not only tempts us to take a frivolous view of literature but also rides roughshod over precisely that crucial point which is everywhere at issue in the book.

Whatever one may think of the complications and confusions of *The Confidence-Man*, one can only admire the bravery of Melville's attempt to assault—on almost every page—the staggering problem of defining the relationship between nature and art, fact and fiction, so-called reality and its presumably unreal reflection in the dark glass of romance. Melville's determination to front the deepest mysteries of the art/life puzzle drove him to writing what must finally be called exponential romance—the kind of book that intellectually, as it were, invites the reader to step between opposed sets of mirrors. Just how bewildering such a stance can be is suggested by numerous incidents in *The Confidence-Man*. Introducing a certain gentleman with gold sleeve-buttons in Chapter VII, for example, the author lets fall an innocent-seeming sentence, wholly typical of the book, the exploration of which involves us in the tightest complexities of Melville's experiment:

> But, considering that goodness is no such rare thing among men—
> the world familiarly know the noun; a common one in every language—
> it was curious that what so signalized the stranger, and made him look
> like a kind of foreigner, among the crowd (as to some it may make him
> appear more or less unreal in this portraiture), was but the expression
> of so prevalent a quality.

The two essential questions that Melville is toying with here—*does the existence of literary constructs, of words, necessarily imply realities?* and *can realities themselves deceive?*—should be immediately apparent, the first in the slyness of his assumption that words validate things ("goodness is no such rare thing among men—the world familiarly know the noun"), the second in his unsettling use of language suggesting that the gentleman may be a fraud ("look like a kind of . . . may make him appear more or less . . . but the expression of . . .").

Stepping back a bit from the sentence, however, the reader may allow himself to speculate more largely on the connotations embedded in it. Is Melville's portrait of this gentleman "unreal" because art should be a true representation of life and there are in fact no good men, in Melville's view of the world? Or does he only *seem* unreal in context because Melville's image in this book of the world as a crowd of cheats is itself a misrepresentation? If the world is a cheating "Fidèle" where all men are liars, Melville's image of the world is *true*, and the gentleman—who is, after all, part of that Melvillian image—may only *appear* unreal because we have not yet learned that his presumed goodness is a fraud. If, on the other hand, there is honesty and goodness in the world, Melville's image of the world is still true in some sense, since he has given us an example of those virtues and implied that we should believe in it precisely because its reality shows up, by contrast, the unreality of a representation of the world that has so far excluded honesty and goodness. Thus art—especially Melville's—tested by the standard of the portrait of the gentleman with gold sleeve-buttons, is shown to be a fake-seeming contrivance that ultimately tells the truth, for whether the world is good or evil, honest or hypocritical, the portrait of this gentleman, as Melville has managed it, variously embodies a reflection of both alternatives.

In spite of the truly satanic ironies which permeate *The Confidence-Man*, verification of Melville's firm belief in the truth of his art, as well as further notes toward a theory of romance, can unequivocally be found in the book. The theoretical backbone of his seemingly formless exercise is provided by three chapters that are clearly linked to one another, not only by similarities of tone and subject, but also by their curious titles—as if the author, by employing parallel devices, had tried to ensure our taking them together as a kind of artistic creed:

XIV.   WORTH THE CONSIDERATION OF THOSE TO WHOM IT MAY PROVE WORTH CONSIDERING

XXXIII.   WHICH MAY PASS FOR WHATEVER IT MAY PROVE TO BE WORTH

XLIV.   ... WHICH WILL BE SURE OF RECEIVING MORE OR LESS ATTENTION FROM THOSE READERS WHO DO NOT SKIP IT

All three headings employ a trick of humorous tautology—a comic version of that momentous statement of self-identity ("I AM THAT I AM") by which God revealed his essence to Moses—suggesting through ironic self-depreciation that each chapter is precisely as serious as it seems to be and will thus reward the scrutiny of readers who know what to look for. Just how seriously Melville himself took the first, and longest, of these chapters may be indicated by the fact that the only surviving manuscript version of any chapter in the book is that of Chapter XIV, and it shows, according to Elizabeth Foster, that the chapter "passed through at least three and possibly six or more versions before Melville achieved the text that he allowed to be published."[15]

Chapters XIV and XXXIII in particular must be considered together.

---

15. *Ibid.*, p. 374. In "Some Notes on the Structure of *The Confidence Man*," *American Literature*, XXIX (1957), 278–288, John G. Cawelti suggests the centrality of the three chapters to Melville's plan in the book. Edward H. Rosenberry, noticing the similarity between the headings of Chapters XXXIII and XLIV, remarks on the possible influence of Sterne and Fielding (*Melville and the Comic Spirit*, p. 147).

Indeed, in the latter, where Melville offers a general apology for having written an apologia—

> Though every one knows how bootless it is to be in all cases vindicating one's self, never mind how convinced one may be that he is never in the wrong; yet, so precious to man is the approbation of his kind, that to rest, though but under an imaginary censure applied to but a work of imagination, is no easy thing

—he refers us back to the former. Both chapters come, significantly, in the midst of or just after the confidence-man's two major attempts at fiction—Goneril and Charlemont—and are clearly offered by Melville as antidotes to the Devil's poisonously superficial attitude toward both art and human character. In the first, Melville is allegedly trying to justify his having created an "inconsistent" character in the good merchant, but this seems only a ruse, since the merchant's final outburst of philosophical despair is hardly inconsistent with his originally gloomy position that there is much inexplicable misery in the world. The really inconsistent character is the confidence-man himself, who tells a tale of misery and then disowns it, who hates and fears his so-called wife and yet mourns her, etc. More importantly, in Goneril the confidence-man had created an image of human character anomalous in the deepest sense and yet had undercut the notion of human inscrutability, first by turning it into farce, and secondly (as the man with the traveling-cap) by trying to rationalize all the apparent mysteries in Goneril's nature.

In Chapter XIV Melville in his own voice makes an impassioned plea for the inscrutable mystery of human nature. (Ultimately, of course, as we find out in Chapter XXXIII, he is defending his diabolically inconsistent confidence-man—which is to say, he is defending both a fictional character created by him and his *own* strange human nature as an author, embodied in that curious figure.) Romance art, he insists, which presents human character in all its strangeness and inexplicable anomaly, is in the profoundest sense faithful to life, whereas "that fiction, where every character can, by reason of its consistency, be comprehended at a glance, either exhibits but sections of character, making them appear for wholes, or else is very untrue to reality." The presentation of "human nature not in obscurity, but transparency, which, indeed, is the practice with most novelists," is a glittering lie. And until "the more earnest psychologists" hit upon "some mode of infallibly discovering the heart of man,"

only that art which says of human nature what is said of the divine—
"that it is past finding out"—can make any claim to truth. Taking a
quasi-religious view of his own function, Melville implies that the romancer presently comes closest to writing a revelation of the soul.

Melville ends this chapter, with a characteristic twist of irony, by
inviting us to return to his comedy—"or, rather, to pass from the comedy
of thought to that of action." The pun on the last word raises an unsettling suggestion that real life partakes of the role-playing associated with
the so-called falsities of art. ("Does all the world act? Am *I*, for instance,
an actor?" asks the confidence-man with deceptive innocence in Chapter
VI, and the canny wooden-legged man replies, "To do, is to act; so all
doers are actors.") This suggestion looks forward directly to Chapter
XXXIII, where Melville refutes the view—to be espoused shortly by
the confidence-man, after he concludes the tale of Charlemont—that the
fantastic theatricalities of his own art imply falsity to reality. Like the
stage, the romance only exaggerates the postures of real life, and in doing
so it exposes, as do dreams, the secret truths which are hidden by the
timidities and hypocrisies of social intercourse—for "the proprieties
will not allow people to act out themselves with that unreserve permitted
to the stage." Thus readers who understand the romancer's assumptions
can expect to find in his fictions even more reality "than real life itself
can show." Such readers of course "want nature . . . but nature unfet-
tered, exhilarated, in effect transformed. . . . It is with fiction as with
religion: it should present another world, and yet one to which we feel
the tie." The other world of romance art, it is suggested, demands of
the reader a willingness to utter the *credo quia absurdum* of the religious
believer if he is to enter into and benefit by the mysteries of the faith.

But, as with all faith, there are dangers. Melville's mention of religion
in this eloquent defense of fantasy establishes an important metaphoric
link between Chapter XXXIII and the final chapter of theory, where
that "originality" everywhere associated with the confidence-man is
essentially defined. Likening an "original character" to "the founder of
a new religion" or "a revolving Drummond light," Melville claims that
"everything is lit by it, everything starts up to it . . . so that, in certain
minds, there follows upon the adequate conception of such a character,
an effect, in its way, akin to that which in Genesis attends upon the beginning of things." Daniel Hoffman's comment on this statement can hardly
be bettered: "The reality Melville creates in this book, then, is to be a

transfiguration of nature, in which an 'original character' sheds the light of its originality upon a world created after its own image."[16]

That other world of fantasy created in the shifting image of the confidence-man is indeed the Devil's realm, its "new religion" the cult of art, whose Bible brings not the pure light of Genesis but the darkness visible of romance, wherein the secrets of the human heart are ambiguously exposed. ("The devil is very sagacious," proclaims the shrewd Missourian Pitch; "he appears to have understood man better even than the Being who made him.") Therefore, *caveat credulus!* For by committing himself to the realm of diabolical fantasy the reader runs many risks. But in this, as in everything else, Melville's comprehensive Devil-as-artist is beforehand, taking it upon himself to warn us (in the words of the Apocrypha!) of the danger lurking in his nature:

> Believe not his many words—an enemy speaketh sweetly with his lips. . . . With much communication he will tempt thee; he will smile upon thee, and speak thee fair, and say What wantest thou? If thou be for his profit he will use thee; he will make thee bear [bare], and will not be sorry for it. Observe and take good heed. When thou hearest these things, awake in thy sleep.

If you fear the danger of being misled—or of being led permanently into the dark, as is the old man at the close of the book—Melville seems to say, launch your yawl no more for fairyland: go not aboard the dreamship "Fidèle." Romance is a journey for intrepid voyagers, willing to cast all havens astern and say with Melville, as he tracks his Pierre into the realm of ultimate ambiguity, "I shall follow the endless, winding way,—the flowing river in the cave of man; careless whither I be led, reckless where I land."

3. The Education of a Romancer

MELVILLE'S belief, embodied theoretically in *The Confidence-Man*, that he who would be initiated into the mysteries of romance must dance to the Devil's tune, is dramatized in the earlier *Pierre*. As in all of Hawthorne's romances (and *Pierre* is Melville's most Hawthornian book), art is used as the touchstone of human development: a man's introduction to the secrets of the self is presented in terms of a maturing artistic con-

---

16. *Form and Fable in American Fiction* (New York, 1965), p. 288.

sciousness. All of the familiar romance themes are included—the inevitable association of a guilty past, sexual awareness, and aesthetic sensibility; the entry into a world of excruciating ambiguity; the terrible uncovering of willful self-delusion; the suggestion of a sinister irrationality lurking beneath the appearances of daylight sanity. Indeed, these themes are intensified, almost grotesquely exaggerated, as if Melville were trying at once to identify himself unmistakably with his fellow romancers and to exorcise their obsessive notions from his exhausted imagination.

No part of the American romancer's standard bag of tricks took more complete control of Melville's mind, received more curious elaboration by him, and was to prove less exorcisable than the dark-fair archetypes that we have traced from Cooper onwards. He had already employed them, of course, in *Mardi* as a method of dramatizing the experiential alternatives available to his protagonist: Taji must choose between Hautia and Yillah. In the womanless world of *Moby-Dick*, Melville brought clearly to the surface the capacity for abstract representation always inherent in these archetypes by using them unexpectedly in a more purely symbolistic mode, setting Ishmael as it were between Queequeg and the Whale. With a truly Poesque flair for startling reversals, however, Melville had made the fair emblem in each of these books stand apparently for the more sinister alternative, the lure to tragedy and self-destruction.[17] In this regard, Melville's handling of the archetypes in *Pierre* is more traditional—one might say more sentimental or stereotypic—since the values normally associated with each figure have been restored. But whatever may be lost in originality is gained in depth and comprehensiveness. Melville's version of the dark and fair ladies in *Pierre* carries the scheme to completion, exposing beneath the surface of literary convention a rich fund of human meaning.

Lucy Tartan, Pierre's fair-haired childhood sweetheart, predictably requires less discussion than her sombre rival (as Milton's Christ invites less critical attention than Milton's Satan). "The world will never see another Lucy Tartan," the author exclaims, and proceeds to offer a description that suggests the world has never seen such a creature at all: "Her cheeks were tinted with the most delicate white and red, the white predominating. Her eyes some god brought down from heaven; her

---

17. Frederic I. Carpenter, "Puritans Preferred Blondes: The Heroines of Melville and Hawthorne," *New England Quarterly*, IX (1936), 253–272, associates Yillah with Moby Dick and suggests how ambiguous is Taji's quest for the "pure" Yillah.

hair was Danae's, spangled with Jove's shower; her teeth were dived for in the Persian Sea." Although the rhetoric here is purely Elizabethan (and seems to cry out for another Shakespeare to parody it), the conception owes more to the polarizations essential to the American romance. As her name suggests and as Pierre himself makes explicit, Lucy belongs "to the regions of an infinite day": she is the representative of that prelapsarian world without darkness from which the fearful journey of Melville's Everyman inevitably begins.

As Lucy "hath nothing but purity to show," she harbors no discoverable sexual impulses within and inspires none in the erotically dormant young Pierre—or rather, she intimidates any such burgeoning feelings in him by forcing him to associate sexuality with sacrilege. ("I to wed this heavenly fleece? Methinks one husbandly embrace would break her airy zone. . . . By heaven, but marriage is an impious thing!") Herself without any suggestion of an inner life and mortally afraid of any hint of mystery in human personality (especially Pierre's), Lucy acts to retain her reverent lover in that phase of unreflective immaturity which enables him to engage innocently in clearly erotic byplay with his mother and to contemplate without trepidation a perpetually chaste marriage of pure "sacrifice." Her influence keeps him "thoughtless of that period of remorseless insight, when all these delicate warmths should seem frigid to him, and he should madly demand more ardent fires."

Entering into the fallen world of dark erotic passion from which the timid spirit of Lucy temporarily bars him, Pierre will also demand a very different kind of expression from the artistic triviality associated with the simple pastoral pleasures of Saddle Meadows. Not unexpectedly, Lucy herself is an artist: we learn late in the book of "her expertness in catching likenesses, and judiciously and truthfully beautifying them; not by altering the features so much, as by steeping them in a beautifying atmosphere." (Melville's fair heroine quite clearly inspired Hawthorne's Hilda.) But undoubtedly more important than Lucy's skill in bringing out the "softest aspects" of things is her significance as Pierre's first muse. Her chaste affection inspires him to begin his career as the author of "fugitive things . . . [which] were the veriest common-place."

Summarizing a great deal of the mythology invariably attached to the fair lady—not the least of which is her association with "pretty" nature as opposed to the natural sublime—Melville develops, with cal-

culated insipidity,[18] a notion of love in connection with Lucy which
is meant to contrast sharply with the terrible sexual passion soon to be
inspired in Pierre by the dark Isabel. Lucy is unequivocally the Vestal of
"the sweetest and the loftiest religion of this earth," the sentimental love
religion: "Love is both Creator's and Saviour's gospel to mankind; a
volume bound in rose-leaves, clasped with violets, and by the beaks of
humming-birds printed with peach-juice on the leaves of lilies." What
this kind of emotional fakery can engender in the way of literature (and
thus Melville's intent here) is made perfectly plain when Pierre's early
productions—especially "that delightful love-sonnet, entitled 'The Trop-
ical Summer' "—are savagely satirized by Melville in the chapter titled
"Young America in Literature." The critics naturally applaud the young
lyrist's efforts ("Perfect Taste . . . it is the glory of this admirable young
author, that vulgarity and vigor . . . are equally removed from him . . .
This writer is unquestionably a highly respectable youth . . . He is blame-
less in morals, and harmless throughout"). But he will learn in good
time that Lucy's religion of love issues invariably in unredeemable
"rubbish." Nor should we overlook the sinister implications lurking in
the cloying religiosity of Melville's metaphor for Lucy's cult—a metaphor
that will undergo a satanic sea change and assume ghastly new meanings
as Pierre's experiences carry him from the sentimental gift-book gospel
of the fair maiden to the "fearful gospel" of Isabel Banford.

Isabel, claims Henry Murray, "is unintelligible to many readers
because she conforms neither to the conventions of allegory and myth
nor to those of naturalism and realism, but is the product of an only
partially realized fusion of these conventions."[19] Such a formulation is
unnecessarily complicated and misleading, for Isabel conforms with a
vengeance to the conventions of the American romance and should be
perfectly intelligible to readers of the authors we have been examining.
She is the dark lady made ten times darker. French by descent (as Lucy
is presumably Scottish), she partakes of the mythology whereby Latinity
—or Negritude (Cora Munro), or Orientalism (Ligeia), or Jewishness
(Miriam)—evokes the notion of wild sexual passion in contrast to the

18. On Melville's parody of gift-book style in *Pierre*, see William Braswell,
"Early Love Scenes in Melville's *Pierre*," *American Literature*, XXII (1950), 283–289.

19. "Introduction" to *Pierre: Or, The Ambiguities*, edited by Henry A. Murray
(New York, 1949), p. lv.

reserve and chastity of the Anglo-Saxon fair maiden (Alice Munro, Rowena, Hilda, Lucy). She is olive-skinned, and her face—"dark-eyed, lustrous, imploring, mournful," and marked by "long-suffering, hopeless anguish"—is full of ineffable "death-like beauty." Her "dark tent of hair," with its "unrestrained" and "attractive" locks, gleams and moves "like a tract of phosphorescent midnight sea." She inspires metaphors of sublime nature only—mountains, oceans, blasted trees, lightning.

Her given name, as Dr. Murray notes, suggests the Phoenician Baal and thus conjures up combined notions of fertility and abomination.[20] But her surname—Banford—is perhaps more directly significant, for it is glossed by the author himself: "The deep voice of the being of Isabel called to him [Pierre] from out the immense distances of sky and air, and there seemed no veto of the earth that could forbid her heavenly claim." Isabel's "heavenly claim," as is made perfectly clear by Melville, is productive of almost total demonism in her enthusiastic protector (and the religious terminology which Pierre habitually uses with regard to Isabel, as we shall see, is the sure sign of both his damnation and his delusion). But what is particularly important here is Melville's definition of the dark lady's function: she leads our hero across that terrible chasm, the incest taboo, which keeps ordinary men from enjoying the darkest of sexual pleasures.

Pre- or post-rational in her mental habits[21] ("I never affect any thoughts, and I never adulterate any thoughts; but when I speak, think forth from the tongue, speech being sometimes before the thought; so, often, my own tongue teaches me new things"), one might say that Isabel's method of drawing Pierre into her realm is to teach him to distrust language and to see that the categories of conventional morality are mere nominalisms. A "ban," after all, is no more than a series of words. "I am called woman, and thou, man, Pierre; but there is neither man nor woman about it. . . . There is no sex in our immaculateness." Lest the reader be tricked into thinking that Isabel is espousing the celibate life à *deux*, Melville devotes an important scene later in the book to demonstrating that this extraordinary couple is preparing to abstain only from the use of misleading terms—"man," "woman," "sex," "brother," "sister"—which unfairly place the passions under a curse.

20. *Ibid.*, p. liv. Cf. Richard Chase, *Herman Melville: A Critical Study* (New York, 1949), p. 115.

21. H. Bruce Franklin speaks of Isabel's "primitive mentality" (*The Wake of the Gods*, p. 126).

"Thou, Pierre, speakest of Virtue and Vice; life-secluded Isabel knows neither the one nor the other, but by hearsay. What are they, in their real selves, Pierre?" Pierre admits the difficulty of the question, but together they decide that these things are "nothing." "Sin" is but "another name for the other name" known as "Vice," and these nothings have power to cause anguish only because they have been given ugly names which seem to confer reality. Henceforth for Pierre and Isabel the "things" they do together will be "the not-to-be-named things." Traveling together "deep down in the gulf of the soul," they enter the realm of pure romance, where all things are known, all things permitted. "How can one sin in a dream?"[22]

The dangerous trance-like state everywhere associated with Isabel ("scarce know I at any time whether I tell you real things, or the unrealest dreams. Always in me, the solidest things melt into dreams, and dreams into solidities") finds its fit accompaniment, and frequent inspiration, in that magic guitar whose music is the only suitable form of artistic expression for the non-rational dark lady. Like Miriam's ominous paintings (or better, like the song Hawthorne's heroine sings, "if song it could be called, that had only a wild rhythm, and flowed forth in the fitful measure of a wind-harp"), Isabel's fantastic guitar embodies and sends forth the inexplicable meaning of her secret nature:

> Mystery! Mystery!
> Mystery of Isabel!
> Mystery! Mystery!
> Isabel and Mystery!
> Mystery!

If Melville's seeming refusal to penetrate the "utter unintelligibleness" of Isabel's performance appears to be no more than an expression of authorial defeat in the face of the undefinable, we should look again; for it is precisely in its furious sound that the "infinite significancies" of Isabel's spastic incantation reside. In the "wonderfully and abandonedly free and bold" rhythm of the syllables Pierre reads the truth of her soul, simultaneously confirmed by her "hair-shrouded form" which "swayed to and fro with a like abandonment, and suddenness, and wantonness."

---

22. "The relationship of Isabel and Pierre suggests the tragedy of introspection, of the mind turning on itself, the last phase of the quest for the Ultimate" (George C. Homans, "The Dark Angel: The Tragedy of Herman Melville," *New England Quarterly*, V [1932], 723).

Isabel's sole inheritance from her presumably licentious French mother, this all but human guitar, the knowledge of whose playing is instinctive in the passionate girl, contains the mystery of Isabel's palpitating sexuality.

Like the specter of Isabel's face which Pierre saw ("vaguely historic and prophetic; backward, hinting of some irrevocable sin; forward, pointing to some inevitable ill"), the guitar, as the girl explains, "knows all my past history" and, as the author implies, predicts Pierre's future involvement. When Isabel invites Pierre literally to explore the inner workings of that instrument which is a symbolic extension of herself, she is offering to let him discover simultaneously the secrets of art and of her own mysterious body. "Bewitched" and "enchanted" by her performance, Pierre remains as if "caught and fast bound in some necromancer's garden"—the victim, subject, and would-be practitioner of romance.

But Pierre is destined to be *only* a would-be romancer, the *artiste manqué* of his soul's secret, perpetually tortured by his own compulsion to give up Lucy's promise of eternal purity and accept the dubious gift of maturity contained in Isabel's dark knowledge. "He seemed placed between them, to choose one or the other," but the necessity of making such a choice—of deciding between the human (and imaginative) possibilities represented by each—remains an unresolved agony.

The struggle, which will have a direct bearing on Pierre's own career as an artist, is reflected first in his attitude toward the works of others. When the earliest premonitions of Isabellian iniquity present themselves to his horrified imagination, he tries to exorcise them by blaming his dark mood on his study of sombre literature. "Damned be the hour I read in Dante!" The singer of night and hell "had first opened to his shuddering eyes the infinite cliffs and gulfs of human mystery and misery," thus preparing the way for a further breach in his armor of innocence, and he reacts defensively with an "ignorant burst of his young impatience, —also arising from that half-contemptuous dislike, and sometimes, selfish loathing, with which, either naturally feeble or undeveloped minds, regard those dark ravings of the loftier poets, which are in eternal opposition to their own fine-spun, shallow dreams of rapturous or prudential Youth."

Pierre's rejection of Dante, however, is as shortlived as the temporary relief from melancholy that it brings, "for as yet he had not seen so far and deep as Dante, and therefore was entirely incompetent to meet the grim bard fairly on his peculiar ground." After his two momentous interviews with Isabel, Pierre finds himself moving inexorably onto that peculiar ground and reads with more comprehension:

> Through me you pass into the city of Woe;
> Through me you pass into eternal pain. . . .

He can no longer reject the *Inferno* as the fantastic ravings of a melancholy madman, any more than he can believe "that *Hamlet*, though a thing of life, was, after all, but a thing of breath, evoked by the wanton magic of a creative hand, and as wantonly dismissed at last into endless halls of hell and night." But what Pierre cannot dismiss he can nevertheless hate and try to destroy. He tears into "a hundred shreds" the fatal copies "of *Hell* and *Hamlet*" and then dashes himself "in blind fury and swift madness against the wall," trying to obliterate the "loathed identity" revealed or confirmed by the serious art of a Dante and a Shakespeare.

A parallel, but much more crucial, use of art objects as indicators of Pierre's development and of his dilemma involves the two portraits of his father to which so much space is devoted in the book. Through them Melville makes the usual distinction (amounting to the romancer's familiar defense of his own art) between superficiality and profundity in art, between the art that provides a blandly respectable public image and the art that reveals the mystery of a human soul. One portrait—like the "fine joyous painting, in the good-fellow, Flemish style," which Pierre set in front of his mother each morning in his carefree youthful days at Saddle Meadows—is preferred by Mary Glendinning and associated with Pierre's early memories of an unimpeachably virtuous father. It depicts a middle-aged married man possessing "all the nameless and slightly portly tranquillities," the image of "devoted wedded love" varnished with a "thousand proprieties and polished finenesses." Such is the Pierre Glendinning *père* who died "leaving behind him, in the general voice of the world, a marked reputation as a gentleman and a Christian."

But the other—the so-called chair-portrait, always "unpleasant and repelling" to Pierre's mother—presents a much more ambiguous image of the presumably spotless father. Painted unbeknownst to its subject by a certain cousin Ralph, "a retired and solitary sort of a youth" who had read a book on physiognomy "in which the strangest and shadowiest rules were laid down for detecting people's innermost secrets by studying their faces," it captures Pierre senior soon after the act, as it were, of gratifying his appetite with a "too lovely young Frenchwoman" who was, we are supposed to understand, the fabled mother of Isabel. Melville makes it more than sufficiently plain in the course of a long tour de force of literary innuendo that the unsettlingly mysterious smile with which the portrait endows Pierre's father amounts to a telltale smirk of lust. Such a revelation, of course, would be anything but acceptable for the fastidious adolescent whose carefully guarded emotional life is built atop his belief in paternal purity, and Pierre willingly shares his mother's preference for the "normal" portrait, despite the undeniable power that the chair-portrait—like all true romance art—occasionally exercises over even his not fully awakened consciousness:

> Sometimes in the mystical, outer quietude of the long country nights; either when the hushed mansion was banked round by the thick-fallen December snows, or banked round by the immovable white August moonlight; in the haunted repose of a wide story, tenanted only by himself; and sentineling his own little closet; and standing guard, as it were, before the mystical tent of the picture; and ever watching the strangely concealed lights of the meanings that so mysteriously moved to and fro within; thus sometimes stood Pierre before the portrait of his father, unconsciously throwing himself open to all those ineffable hints and ambiguities, and undefined half-suggestions, which now and then people the soul's atmosphere.

This, as any reader of Hawthorne should recognize, is the time and place—the total aura—of romance, and the young Pierre instinctively protects himself from its disturbing suggestions: "starting from these reveries and trances, Pierre would regain the assured element of consciously bidden and self-propelled thought; and . . . upbraiding himself for his self-indulgent infatuation, would promise never again to fall into a midnight revery before the chair-portrait of his father." Pierre's refusal to plumb the sordid depths of his father's nature as revealed by the magic picture is equivalent to the good boy's promise never to become a romancer—never to allow the dreams and fantasies embodied in and inspired by this dark art permanently to darken his imagination and his life.

With the arrival of Isabel's letter, however, the veil of innocence is forever removed from Pierre's soul, "and forth trooped thickening phantoms of an infinite gloom." Romance is upon him, for "on all sides, the physical world of solid objects now slidingly displaced itself . . . and he floated into an ether of visions," whence he sees with utter clarity the horrible meaning of the chair-portrait, soon to be confirmed by the burning presence of Isabel. As with the *Inferno* and *Hamlet*, Pierre can no longer argue away the insistent dark visions, but he will try once again to obliterate them by venting his blind rage on their source. In an orgy of ambiguous fury, Pierre burns the chair-portrait before racing off irrevocably to the precincts of hell (otherwise identified as New York City), where he will take the dark lady to wife.

This complex scene of ritual destruction represents Pierre's ambivalent response to the romance world that has encroached upon him. In the very act, presumably, of casting from himself the mysterious memorial of his father's lustful past, he binds himself to a gloomy future based on that past, thus ensuring the perpetuation of what he supposedly wishes to destroy. Ostensibly he burns the portrait—"the one great, condemning, and unsuborned proof" of his father's nastiness—in order to be able to "hold his [father's] public memory inviolate." But the flimsiness of this rationalization is obvious, for he admittedly is attempting to wipe out one nightmare only that he might be at liberty to act out another, related one; he is setting himself "free to do his own self-will and present fancy to whatever end!" That "fancy" is startlingly Freudian: having "killed" the hated Oedipal father—who, while indulging himself, has always thundered Thou Shalt Not!—Pierre becomes free to supplant him by converting his own sister into a wife (thus completing the incestuous process begun, as Melville tells us flatly, when Pierre "only innocently and pleasantly as yet" had converted his mother into a "sister").

This dark meaning of Pierre's act he must of course repress from consciousness at all costs. Desperately needing to believe that his "intense and fearful love" for Isabel is pure, he naturally finds "loathsome . . . the smiling and ambiguous portrait" in which he sees "her sweet mournful image . . . sinisterly becrooked, bemixed, and mutilated." Like Hawthorne's Hilda, he cannot accept the knowledge of moral ambiguity embodied in the fateful picture. What is even worse for Pierre than the universal taint of sexuality (his father's, Isabel's, his own) reflected in the portrait is its terrible coexistence with an image of virtue. That good and evil, love and lust, are inextricably mixed—making us all, like Donatello, "worthy of Death, but not unworthy of Love"—is the final ambiguous horror which Pierre struggles to banish from his wounded soul.

But the romance truth of our fallen humanity can hardly be exorcised from consciousness permanently by the tearing of books or the burning of pictures. The repressed must always return. Wandering through a picture gallery at the end of the book in the company of both Lucy and Isabel—the twin poles of his divided soul[23]—Pierre is filled with agonized surprise to discover in a painting of "a stranger's head, by an unknown hand," the double of the disturbing face in the chair-portrait. And as for a crowning horror, Melville reports that a copy of Guido Reni's portrait of the infamous Beatrice Cenci—radiating more strongly than ever its anomalous mixture of seraphic beauty, incest, and parricide—was hung facing the mysterious reincarnation of Pierre senior, "so that in secret they seemed pantomimically talking over and across the heads of the living spectators below." Thus do the sins of all the fathers return, in the silent conspiracy of art, to hound Pierre to his grave with reduplicated force.

The implications for Pierre's career of the twin images of his father (so to speak, as saint and as lecher) are brilliantly illuminated by Melville's use of a "religious" metaphor—or rather of a metaphor combining notions of religion, art, and love—whose development throughout the book is a major key to meaning. Pierre's starting point, corresponding to his adherence to Lucy's love gospel, is described in an elaborate figure whose significance is far from being merely rhetorical:

> There had long stood a shrine in the fresh-foliaged heart of Pierre, up to which he ascended by many tableted steps of remembrance; and around which annually he had hung fresh wreaths of a sweet and holy affection. Made one green bower of at last, by such successive votive offerings of his being; this shrine seemed, and was indeed, a place for the celebration of a chastened joy, rather than for any melancholy rites. But though thus mantled, and tangled with garlands, this shrine was of marble—a niched pillar, deemed solid and eternal, and from whose top radiated all those innumerable sculptured scrolls and branches, which supported the entire one-pillared temple of his moral life; as in some beautiful Gothic oratories, one central pillar, trunk-like, upholds the roof. In this shrine, in this niche of this pillar, stood the perfect marble form of his departed father; without blemish, unclouded, snow-white, and serene; Pierre's fond personification of perfect human goodness and virtue. Before this shrine, Pierre poured out the fullness of all young life's most reverential thoughts and beliefs. Not to God had Pierre ever gone in his heart, unless by ascending the steps of that shrine, and so making it the vestibule of his abstractest religion.

---

23. Cf. E. L. Grant Watson, "Melville's *Pierre*," *New England Quarterly*, III (1930), 200–202.

Like the "green vines" which symbolize Lucy's heart for Pierre and are supposed to surround her easel (contrasted, at the end of the book, to the "ebon vines" of Isabel's hair, the "tent" within which she plays her guitar), this verdant niche is the setting for a religious work of art, a sculpture imaging his father's supposed purity, which Pierre identifies with "the marble of the tomb of him of Arimathea." Of this Christ-inspired shrine Pierre is the reverent devotee, until his moral life is overturned by Isabel's revelation of his father's secret iniquities, which "stripped his holiest shrine of all overlaid bloom, and buried the mild statue of the saint beneath the prostrated ruins of the soul's temple itself." Forthwith Pierre becomes manifestly irreligious, determined to release his secret self from the smothering influence of sentimental piety: "Let me go, ye fond affections; all piety leave me;—I will be impious, for piety hath juggled me, and taught me to revere, where I should spurn. From all idols, I tear all veils; henceforth I will see the hidden things; and live right out in my own hidden life!" The metaphoric suggestion of a ghastly exposure of his father's private parts is not amiss here, since Pierre's new life, in art as in religion (the two are inseparable), will be based upon knowledge of his father's—and, by inheritance, his own—sexuality, as his past life was based upon belief in his father's unsullied virtue.

But the obvious fact that Pierre's new career is fundamentally diabolic —or priapic—he dares not face unwaveringly. Instead, he compounds his sins by indulging in a blasphemous delusion of holiness, which guarantees his failure as a conscious artist and his ultimate damnation. Where, Melville asks for his hero, could he find "the Church, the monument, the Bible, which unequivocally said to him—'Go on; thou art in the Right; I endorse thee all over; go on' "? After the collapse of his old gospel and shrine, the only thing Pierre finds approaching a religious manifesto is the treatise on "Chronometricals and Horologicals" by Plotinus Plinlimmon, which specifically warns that the worst acts of deviltry are those done in the name of the Lord. Any man who arrogates to himself the character and prerogatives of Christ is apt somehow to involve himself "eventually in strange, *unique* follies and sins." (Pierre seems not to understand this, but although he loses the paper, it later turns out to have fallen into the lining of his coat—and the warning is therefore always with him, whether he is aware of it or not.) Finding no endorsement of his program in the pamphlet, Pierre is forced to create his own church, monument, and bible with which to justify and commemorate his actions; and though this "religious" project is founded on the darkest principles, he will attempt to convince himself that it is purely Christ-inspired.[24]

Leaving behind the love gospel of the fair maiden (which metaphorically conjoins ideas of orthodox religion, unsexual love, and insipid art), Pierre moves on to the dark lady's "fearful gospel" with its metaphoric association of blasphemy, sexual passion, and bitterly profound art. At first Isabel's face haunts Pierre as an "ideal Madonna's haunts the morbidly longing and enthusiastic, but ever-baffled artist." He is frightened by a presentiment that seems a "foetal fancy" beckoning him into "the infernal catacombs of thought." Soon, however, he convinces himself that the things "foetally forming in him" are "impregnations from high enthusiasms" and that "the now incipient offspring which so stirred, with such painful, vague vibrations in his soul" would "in its mature development . . . at last come forth in living deeds" as "the heaven-begotten Christ." Baptized by Isabel's tears (which he himself has conjured from the skies), Pierre invites her to his own celebration of the Eucharist ("I do dare to call this the real sacrament of the supper.—Eat with me") and unites himself to her in "marriage" in an erotic ceremony ("He held her tremblingly; she bent over toward him; his mouth wet her ear; he whispered it"). Ultimately Isabel even provides extreme unction for them both (efficacious, of course, for damnation only) with the "death-milk" hidden in her bosom.

But at the outset of his adventure Pierre sees his choice as lying between "Lucy or God." Carrying Isabel off (on a coach driven by one who seemed ominously to belong to the "hideous tribe of Charon ferry-men to corruption and death"), Pierre sets up his household in an artists' colony—formerly a religious edifice—called the Church of the Apostles. ("When the substance is gone, men cling to the shadow," Melville laments. "Places once set apart to lofty purposes, still retain the name of that loftiness, even when converted to the meanest uses.") Here, giving himself up to "mystic and transcendental persuasions" born, he later realizes, "purely of an intense procreative enthusiasm," Pierre vows to the

24. "The story of Pierre," says H. Bruce Franklin, is that "of a Christian youth, who, by trying to become symbolically and ethically a new Christ, becomes symbolically and ethically a pagan god; who, in trying to be a savior, becomes the destroyer of all that he tries to save. . . . Isabel's mysterious influence leads Pierre into a primitive worship, the tragic sacrifice of himself, and his own ironic deification in that sacrifice" (*The Wake of the Gods*, pp. 99, 119–120).

woman whose mysterious power inspires him that he will bring forth a bible: "Isabel, I will write such things—I will gospelize the world anew, and show them deeper secrets than the Apocalypse!—I will write it, I will write it!" Night after night Isabel "sat by him in the twilight, and played her mystic guitar till Pierre felt chapter after chapter born of its wondrous suggestiveness."

We have, however, good reason to suspect that Pierre's sacred book will never see the light of day—and not, as it is suggested, simply because the secret of the guitar was "eternally incapable of being translated into words." It may indeed be that the ultimate romance of the self is literally unwritable—that as Poe insisted, "No man dare write it. No man ever will dare write it. No man *could* write it, even if he dared." But in any case the would-be romancer who deludes himself into believing that the darkest mysteries of the soul can come forth as "the heaven-begotten Christ"— who "with the soul of an Atheist" writes down "the godliest things"—is doomed to produce only a literary and spiritual monstrosity. Thus Pierre, imprisoned in the Tombs, meditates: "Here, then, is the untimely, timely end;—Life's last chapter well stitched into the middle! Nor book, nor author of the book, hath any sequel, though each hath its last lettering! —It is ambiguous still. . . . now, to my soul, were a sword my midwife!" Pierre's "incipient offspring," the creature that sin begot upon self-deception, is stillborn—no Christ child, but only an abortive romance.

"Circumstances have so decreed," Melville writes, that a man cannot produce a "deep book" for the eyes of others until he has inscribed its truth first in his own heart. "The one can not be composed on the paper, but only as the other is writ down in his soul." Incapable of bringing to full awareness the truth of his illicit passion for Isabel, Pierre must fail as the conscious artist of his own heart's abysses. But what he cannot utter he can at least dream. In a "state of semi-unconsciousness, or rather trance," Pierre manages unvolitionally and evanescently to produce the romance that eludes his waking skill. It is the myth of Enceladus—Pierre himself allegorized—the "doubly incestuous" Titan who tried to assault heaven with his limbless stump of a body, turning "his vast trunk into a battering-ram" with which to vanquish the "invulnerable steep." Such is the unspeakable satanic truth of Pierre's obscure voyage into his buried life: a fantasy of phallic potency capable of assaulting even the universe itself.

"Ye knew him not!" exclaims Isabel—one cannot tell whether in despair or triumph—at the corpse-strewn conclusion to Pierre's tragedy.

And we might truly respond: he knew not himself. It is, as Conrad's Marlow would say, too dark altogether, a terrible revelation of human sin and sorrow perhaps mercifully left unrevealed: whereby Melville seems to suggest, once again, that—for the cautious writer as for the timid reader—the deepest romance is a book not to be attempted at all.[25]

4. "Aren't It All Sham?"

"Who in the rainbow," Melville asks in *Billy Budd*, "can draw the line where the violet tint ends and the orange tint begins? Distinctly we see the difference of the colors, but where exactly does the one first blendingly enter into the other?"[26] The habit of exploring the perplexities and complications of experience in terms of an ambiguous color symbolism is, as we have seen, characteristic of the American romance generally. But surely only a Melville could have conceived the startling notion, in his last work of fiction, of embodying the familiar figures of the fair and dark ladies in a handsome young sailor and a sinister Master-at-arms. Incorrigibly innocent, with his "welkin eyes," "yellow curls," and purely Saxon appearance (presumably free "of any Norman or other admixture") —he is likened to one of Fra Angelico's seraphs, with their "faint rosebud complexion of the more beautiful English girls"—Billy Budd seems to be as much the exemplar of blonde, blue-eyed purity as any Lucy Tartan. Claggart, on the other hand, is unmistakably a version of the diabolically clever, destructively passionate brunette. His mesmeric eye, of an unsettlingly rich violet color, "could cast a tutoring glance"; and his brow, "of the sort phrenologically associated with more than average intellect," had "silken jet curls partly clustering over it, making a foil to the pallor below," a result of his "official seclusion from the sunlight." Predictably, he is dubiously English, for "there lurked a bit of accent in his speech."

Melville's major purpose in *Billy Budd* amounts to a final attempt to fathom the ultimate significance of these apparent embodiments of ab-

---

25. Charles Feidelson's remark on *Moby-Dick* seems apposite here: "the inconclusive fate of Ishmael evinces a double attitude in Melville—an acceptance of 'voyaging' and a fear of its full implications" (*Symbolism and American Literature* [Chicago, 1953], p. 33).

26. For all citations I have used the invaluable *Billy Budd Sailor (An Inside Narrative)*, edited by Harrison Hayford and Merton M. Sealts, Jr. (Chicago, 1962), which contains an excellent bibliography on Melville's last work.

solute good and absolute evil. And as in *Pierre*, and many of the other romances we have examined, the author's dilemma becomes at least partly the problem of a protagonist who is set between these opposed figures. Captain the Honorable Edward Fairfax Vere, whose notably gray eyes seem to mark his position as adjudicator between the light and the dark, has no less a task than that of demarcating the tints of the rainbow. The difficulties of this task, at least as regards Billy Budd, are hinted at by Melville's presentation, at the beginning of the tale, of an archetypal "Handsome Sailor" whose very being is a striking symbol of color ambiguities. (He was "intensely black," but "the two ends of a gay silk handkerchief . . . danced upon the displayed ebony of his chest, in his ears were big hoops of gold, and a Highland bonnet with a tartan band set off his shapely head.") The imagination that created *Moby-Dick*, as Richard Chase has remarked, "does not settle ultimate questions; it leaves them open." And although many critics have read Melville's last tale as unequivocally the fable of a hanged and resurrected god, "the final impression we get from Melville's story," as Chase puts it, concerns "less the mystery of incarnation than the mystery entailed in the eternal contradiction of good and evil."[27] That mystery, one should add most emphatically, also involves the *internal* contradictions of those inscrutable absolutes themselves.

Although Melville undeniably presents "Baby" Budd as an example of radical innocence, the interest of his handling of Billy lies precisely in the subtle suggestion, developed inexorably as the tale proceeds, that in human life total *innocence* is by no means equivalent to total *good*. (Melville's treatment of his blonde hero thus allies him to Hawthorne with his Hilda, on the one side, and to James with his Maggie Verver, on the other.) Billy, "who in the nude might have posed for a statue of young Adam before the Fall," has not yet "been proffered the questionable apple of knowledge"; he is illiterate, lacks self-consciousness, and is incapable of understanding the will to malice or the turnings of a duplex nature. Yet not for all this is Billy himself entirely free of violent instincts or impulses. He is decidedly a postlapsarian creature, whose inner nature has been touched by "the envious marplot of Eden"—Satan's sign being Billy's tendency to stutter when excited (the prelude to an explosion of dangerously bottled-up emotions).

27. Richard Chase, *The American Novel and Its Tradition* (New York, 1957), p. 115.

Thus, although Billy is *unaware* of evil, he is not unaffected by it. Speculations on its nature are "so disturbingly alien to him" that he does "his best to smother them." Recoiling in disgust from things "which, though he but ill comprehended, he instinctively knew must involve evil of some sort," Billy keeps from himself precisely the kind of conscious enlightenment that might enable him to respond to the malign with human understanding and measured effect. Innocence, as Melville says, "was his blinder." And like the wildly released spirit of the French Revolution which, at the time of the Nore Mutiny, ignited "reasonable discontent growing out of practical grievances . . . into irrational combustion," Billy's reactions, when finally unleashed, lead to total disaster. Faced with Claggart's ugly accusation, he responds with an un-Christlike violence from which there is no appeal, whence the "peacemaker" of the "Bellipotent" threatens chaos aboard the ship, and "innocence and guilt personified in Claggart and Budd in effect changed places." Writing early in the story of the Master-at-arms' insane suspicion that Billy was trying to injure him, Melville warns that in such cases "the retaliation is apt to be in monstrous disproportion to the supposed offence; for when in anybody was revenge in its exactions aught else but an inordinate usurer?" Ironically, the words also apply to Billy's retaliation for Claggart's malevolence. "Such innocence as man is capable of," reflects the wise old Dansker, "does yet in a moral emergency not always sharpen the faculties or enlighten the will."

As for Claggart, it would certainly seem far more difficult to whiten his "natural depravity" than to bring out the dark side of Billy's innocence, yet Melville succeeds to a surprising degree in suggesting that there is a pathetic, even humanly poignant side to a personality apparently devoted to pure malice. Like the complicated hatred that Milton's Satan nourishes toward Adam, Claggart's antipathy to Billy is at least partly the expression of a profoundly despairing love. As an irrevocably fallen creature whose experience and insight will never allow him to forget the value of what he has lost, Claggart is in a position to entertain more comprehensive feelings toward Billy than Billy is toward him. ("One person excepted, the master-at-arms was perhaps the only man in the ship intellectually capable of adequately appreciating the moral phenomenon presented in Billy Budd.") A nature such as Billy's, which "had in its simplicity never willed malice or experienced the reactionary bite of that serpent," is bound to engender ambivalent feelings in a man "apprehending the good, but powerless to be it . . . what recourse is left to it [Claggart's nature] but to recoil upon itself and . . . act out to the end the part allotted it."

Claggart's tortured hatred of Billy is thus the result of a self-loathing so profound that it verges on the tragic, as Melville suggests in his complex portrait of the baffling Master-at-arms: "When Claggart's unobserved glance happened to light on belted Billy . . . that glance would follow the cheerful sea Hyperion with a settled meditative and melancholy expression, his eyes strangely suffused with incipient feverish tears. Then would Claggart look like the man of sorrows." Billy Budd's opponent, as F. O. Matthiessen remarks, "is not wholly diabolic . . . the felt recognition of its miserable isolation by even the warped mind partakes in the suffering of the Christ."[28] Melville's tale, then, has two "Christs"—at least, for we should not forget Captain Vere.

Setting the Captain aside temporarily, along with numerous perplexities and ambiguities, we may read *Billy Budd* as the tragedy of the "Handsome Sailor"—a fable of subversion in which the innocent fair "lady" is inexorably drawn by the knowing dark "lady" into a fallen world of painful experience that issues inevitably in death. Moving from "his former and simpler sphere to the ampler and more knowing world," where his position "was something analogous to that of a rustic beauty transplanted from the provinces and brought into competition with the high-born dames of the court," Billy finds himself hopelessly out of his depth. His first experience of crime and punishment (seeing a young afterguardsman scourged for dereliction of duty) horrifies him, and he resolves "that never through remissness would he make himself liable to such a visitation or do or omit aught that might merit even verbal reproof." But Billy has moved into a realm where good intentions count for very little. What can he possibly do to protect himself against a man who, like the Maules in *The House of the Seven Gables*, seems to exercise control over the more sinister aspects of human experience? Claggart's hand is on "various converging wires of underground influence . . . capable when astutely worked . . . of operating to the mysterious discomfort, if nothing worse, of any of the sea commonalty." Culminating his use of just such powers against Billy with an allegation of capital crime, Claggart succeeds in bringing an

---

28. *American Renaissance: Art and Expression in the Age of Emerson and Whitman* (New York, 1941), p. 507.

aspect of "white leprosy" to the innocent foretopman's normally rose-tan cheek. In the moment of accusation Billy's face wears an expression "like that of a condemned vestal priestess in the moment of being buried alive, and in the first struggle against suffocation." Thus, presumably, does death enter Billy's world, as the vicious influence of the corrupter permanently corrodes our young Adam's purity, tragically deepening his consciousness.

Such a reading of Melville's story immediately runs into some interesting difficulties. First, the death most immediately brought about by Claggart's machinations is his own, not Billy's. (In his description of Billy's punch, "quick as the flame from a discharged cannon at night," which took "effect full upon the forehead, so . . . intellectual-looking a feature in the master-at-arms," Melville seems actually to suggest a triumph of heart over head.) But, more importantly, the innocent sailor is shown to be incapable of any sustained tragic reaction to his dire experience: "True, Billy himself freely referred to his death as a thing close at hand; but it was something in the way that children will refer to death in general, who yet among their other sports will play a funeral with hearse and mourners." Billy's agony, Melville tells us, "mainly proceeding from a generous young heart's virgin experience of the diabolical incarnate and effective in some men," did not last very long. "It survived not the something healing in the closeted interview with Captain Vere."

Leaving his private talk with Billy after the foretopman's conviction, Captain Vere bears a look—"a startling revelation" to the senior Lieutenant who encounters him—"expressive of the agony of the strong." It is Vere, not Billy or Claggart, who is the true protagonist and suffering martyr of the episode aboard the "Bellipotent." "That the condemned one suffered less than he who mainly had effected the condemnation," Melville asserts, "was apparently indicated by the former's exclamation" —"God bless Captain Vere!"—just before he is hanged. Thus one meaning of Billy's benediction is made clear: it is Vere, condemned to live on in a fallen world bearing the burden of dark knowledge, who is truly in need of a blessing. Forced to witness, and finally to take part in, the excruciatingly incomprehensible struggle between good and evil, he is constrained to accept a difficult position of moral neutrality. Vere has learned how to compromise (as distinct from Billy, goodness elevates without dehumanizing him; as distinct from Claggart, knowledge of evil humanizes without degrading him), and it is precisely his conscious awareness of the necessity of making moral compromises that defines his tragedy.

Captain Vere's conscious adherence to the middle way defines, however, not only his essential human understanding but also—and more
negatively—his normal human timidity. In this regard, Vere represents
Melville's final fictional embodiment of a human and artistic dilemma
that occupied him throughout his career. Like the narrator of *Moby-Dick*
and like so many of the narrators of Poe's tales, Captain Vere learns to
fear the dangers of any passion (passionate goodness as well as passionate
malice) that proves itself to be absurd—that is, contrary to reason and to
the usual conditions of human existence. Faced with an extraordinary
clash of absolutes, in which an apparent embodiment of diabolism is
"struck dead by an angel of God" and "yet the angel must hang," Vere
understandably retreats behind law and order—reason and control. Not
that he lacks interest in large questions; he is, in fact, widely and deeply
read, and his occasional "dreaminess of mood" seems to betray a concern
with philosophical ultimates. But (to use Melville's terms in *Pierre*) though
he is aware of chronometricals, he chooses to abide by horologicals. As
Melville's use of Marvell's lines from "Appleton House" makes clear, the
Captain is indeed a "starry Vere," but his proper realm of action is a
"domestic heaven" characterized by "discipline severe." Human life, Vere
seems to feel, if it is to be gotten through sanely, must be based upon
reason and the containment of the irrational.[29] Accordingly, for the sake
of sanity and peace he painfully decides to turn away from the deepest and
most disturbing problems of the human heart.

Such problems, of course, are the stock in trade of the committed
romancer, for they point to something ineluctably and terrifyingly mysterious at the bottom of human experience. Refusing to indulge himself
in creating some fatuous "romantic incident" as an explanation of the
antagonism between Claggart and Billy, Melville argues in his last work
for a serious definition of his chosen genre—a definition that equates the
mystery of romance with that which is most profoundly *real*:

> The cause necessarily to be assumed as the sole one assignable is in its
> very realism as much charged with that prime element of Radcliffian
> romance, the mysterious, as any that the ingenuity of the author of *The
> Mysteries of Udolpho* could devise. For what can more partake of the mys-

---

29. "Control," writes Merlin Bowen, "is perhaps his [Vere's] most marked
characteristic" (*The Long Encounter: Self and Experience in the Writings of Herman
Melville* [Chicago, 1960], p. 221).

terious than an antipathy spontaneous and profound such as is evoked in certain exceptional mortals by the mere aspect of some other mortal, however harmless he may be, if not called forth by this very harmlessness itself?

"Passion in its profoundest," Melville makes clear, is the truly mysterious subject of *Billy Budd*, as it is of all serious romance, and such a subject demands for its full elucidation a kind of writing which, in its form and methods, approaches the Scriptures. "Coke and Blackstone," Melville asserts in discussing Claggart, "hardly shed so much light into obscure spiritual places as the Hebrew prophets." But what good will it do Melville as a modern author to attempt in *Billy Budd* to imitate the inspired writers of the Old Testament? "Dark sayings are these, some will say. But why? Is it because they somewhat savor of Holy Writ in its phrase 'mystery of iniquity'? If they do, such savor was far enough from being intended, for little will it commend these pages to many a reader of today." Hiding his true intentions behind a thick layer of irony, Melville constrains himself to return to the usual plausibilities of adventure fiction, just as Captain Vere, in front of the drumhead court, forcibly suppresses a hazardous interest in moral conundrums for the sake of military expediency: "Ay, there is a mystery; but, to use a scriptural phrase, it is a 'mystery of iniquity,' a matter for psychologic theologians to discuss. But what has a military court to do with it?" Vere must content himself with the rationalities of Coke and Blackstone, as embodied in the Mutiny Act, just as Melville must appear to content himself with writing a seemingly conventional tale of life at sea.[30]

"With mankind," Captain Vere is reported to have said, "forms, measured forms, are everything; and that is the import couched in the story of Orpheus with his lyre spellbinding the wild denizens of the wood." Thus, presumably, does Melville justify Vere's insistence on tradition and convention as a way of controlling the otherwise uncontrollable —of reducing the abnormal to the normal, the wild to the tame. But

---

30. One of the more judicious of the many essays on *Billy Budd*, Richard Harter Fogle's "*Billy Budd:* The Order of the Fall," *Nineteenth-Century Fiction*, XV (1960), 189–205, focuses steadily on Vere's role in the tale and suggests parallels between Vere's position and Melville's. Richard Chase argues that Vere "is the tragic hero of the story" and that there are similarities between Vere's situation and Melville's plight as a writer. See *Herman Melville: A Critical Study*, pp. 276–277.

surely Melville expected his readers to recall that Orpheus himself was finally overwhelmed and destroyed by the bacchantes. The forces of irrationality are never so easily nor so permanently put down (Captain Vere, we notice, is ultimately killed in an engagement with the "Athée"),[31] and this eternal struggle between the Dionysian and the Apollonian affects not only Captain Vere in the daily conduct of life, but also Melville the author, who can hardly hope to succeed in containing the "wild denizens" of his unsettling *Billy Budd* in a speciously neat fictional package.

> The symmetry of form attainable in pure fiction cannot so readily be achieved in a narration essentially having less to do with fable than with fact. Truth uncompromisingly told will always have its ragged edges; hence the conclusion of such a narration is apt to be less finished than an architectural finial.

The "fact" of human passion—the truth of the human heart—necessarily spills over the confines of orderly story-telling, forcing Melville to end his last romance on a note of mysterious ambiguity.

The final two chapters of *Billy Budd*, with their implicit offer of alternative versions of the tale just related, leave to the reader the questions of what to make of the career of Billy Budd and what narrative form can best convey the truth of that career. The first of these alternative treatments is a journalistic account—"doubtless for the most part written in good faith, though the medium, partly rumor, through which the facts must have reached the writer served to deflect and in part falsify them"— which represents the foretopman as a scheming villain who "vindictively stabbed to the heart" a "middle-aged man respectable and discreet" notable for his fidelity and patriotism. Bluejacket tradition, however, takes a diametrically opposed view, remembering Billy as a martyred holy innocent, a chip of whose scaffold is thought of "as a piece of the Cross." But from the "Bellipotent" itself comes a third version, a ballad composed by another foretopman gifted "with an artless *poetic* temperament," which provides an inner view of Billy's experience. (*Billy Budd*, we must remember, is meant to be "An inside narrative.") The ballad provides us with the handsome sailor's own interior monologue:

---

31. "Vere's preservation of martial order leads to the symbolic defeat of chaos, but this chaos kills him," says Bruce Franklin (*The Wake of the Gods*, p. 202).

> Ay, ay, all is up; and I must up too,
> Early in the morning, aloft from alow.
> On an empty stomach now never would it do.
> They'll give me a nibble—bit o'biscuit ere I go.
> Sure, a messmate will reach me the last parting cup;
> But, turning heads away from the hoist and the belay,
> Heaven knows who will have the running of me up!
> No pipe to those halyards.—But aren't it all sham?
> A blur's in my eyes; it is dreaming that I am.
>
> . . . .
>
> . . . they'll lash me in hammock, drop me deep.
> Fathoms down, fathoms down, how I'll dream fast asleep.
> I feel it stealing now. Sentry, are you there?
> Just ease these darbies at the wrist,
> And roll me over fair!
> I am sleepy, and the oozy weeds about me twist.

It might seem an abdication of Melville's responsibility as an artist in quest of truth that he should have finished his writing career by suggesting that life is no more than a dream. Perhaps such a conclusion does constitute a kind of evasion. But dreams—seemingly formless, ambiguous, largely inscrutable—have their truth as well as their confusion, and are, as we have seen, the American romancer's most persistent metaphor for his art. It is a perplexing view of experience. But Melville must have felt himself joining hands with Shakespeare as, preparing like Prospero to drown his book, he admitted that human experience and reflections on it finally dissolve in a perplexity:

> We are such stuff
> As dreams are made on, and our little life
> Is rounded with a sleep.—Sir, I am vex'd:
> Bear with my weakness; my old brain is troubled.

If to remind us of Prospero's words was Melville's intent, the poetic finale of *Billy Budd* is indeed the fitting testament of a writer who devoted his career to seeking the "ungraspable phantom of life" in the "baseless fabric" of a romancer's shifting vision.

V

JAMES

1. *A Rich Passion for Extremes*

ANY discussion of Henry James as a romancer is bound to face the immediate objection that James wrote novels, not romances—or, in Richard Chase's more conciliatory view, that he was "a novelist to the finger tips"[1] whose fictions contain, variously, assimilated or unassimilated elements of romance. Such a view must contend, however, with the strong suggestion James himself immodestly provides in the Preface to *The American* that he, unlike Scott, Balzac, or even "the coarse, comprehensive, prodigious Zola," exhibited the "general wealth" and great interest of his genius by committing "himself in both directions; not quite at the same time or to the same effect, of course, but by some need of performing his whole possible revolution, by the law of some rich passion in him for extremes."

Thus James seems to license us to take a cyclical view of his career: beginning as a practitioner of romance in the '70's with *Roderick Hudson* and *The American*, he moved through a period of concern with the actual fabric of society, represented most notably by *The Princess Casamassima*, only to return in his major phase to the extravagances of symbolism and allegory, thereby completing his whole possible revolution. This formulation is, of course, overly schematic, but it does underline the fact that James, unlike most other fictionists of his period, indulged himself in distinctly different kinds of writing during the course of his career, revealing a rich passion for extremes that would always perplex his critics.

But perhaps a temperamental, rather than a developmental, view of

---

1. *The American Novel and Its Tradition* (New York, 1957), p. 135.

James's work illuminates best his curious oscillation between romance and novel. Although he was early attracted to the growing school of fictional realism, James seems to have been by bent and background always strongly drawn to the traditions of non-realistic representation. In his critical writings he would think of romance, not as one of the easy exercises associated with a novelist's artistic apprenticeship, but as another, equally valid way of dealing with experience in the world of fiction. (Calling a work a romance, he insists in "The Art of Fiction," will not "make the difficult task any easier. . . . I can think of no obligation to which the 'romancer' would not be held equally with the novelist; the standard of execution is equally high for each.")

Whatever justification is needed for associating James's manifest interest in the theory and practice of romance with a peculiarly *American* tradition, however, can probably only be supplied by considering several of his productions in such a context as the foregoing studies of Cooper, Poe, Hawthorne, and Melville have hopefully provided.[2]

2. *Newman's Moon-Borne Madonna*

"By what art or mystery," James asks, "what craft of selection, omission or commission, does a given picture of life appear to us to surround its theme, its figures and images, with the air of romance while another

---

2. One of the earliest "apologies" for James as a romancer is still among the best: Joseph Warren Beach, *The Method of Henry James* (New Haven, 1918), pp. 120–130. James's vacillating opinions on romance versus the novel (as well as his critical views generally) are concisely summarized by René Wellek in "Henry James's Literary Theory and Criticism," *American Literature*, XXX (1958), 293–321. A good discussion of James's interest in and practice of "metaphysical romance," touching also on his relations with Poe and Hawthorne, is Earl Roy Miner, "Henry James's Metaphysical Romances," *Nineteenth-Century Fiction*, IX (1954), 1–21. Edward Stone's *The Battle and the Books: Some Aspects of Henry James* (Athens, Ohio, 1964) is an eminently readable presentation of James's work and the critical positions to which it has given rise. Especially relevant here are Stone's chapters on "The Art" (pp. 13–26) and "The Tug of the Fairy-Tale" (pp. 137–162). A probing and suggestive recent attempt to define James's peculiar genre and his formal and stylistic concerns, and to relate him to an American literary tradition, is Laurence B. Holland, *The Expense of Vision: Essays on the Craft of Henry James* (Princeton, 1964). Holland argues that James's "grasping" or "penetrating" imagination transformed the traditional novel of manners into a self-conscious and exaggerated art form which is at once "expressionistic" and "manneristic." See especially pp. 57–89, "The Makers of Manners."

picture close beside it may affect us as steeping the whole matter in the element of reality?" The answers he offers in connection with his "arch-romance," *The American*, demand, for all their familiarity, a certain amount of nuancing. What true romance is *not* he can announce with lucid assurance, disposing wittily of such "stalest stuff of romance" as conventionally jilted lovers, "bold bad treacheries" set in Paris, or "immense and flagrant dangers" decked out in all the gaudy trappings of history or exotic location. For a positive definition of romance—one that seems to ally it inextricably with the imagination itself—James reaches beyond the extrinsic to the subtleties of epistemology and psychology:

> The real represents to my perception the things we cannot possibly *not* know, sooner or later, in one way or another; it being but one of the accidents of our hampered state, and one of the incidents of their quantity and number, that particular instances have not yet come our way. The romantic stands, on the other hand, for the things that, with all the facilities in the world, all the wealth and all the courage and all the wit and all the adventure, we never *can* directly know; the things that can reach us only through the beautiful circuit and subterfuge of our thought and our desire.

The distinction that James seems to be driving at touches, not only the nature of whatever things may be experienced, but also the *quality* of our experience of things. The real, involved with accidents and incidents, is that which is objectively verifiable, unavoidably offered to the senses. Whether or not we have come across them, and even if, like Bishop Berkeley, we wish theoretically to dispute their existence, banknotes and bananas are insistently present to the unreflecting consciousness. The romantic, on the other hand, is not verifiable in ordinary ways; it comprises those things, like art and religion, which require (in Keats's phrase) a "greeting of the spirit" for their discovery and authentication. Without the presence of a developing consciousness, capable of responding to experience with imagination, "particular instances" of the romantic will never come our way at all, for they can hardly exist apart from the circuits and subterfuges of thought and desire.

The romance, according to James's definition of the romantic, must therefore deal with the spiritual adventures of the inner life, dramatized in terms dictated solely by such experience and accountable to no other standard.

The only *general* attribute of projected romance that I can see, the only one that fits all its cases, is the fact of the kind of experience with which it deals—experience liberated, so to speak; experience disengaged, disembroiled, disencumbered, exempt from the conditions that we usually know to attach to it and, if we wish so to put the matter, drag upon it, and operating in a medium which relieves it, in a particular interest, of the inconvenience of a *related,* a measurable state, a state subject to all our vulgar communities.

Così è se vi pare, James can truly say to his hero, stressing the interiority and subjectivity of romance experience. Extravagances of response, of conception, of expression, are thus justified for the protagonist of romance, as for the artist, if he should wish to indulge in them, since "it is a case of Newman's own intimate experience. . . . the thing constitutes itself organically as *his* adventure. . . . the interest of everything is all that it is *his* vision, *his* conception, *his* interpretation. . . . He therefore supremely matters; all the rest matters only as he feels it, treats it, meets it." *The American,* James concludes in a sentence that provides a clear link to our other authors, is an example of "the romantic *tout craché*" because it portrays "the fine flower of Newman's experience blooming in a medium 'cut off' and shut up to itself." Like so many of the romances treated in previous chapters, in which *vraisemblance* of social existence is sacrificed for the sake of psychological intensity, James's book concerns itself with exhibiting the process whereby an innocent consciousness blooms darkly under the pressure of being "insidiously beguiled and betrayed." And, again as in many of the works already examined, that process extravagantly but expressively images itself to the developing consciousness in terms of an exposure to the deepest secrets of art and religion.

We first see Christopher Newman "staring at Murillo's beautiful moon-borne Madonna" in a scene in the Louvre which prefigures his whole European experience and establishes its conditions.[3] A genial young businessman, James's expectant American hero is described as an "undeveloped connoisseur" who by his own admission is "not cultivated . . .

---

3. My analysis of *The American*, as will appear (especially with regard to the ending), is predicated on the original edition, in which James by his own admission was working freely and fully under "the emblazoned flag of romance." A generation later he would claim a desire to furl that flag. (The text used here is that of the 1877 Osgood edition as presented in *The American*, edited by Joseph Warren Beach [New York, 1949].)

not even educated." He has come abroad for knowledge of the world. "I know nothing about history, or art, or foreign tongues, or any other learned matters," he explains to his confidante, Mrs. Tristram: "But I am not a fool, either, and I shall undertake to know something about Europe by the time I have done with it." Newman is indeed "shrewd and capable," but his capabilities have thus far had to deal only with accounts and transactions. Now, despite his eagerness to learn, he finds himself facing a kind of experience which portends difficulties and dangers that make him uneasy: "Raphael and Titian and Rubens were a new kind of arithmetic, and they inspired our friend, for the first time in his life, with a vague self-mistrust." For one thing, Newman has entered a world where the ability to tell a copy from the original, or even a good copy from a bad one—in short, to tell the authentic from the false—is at a premium. ("They imitate, you know, so deucedly well," warns his American friend, Mr. Tristram.) Newman lacks precisely this ability. He also, and more importantly, lacks an awareness that the mysteries of European culture cannot be purchased for a sack of napoleons. They can be learned only, if ever, at the cost of painful inner development.

What Newman *can* buy, as well as his intense naiveté, is immediately dramatized by his encounter in the museum with the coquettish French copyist Mademoiselle Noémie Nioche and her father, who together suggest a tinsel version of the soon-to-be-encountered Bellegardes and foreshadow, by ironic parallel, all of Newman's difficulties with that mysterious clan. Newman's attention shifts from the moon-borne Madonna to her apparent admirer, a young lady engaged in making a "squinting" copy of Murillo's painting. Instantly the American expresses a desire to purchase Noémie's production ("I am not a Catholic, but I want to buy it. Combien?"), and the amazed amateur, swallowing her incredulity at Newman's offering to pay good money for her poor effort, puts on the face of a professional ("the young lady's aptitude for playing a part at short notice was remarkable") and demands 2,000 francs. Surprised, but reassured by her insistence that the copy "has remarkable qualities" and "is worth nothing less," Newman agrees, stipulating only that she complete it, for he insists on receiving a *finished* article:

> "Oh, it shall be finished in perfection; in the perfection of perfections!" cried mademoiselle; and to confirm her promise, she deposited a rosy blotch in the middle of the Madonna's cheek.

But the American frowned. "Ah, too red, too red!" he rejoined. "Her complexion," pointing to the Murillo, "is more delicate."

"Delicate? Oh, it shall be delicate, monsieur; delicate as the Sèvres *biscuit.* I am going to tone that down; I know all the secrets of my art."

As this fine comic interchange makes clear, Noémie's Madonna (the *purchasable* Madonna) is, like herself, an accommodating piece of fakery that can be adjusted to Newman's present taste—made shockingly rouged or delicately powdered, just as he wishes. Like her painting, Noémie is for sale, and she believes she knows what Newman wants. At least she suspects that she is certainly the mistress of any art which Newman is at the moment capable of appreciating, and as far as the painting is concerned she is undoubtedly correct. When it is finally delivered by Noémie's father, Newman's unsophisticated response to his tasteless treasure is ludicrously clear:

> It had been endued with a layer of varnish an inch thick, and its frame, of an elaborate pattern, was at least a foot wide. It glittered and twinkled in the morning light, and looked, to Newman's eyes, wonderfully splendid and precious. It seemed to him a very happy purchase, and he felt rich in the possession of it.

This purchase—decidedly "happy" because it is innocent of any artistic depth—is turned over to Newman by Monsieur Nioche with an apology for their having kept Newman waiting ("You accused us, perhaps, of inconstancy, of bad faith") which looks forward ominously to the Bellegardes' startling reversal with regard to Claire that will baffle Newman so later on. Now, however, all goes off without a hitch. Like the ridiculously shallow "French conversation" that Newman arranges to learn from Monsieur Nioche (" 'Our French conversation is famous, you know,' M. Nioche ventured to continue. 'It's a great talent.' 'But isn't it awfully difficult?' asked Newman, very simply. 'Not to a man of *esprit*, like monsieur, an admirer of beauty in every form!' and M. Nioche cast a significant glance at his daughter's Madonna"), Noémie's vapid painting glosses over precisely those depths and difficulties in which Newman is shortly to find himself.

Forever innocent and happy might Newman remain if he could truly content himself with an ersatz representation or a cheap and worldly disciple of the Blessed Virgin. But Newman wants to possess "the best article in the market." He "found his metaphysical inspiration in a vague acceptance of final responsibility to some illumined feminine brow," and it is not a mundane but a moon-borne Madonna that kindles his imagination. Oblivious of danger and unaware that he can never hope to understand, let alone possess, this mysterious representative almost of another planet, Newman plunges ahead in pursuit of Claire de Cintré, the ultimately unfathomable woman who "seemed enveloped in a sort of fantastic privacy" and around whom Newman "seemed to see the vague circle which sometimes accompanies the partly-filled disk of the moon." (Lunar metaphor follows Claire throughout the book. When the young Madame de Bellegarde appears at a party "dressed in an audacious toilet of crimson crape, bestrewn with huge silver moons," she tells Newman that she is "not a heavenly body" and has chosen crimson because it is "amusing," but that her "sister-in-law [Claire] would have chosen a lovely shade of blue, with a dozen little delicate moons." At Newman's last interview with Claire, "her eyes looked like two rainy autumn moons.")[4] If Newman wanted to see more of the world, James asks, "should he find it in Madame de Cintré's eyes? He would certainly find something there, call it this world or the next."

What Newman finds, as his passion for Claire draws him into the queer circle of the Bellegardes, is a world whose mingled mysteries of art and religion are utterly alien to anything he knows. "He had never read a novel!" the author exclaims of his hero ("I am not fond of books," Newman himself admits to Urbain de Bellegarde), and his adventure with Claire figures as an introductory course in strange literature. "He had opened a book and the first lines held his attention." Mrs. Bread's relation of the family's dark history, told as if by "the most artistic of romancers," will make him feel "as if he were turning over the page of a novel." And when Claire decides to become a nun, it will prove "too strange and too mocking to be real . . . like a page torn out of a romance, with no context in his own experience."

Similarly, during his earliest visits to the Bellegarde house Newman "sat by without speaking, looking at the entrances and exits, the greetings and chatterings, of Madame de Cintré's visitors. He felt as if he were at the play, and as if his own speaking would be an interruption; sometimes he wished he had a book, to follow the dialogue; he half expected to see a

4. In "James's Revisions of the Love Affair in *The American*," *New England Quarterly*, XXIX (1956), 53, Isadore Traschen notes that the moon metaphor is used "to represent the mystery and romance Newman saw in Claire."

woman in a white cap and pink ribbons come and offer him one for two francs."⁵ Unfortunately, such an offer is never made him. Claire herself "was part of the play that he was seeing acted, quite as much as her companions," and he finds her performance superlative; but what interests him most is to learn "what she was off the stage." Her manner seems to him "like an accomplishment, a beautiful talent, something that one might compare to an exquisite touch in a pianist," and it "especially impressed and fascinated Newman":

> The only trouble, indeed, was that when the instrument was so perfect it seemed to interpose too much between you and the genius that used it. Madame de Cintré gave Newman the sense of an elaborate education, of her having passed through mysterious ceremonies and processes of culture in her youth. . . . All this . . . made her seem rare and precious—a very expensive article, as he would have said, and one which a man with an ambition to have everything about him of the best would find it highly agreeable to possess. But looking at the matter with an eye to private felicity, Newman wondered where, in so exquisite a compound, nature and art showed their dividing line.

What Newman must learn is that for the Bellegardes there is no such dividing line: nature and art are one. He has entered "a strange corner of the world," where art is not merely an amusement, a leisure-time diversion, but a complex representation of reality to the condition of which the most cultured people themselves aspire. Thus, Claire's training was not intended simply to coat her with a patina of grace and good manners, but to enable her to act out her life roles with a feeling for their inner meaning. To be, like Newman at the start of his adventure, no more than natural is to be unformed, incapable of penetrating to the heart of things, excluded from the "romantic." Accordingly, Newman's introduction

---

5. The implications of James's theater metaphors in *The American* are touched on by Henry Popkin in "The Two Theatres of Henry James," *New England Quarterly*, XXIV (1951), 69–83. James's desire to liken Newman's experience of the Bellegarde circle to that of the world of literature was strengthened in revision. In "An American in Paris," *American Literature*, XXVI (1954), 67–77, Isadore Traschen points out, for example, that at the Bellegardes' engagement party the friends to whom Urbain introduces Christopher Newman are called "*beaux noms*" in the original edition, whereas in the revised version we are told that "these pronouncements [their names] again affected Newman as some enumeration of the titles of books, of the performers on playbills."

to the secrets of art amounts to an education in recognizing the importance of those symbolic gestures which reveal the inner life. He must learn that Claire's life is always a "play" and that it signifies immensely.

Similarly with religion. For Claire, Roman Catholicism, like art, is a mysterious dramatization of human experience which she takes seriously. If he hopes ever to understand her, he must undertake to fathom—as he finally cannot—the intense significance of her religious feeling. Newman is "struck with the gravity of her tone" when Claire tells him she is a Catholic, but he is obviously not sufficiently aware of what is implied by that gravity: her capacity for obedience, for renunciation, and for devotion to a spiritual ideal in the face of worldly disappointment. Her decision to become a Carmelite will seem to Newman "too dark and horrible for belief" and make "him feel as he would have done if she had told him that she was going to mutilate her beautiful face, or drink some potion that would make her mad." Her explanations will mean nothing to him:

> She laid her hand upon his arm, with a tender, pitying, almost reassuring gesture. "You don't understand," she said. "You have wrong ideas. It's nothing horrible. It is only peace and safety. It is to be out of the world, where such troubles as this come to the innocent, to the best. And for life—that's the blessing of it! They can't begin again."

For Newman however:

> That this superb woman, in whom he had seen all human grace and household force, should turn from him and all the brightness that he offered her—him and his future and his fortune and his fidelity—to muffle herself in ascetic rags and entomb herself in a cell, was a confounding combination of the inexorable and the grotesque . . . a reduction to the absurd of the trial to which he was subjected.

We may observe, as Newman cannot, that Claire's act also reduces to comprehensibility the fascination she has exercised over him—a fascination clearly based on her mysterious spiritual depths. Paradoxically, if she were not capable of a decision of this sort, she could hardly be the superb woman whom he feels compelled to pursue with such blind intensity. ("Madame de Cintré's conduct . . . struck him with a kind of awe, and the fact that he was powerless to understand it or feel the reality of its motives only deepened the force with which he had attached himself to her.") But Newman's mistake was to assume facilely that he could separate

Claire's "religious feelings" from her reality as a woman (just as he assumed wrongly that he could come to know her "off the stage"):

> He had never let the fact of her Catholicism trouble him; Catholicism to him was nothing but a name, and to express a mistrust of the form in which her religious feelings had moulded themselves would have seemed to him on his own part a rather pretentious affectation of Protestant zeal. If such superb white flowers as that could bloom in Catholic soil, the soil was not insalubrious. But it was one thing to be a Catholic, and another to turn nun—on your hands! . . . To see a woman made for him and for motherhood to his children juggled away in this tragic travesty—it was a thing to rub one's eyes over, a nightmare, an illusion, a hoax.

What strikes Newman as no more than a nightmarish travesty is actually, in James's phrase, simply a "dusky old-world expedient"—a solution to a human problem which, however sad, is nevertheless comprehensible in terms of Catholic European culture. It appears incomprehensibly grotesque only to a mind incapable of understanding such a culture or of taking it seriously.

Ironically—how much so, one can realize only after completing the book—it is in fact the exaggerated "Protestant zeal" of Benjamin Babcock (the Unitarian minister from Dorchester, Massachusetts, who travels with Newman early in the story) that stumbles upon a truth which Newman's good humor blinds him to. Ridiculously, Babcock attempts to warn Newman of the "dangers" of European culture and worries himself sick trying to come to terms morally with European art. Uncertain what kind of judgment to pass on the paintings of Luini, he is deeply distressed by Newman's easygoing reaction, which splendidly (but—as Newman's simile may seem to us later—ominously) glides over all difficulties: "Luini? . . . why, he's enchanting—he's magnificent! There is something in his genius that is like a beautiful woman. It gives one the same feeling." Babcock returns alone to Milan for further study, whence he writes his erstwhile companion a letter in which, besides pronouncing himself "greatly perplexed by Luini," he offers some pastoral advice: "Art and life seem to me intensely serious things, and in our travels in Europe we should especially remember the immense seriousness of Art . . . . I hope you will continue to enjoy your travels; only *do* remember that Life and Art *are* extremely serious."

Babcock's moral intensity of course seems to Newman (and to us, at this point in James's narrative) absurdly overdone, but its unexpected application to Newman's adventure gradually becomes clear, as does the true but presently unsuspected meaning of Newman's response:

> He wrote no answer at all, but a day or two afterward he found in a curiosity shop a grotesque little statuette in ivory, of the sixteenth century, which he sent off to Babcock without a commentary. It represented a gaunt, ascetic-looking monk, in a tattered gown and cowl, kneeling with clasped hands and pulling a portentously long face. It was a wonderfully delicate piece of carving, and in a moment, through one of the rents of his gown, you espied a fat capon hung round the monk's waist. In Newman's intention what did the figure symbolize?

The author professes not to know exactly, and contents himself with suggesting that the statue was meant as a kind of general satire on human efforts to be "high-toned." Its more immediate reference to Babcock's sermonizing, however, seems clear: Newman has sent his earnest friend an example of the jolly hypocrisy of European religious life and art as an antidote to Babcock's high seriousness. But the figure also appears to symbolize Newman's dangerously easygoing acceptance of a stereotypic view of Catholicism that predisposes him to seeing it as "nothing but a name"—grave and mystical in appearance, but essentially familiar and accommodating, and reducible to a joke. That joke, however, becomes tinged with seriousness, a flippant seriousness (reminiscent of the gay desperation of an Ivan Karamazov) which Newman seems not to appreciate, when Claire's brother announces, apropos of his pursuit of pleasure:

> "I am good for another five years, perhaps, but I foresee that after that I shall lose my appetite. Then what shall I do? I think I shall turn monk. Seriously, I think I shall tie a rope round my waist and go into a monastery. It was the old custom, and the old customs were very good. People understood life quite as well as we do. They kept the pot boiling till it cracked, and then they put it on the shelf altogether."

Newman's response is a measure of his incredulity: " 'Are you very religious?' asked Newman, in a tone which gave the inquiry a grotesque effect." But the portentous significance of Valentin's remark, as of Newman's statuette, lies in its clear reference to Claire's decision to become a nun. As Mrs. Bread explains to Newman:

> "There is no rule so strict as that of the Carmelites. . . . They sleep on the ground. . . . They give up everything. . . . father and mother, brother and sister,—to say nothing of other persons. . . . They wear a shroud

under their brown cloaks and a rope round their waists, and they get up on winter nights and go off into cold places to pray to the Virgin Mary. The Virgin Mary is a hard mistress!"

Whereupon Newman can only utter a "melancholy groan."

Thus does Claire, who might herself be called a good example of French religious art, lead Newman's imagination into total perplexity ("You are a mystery to me; I don't see how such hardness can go with such loveliness"), as his fascination with the "moon-borne Madonna" culminates in the "bottomless depth" of Madame de Cintré's nature. Her final "performance" figures itself to Newman's agitated soul, when he visits her convent, as the "confused, impersonal wail" which "arose from the depths of the chapel, from behind the inexorable grating . . . a strange, lugubrious chant, uttered by women's voices. . . . the chant of the Carmelite nuns, their only human utterance. . . . their dirge over their buried affections and over the vanity of earthly desires." This may stand for Newman's ultimate experience of European culture: something "hideous" and "horrible" that leaves him "bewildered—almost stunned."

James's comprehensive vision of his hero's adventure as a journey into the depths and complexities of art governs not only Newman's way of seeing the people with whom he comes into contact—all of the Bellegardes and their friends are, at one point or another, compared to objets d'art or described as actors and actresses—but also his own role. Newman is first presented in the role of protagonist in a mere fairy tale or fable, viewed by turns as a hero "in seven-league boots," the "Beast" who tries for the Beauty's hand, and the "young prince" who "married the beautiful Florabella . . . and carried her off to live with him in the Land of the Pink Sky." He ends by exchanging such happy simplicities for a part in something more nearly approaching tragedy, or at least "lugubrious comedy." One suggestion comes from Newman himself. Seeing *Don Giovanni* for the first time, he is reminded of his own situation:

> "I am very curious to see how it ends," said Newman.
> "You speak as if it were a feuilleton in the 'Figaro,'" observed the marquis. "You have surely seen the opera before?"
> "Never," said Newman. "I am sure I should have remembered it. Donna Elvira reminds me of Madame de Cintré; I don't mean in her circumstances, but in the music she sings."
> "It is a very nice distinction," laughed the marquis lightly. "There is

no great possibility, I imagine, of Madame de Cintré being forsaken."

"Not much!" said Newman. "But what becomes of the Don?"

"The devil comes down—or comes up," said Madame de Bellegarde, "and carries him off. I suppose Zerlina reminds you of me."

"I will go to the foyer for a few moments," said the marquis, "and give you a chance to say that the commander—the man of stone—resembles me." And he passed out of the box.

We may take the episode merely as an illustration of Newman's naiveté and Urbain's biting ill-humor, or we may follow Newman's lead and allow ourselves to construct those rough parallels, direct or ironic, by which alone the individual human situation finds itself mirrored in universal art. Claire is indeed betrayed and left forlorn (though not directly by Newman), as Newman's good humor is turned to horror (though not strictly through the agency of the devil). But the conclusion of the opera will enlighten Newman only obliquely, since the transcendently gay coda of Mozart's work is missing from Newman's own performance. Leporello ("nowadays," admits Valentin, "we see a great strapping democrat keeping a count about him to play the fool") will die for his pains, and our democratic hero will be left living to bear as best he can the perplexities of his permanently transformed consciousness.

A more sinister literary paradigm for the situation in which Newman finds himself embroiled is provided by Valentin. "We are such a brother and sister as have not been seen since Orestes and Electra," he says of himself and Claire, hinting at some obscure drama of ancient guilt and retribution which binds the two younger Bellegarde children closely together. Later this suggestion will be confirmed both by Claire, when she announces mysteriously in her last interview with Newman, "There's a curse upon the house," and by Mrs. Bread, who relates to Newman the sombre tale of iniquity connected with the house. (In that tale Bellegarde *mére* figures as the Clytemnestra who did away with Bellegarde *père*/Agamemnon. Mrs. Bread, having in her youth inspired the wrath of Lady Emmeline by attracting the roving eye of her husband, plays the role of Cassandra, now grown old and bitter in ignominious service.)

By allowing his candid American hero to be drawn into this modern version of an old tragedy, James exposes Newman to the dangers of its motif: the contagion of desired revenge for real or imagined insult. It is the growth of precisely this dark desire, the revelation of Newman's capacity for such feeling, that defines the lethal effect of his contact with the Bellegarde world. "You may depend upon it that there are things going on inside of us that we understand mighty little about," Newman exclaims all too innocently to his compatriot Tristram at the start of the book, hardly suspecting that he is suggesting his capacity for painful as well as pleasurable spiritual growth. Arriving in Europe, he had indeed been possessed by "a vague sense that more answers were possible than his philosophy had hitherto dreamt of," but this sense is represented at the beginning as an unequivocally happy one. Feeling himself to be unqualifiedly a creature of sunshine, he sees all the world in that bright image, or at least believes himself potent to dispel any hint of darkness. Claire, he decides on first meeting her, "was a woman for the light, not for the shade; and her natural line was not picturesque reserve and mysterious melancholy, but frank, joyous, brilliant action. . . . To this, apparently, he had succeeded in bringing her back. He felt, himself, that he was an antidote to oppressive secrets; what he offered her was, in fact, above all things a vast, sunny immunity from the need of having any." In this connection, his final failure will be stated simply by Mrs. Bread: "You pushed her into the sunshine, sir. . . . Then they pulled her back into the shade." But his loss in this metaphoric tug of war is even more complete than Mrs. Bread's words indicate, for he is himself pulled into the shade, losing his cherished immunity from "oppressive secrets" and the destructive emotions that accompany them. "You can't hurt me unless you kill me by some violent means," Newman assures Valentin confidently, still unaware of how painful can be the inner wound that marks a fall from innocence.

The change that Newman undergoes can be easily gauged. In the pre-Bellegarde state his most notable quality is his unshakable good humor, his seemingly total incapacity for malicious response. Early in the book Mrs. Tristram announces her belief that Newman is "a man of no feeling" (she means love), and he admits that so far in life he has had no time to *feel* things; but Mrs. Tristram remains incredulous at his insistence that he also lacks the darker passions:

> "When you are in a fury it can't be pleasant."
> "I am never in a fury."
> "Angry, then, or displeased."
> "I am never angry, and it is so long since I have been displeased that I have quite forgotten it."

Mrs. Tristram's shrewd response to Newman's words—she says that he is "neither good enough nor bad enough" to lack temper—is reminiscent of *Billy Budd* in its suggestion that the liability to anger is a sign of normal postlapsarian humanity. Newman's description of himself, especially as he repeats it to Claire, seems almost a denial of any inner life: "What there is you see before you. I honestly believe I have no hidden vices or nasty tricks. I am kind, kind, kind!" In this regard, Newman's experience with the Bellegardes might be considered an introductory journey along precisely that dark circuit and subterfuge of thought and desire which James, in his Preface, associates generally with romance. The possibility that Newman might actually think of and finally wish to enjoy the satisfactions of vengeance only appears when, "angry," "sore," and "sick" at being rejected by the Bellegardes, he accepts with guilty excitement Valentin's tempting offer of secret information:

> "A secret!" Newman repeated. The idea of letting Valentin, on his death-bed, confide him an "immense secret" shocked him, for the moment, and made him draw back. It seemed an illicit way of arriving at information, and even had a vague analogy with listening at a key-hole. Then, suddenly, the thought of "forcing" Madame de Bellegarde and her son became attractive, and Newman bent his head closer to Valentin's lips.

Well might all nature (at least American nature) groan at the end of this scene, as it does in *Paradise Lost* when Adam falls, for the scene represents James's version of a truly Miltonic calamity—Newman's conscious accession to what he feels to be evil. Aware that he is fumbling in "a horrible rubbish-heap of iniquity," Newman nevertheless plunges ahead passionately in search of ancient skeletons to flourish in the service of revenge—so passionately that even Mrs. Bread, who like Tiresias seems to have seen and suffered all, is surprised by his vehemence: "Mercy on us ... how wicked we all are!" Newman's response exhibits the full bloom of his transformed nature:

> "I don't know," said Newman; "some of us are wicked, certainly. I am very angry, I am very sore, and I am very bitter, but I don't know that I am wicked. I have been cruelly injured. They have hurt me, and I want to hurt them. I don't deny that. . . . I want to bring them down,—down, down, down! I want to turn the tables upon them—I want to mortify them as they mortified me. They took me up into a high place

and made me stand there for all the world to see me, and then they stole behind me and pushed me into this bottomless pit, where I lie howling and gnashing my teeth! I made a fool of myself before all their friends; but I shall make something worse of them."

Injured pride and thwarted desire for his moon-borne Madonna have elicited from James's "extremely good-humored" hero a furious reaction of cosmic proportions. Head thrown back, "gazing at all the stars," Newman feels as if he were "riding his vengeance along the Milky Way." He luxuriates grandly in the destructive potential newly discovered within himself:

> He was nursing his thunder-bolt; he loved it; he was unwilling to part with it. He seemed to be holding it aloft in the rumbling, vaguely-flashing air, directly over the heads of his victims, and he fancied he could see their pale, upturned faces. Few specimens of the human countenance had ever given him such pleasure as these, lighted in the lurid fashion I have hinted at, and he was disposed to sip the cup of contemplative revenge in a leisurely fashion.

Thus does our "kind, kind, kind" Christopher Newman, corrupted by contact with the malevolent, indulge his now lurid imagination in the projected joys of pure malice.

In his Preface to *The American* James insists that the "point" of his romance lies in the protagonist's suffering "at the hands of persons pretending to represent the highest possible civilisation and to be of an order in every way superior to his own," but proving his own moral superiority by finally not deigning "all triumphantly and all vulgarly" to exercise the power of revenge. Newman's sense of moral revulsion, James explains, would overcome "the bitterness of his personal loss": "All he would have at the end would be therefore just the moral convenience, indeed the moral necessity, of his practical, but quite unappreciated, magnanimity. . . . there would be no subject at all, obviously,—or simply the commonest of the common,—if my gentleman should enjoy his advantage." One wonders to what extent James's sense of his "subject" here betrays a kind of nostalgic revisionism, the charmingly shortsighted national pride of an aging and exiled American romancer (the parallel with Hawthorne's preface to *The Marble Faun* is striking). D. H. Lawrence's warning that in dealing with American literature we should trust the fable rather than the author seems especially necessary here, for James's view of the meaning of a story he had written more than thirty years before seems egregiously, albeit patriotically, beside the point.

James stresses the fact that Newman finally does not "enjoy" his advantage, but what matters is that Newman is manifestly *changed* by his experience. Having tasted "the treachery of the Bellegardes," he finds that his old occupations in America appear "unreal"—"do what he would he somehow could not believe in them"—and we feel that their reality will forever remain qualified for him. Returning to Europe, Newman of course decides not to try to expose the Bellegardes and in that mood throws his little scrap of paper, with its damning evidence, into Mrs. Tristram's fire. But the last page of the book makes a telling point. Having burned his "revenge," he learns from Mrs. Tristram that the Bellegardes had undoubtedly calculated that he would not use his information and have thus taken the last trick. "Their confidence, after counsel taken of each other, was not in their innocence, nor in their talent for bluffing things off; it was in your remarkable good nature!" Whereupon—as a kind of ironic commentary on the final condition of Newman's "remarkable good nature"—James gives us the ultimate sentence: "Newman instinctively turned to see if the little paper was in fact consumed; but there was nothing left of it." That final movement, that instinctive impulse toward revenge, is the mark of his wound, the forever ineffaceable evidence of moral uncertainty that testifies to Newman's changed state.[6]

He has come to Europe, he explains to Tristram at the beginning of the book, because, "sick of business," he had felt "a new man" inside his old skin and "longed for a new world." Like his "patron-saint," Columbus, James's hero discovers a "new world" which is in truth very old. His exploration proves himself to be, not really a "new man," but simply the familiar old Adam, growing painfully and irrevocably into maturity.

3. The "Darkest Abyss of Romance"

IN view of the ample discussion which James's most famous tale has aroused, it might seem an act of particular cruelty to subject *The Turn of the Screw* to another twist on the critical rack. But since the inquisitional

---

6. The discrepancy between James's view of his hero's "good nature" and Newman's impulse at the end is discussed in Floyd C. Watkins, "Christopher Newman's Final Instinct," *Nineteenth-Century Fiction*, XII (1957), 85–88. In the revised version James completely changed the conclusion of the book, clearly bringing the text in line with his latest idea about Newman's character.

ferocity visited on the story has almost invariably involved an attempt to extract from it a confession concerning the metaphysical status of the ghosts (the Big- and Little-Endians in this case being the apparitionists and non-apparitionists[7]), we can sidestep the bitterness of factional dispute and perhaps avoid doing any further violence to James's "*amusette*" by treating it, as much as possible, in terms of technique and literary theory. *The Turn of the Screw*, James gives us ample reason to believe, may be viewed as an exercise in "pure romance."

What we should expect such an item to be, James makes reasonably clear in his Preface to the tale, where he spins out a theory which is unmistakably allied to that offered in the Preface to *The American*. His "sinister romance," James repeatedly insists, is such by virtue of its being an egregious case of "experience disengaged" (to use a key phrase from the earlier Preface). "The thing had for me the immense merit," he explains, "of allowing the imagination absolute freedom of hand, of inviting it to act on a perfectly clear field, with no 'outside' control involved." The tale is "a perfect example of an exercise of the imagination unassisted, unassociated—playing the game, making the score . . . off its own bat"; and it is precisely its status as an exercise of "the imaginative faculty acting with the *whole* of the case on its hands" that strikes James as "the interesting thing." In other words, the author says, his "exhibition" is "a fairy-tale pure and simple," the charm of which "for the distracted modern mind is in the clear field of experience . . . over which we are thus led to roam; an annexed but independent world in which nothing is right save as we rightly imagine it."

James thus evinces a deep interest in exploring the realm of *pure* imagination, a realm in which images of the world are strictly ideal because they are freed of responsibility to the way things generally happen. Such a realm corresponds of course to the interior, or underside, of every human consciousness, where fantasy is liberated from the necessity of reality testing. James invites us to wander in (as he invites himself to experiment

---

7. For an entertaining summary (including a very useful bibliography) of this endless controversy, admittedly written from the non-apparitionist point of view, see Thomas Mabry Cranfill and Robert Lanier Clark, Jr., *An Anatomy of The Turn of the Screw* (Austin, Texas, 1965). Generous selections from the voluminous criticism on James's "shameless pot-boiler" are offered in *A Casebook on Henry James's The Turn of the Screw*, edited by Gerald Willen (New York, 1960), and *The Turn of the Screw*, edited by Robert Kimbrough (New York, 1966).

with) this independent world of total subjectivity—this "little firm fantasy"—mainly, it would seem, for the sake of amusement. But there is a vitally serious side to the experiment. For everywhere in his theorizing, as in the tale itself, he suggests an important question: *what is the status of pure romance in the real world, its relationship to public experience?* In strictest terms, of course, he would make absolutely no claims for the *truth* of so patent a contrivance. But the deepest implication of an experiment of this kind is that innocent questions about veridicality are quite irrelevant. One can in fact hardly dispute the validity of any such image of experience, for to the individual consciousness its own image of reality *must* be valid.[8]

One should ask, rather, about the *effect* of such admittedly self-contained, private constructions. Pure art (i.e., romance) may be false to the public mind, but it can have a real influence on the world we all share. What, we might finally ask, is that world, anyway, if not something fabricated out of our pooled subjectivities? We scarcely need to argue, in defense of romance, that truth is stranger than fiction if we can establish that truth is largely *composed* of fiction. James's governess, Richard Chase notes astutely, is "a human being whose pathos is that of everyone—namely, that she has in terror, joy, and anxiety spun out in her mind a precious image of reality . . . . Her fantasied version of reality is only in degree different from the false but precious and jealously guarded version we all form in our minds." The tale itself, we may say, is mainly an object lesson in the very process by which the mind attempts to create a model

---

8. Appearance and reality are separated to such an "appalling extent" in this story, writes Marius Bewley, that "what James has, in effect, accomplished, is an undermining of the laws of evidence, and a destructive foray into the grounds for moral judgment" ("Appearance and Reality in Henry James," *Scrutiny*, XVII [1950], 113). If I may be allowed to translate Bewley's "appearance" and "reality" into "narrative world" and "truth," his statement seems a good summary of my own argument. Amplifying his remark in a reply to F. R. Leavis, Bewley makes a connection that has further relevance to this study: "When I called *The Turn of the Screw* 'appalling' I had in mind something different from the mere Gothic horror which, I believe, Mr. Leavis credits me with. . . . [By 'metaphysically appalling'] what I meant was that the dissolution of the ties between appearance and reality which seems to threaten in many of James's stories was here realized with peculiar violence and intensity, and that what it signified was a lack of faith in the grounds of creation, and hence a denial of the possibility of strict moral action. In one guise or another this is a theme of many American writers. Melville wrote a variation on it in *The Confidence Man*" ("Maisie, Miles and Flora, the Jamesian Innocents: A Rejoinder," *Scrutiny*, XVII [1950], 255–263).

of experience, as well as a demonstration of how dangerously effective
that process can be when the imagination is subjected to extraordinary
turns of the artistic screw.

For James himself, as he saw it, "this full-blown flower of high fancy"
amounts largely to an experiment in compelling belief in a "perfectly
independent and irresponsible little fiction." "It is a piece of ingenuity
pure and simple," he argues in Poesque fashion, "of cold artistic calcula-
tion, an *amusette* to catch those not easily caught (the 'fun' of the capture
of the merely witless being ever but small), the jaded, the disillusioned,
the fastidious."[9] He thus set out ostensibly to produce a tour de force
capable of tricking even the sophisticated into crediting the extravagances
of romance. But his success goes far beyond mere fun, proving finally
that fantasy—especially that involved with "the dear old sacred terror"—
has a permanent place in the geography of every mind. Indeed, James's
method of achieving his effect is based on an assumption that an audience
hardly needs to be coerced at all into conceiving of unusual horrors, no
matter how implausible or inscrutable, since their own creative spirits
will rise to the occasion: "Only make the reader's general vision of evil
intense enough . . . and his own experience, his own imagination . . . will
supply him quite sufficiently with all the particulars. Make him *think* the
evil, make him think it for himself, and you are released from weak speci-
fications." Proof of how responsive—and sinister—a chord the fantastic
music of pure romance sounds in the soul of general humanity can be
seen, James assures us, in the reader's "droll" response to a make-believe
world that he has himself helped to create:

> How can I feel my calculation to have failed, my wrought suggestion
> not to have worked, that is, on my being assailed, as has befallen me, with
> the charge of a monstrous emphasis, the charge of all indecently ex-
> patiating? There is not only from beginning to end of the matter not an
> inch of expatiation, but my values are positively all blanks save so far as
> an excited horror, a promoted pity, a created expertness—on which punc-
> tual effects of strong causes no writer can ever fail to plume himself—
> proceed to read into them more or less fantastic figures. Of high interest
> to the author meanwhile—and by the same stroke a theme for the moral-
> ist—the artless resentful reaction of the entertained person who has

---

9. *The Turn of the Screw* "is a triumph, conceived in a spirit that Poe might have
applauded, of calculating contrivance," says F. R. Leavis ("James's 'What Maisie
Knew': A Disagreement," *Scrutiny*, XVII [1950], 115–127).

abounded in the sense of the situation. He visits his abundance, morally, on the artist—who has but clung to an ideal of faultlessness.

There is surely more than a touch of disingenuousness in James's insistence that his hands are totally clean, that he has only discovered the perfect equation for producing romance answers in the reader's imagination. Romance truth is thus nobody's fault! Perhaps the romancer's "artless" unwillingness to accept responsibility for the fantasies he has triggered is equally a theme for the moralist. But James's point is nevertheless well taken: the reaction of the entertained person, which represents to some extent the kick of the reader's own gun, gives proof both of the power of romance and of the universal reluctance to admit that such power has its source in fantasies which we all share.

The controlling symbol of James's experiment, signalled by the title, perfectly expresses both the author's intent and his method of carrying out that intent. The purpose of this romance is to exhibit human imagination under pressure but not completely broken down—twisted but not torn. Technically it is a problem in presenting experience at once lurid and credible—beyond what is publicly ordinary and probable, but not beyond what is privately conceivable. James solved that problem here in his choice of a narrative method and a narrator. "The romantic privilege of the 'first person,'" he tells us in his Preface to *The Ambassadors*, represents the "darkest abyss of romance." Setting us afloat in a version of reality totally constructed by a single consciousness, James has cast us into a world incapable of being verified or clarified through outside reference. "I had the fancy of our being almost as lost as a handful of passengers in a great drifting ship," the governess says in her first chapter. "Well, I was strangely at the helm!"[10]

We are not, however, in a certifiedly mad world, for our narrative guide is by no means presented as an example of aberrant human nature, but only of normal human consciousness tightened a few notches beyond what is usual. The governess's world is entirely self-consistent, and she herself is mainly characterized by her love of lucidity. She has "authority," as James says, the considerable ability "to make her particular credible statement of . . . strange matters." And if it is just the extreme insistence of

10. The governess's metaphoric reaction to the "castle of romance" in which she finds herself looks back to Melville's dream-ship "Fidele," as well as forward to James's own Preface to *The American*.

her logic that makes us most uneasy (as frequently with the narrative voices of Poe's tales), we may notice by how scarcely perceptible an incline James has conducted us to the deepest part of his romantic abyss. For it is reason, after all, which (as Poe said) constitutes "man's chief idiosyncrasy" in his "natural" state. The governess herself explains:

> What I had to deal with was, revoltingly, against nature. I could only get on at all by taking "nature" into my confidence and my account, by treating my monstrous ordeal as a push in a direction unusual, of course, and unpleasant, but demanding after all, for a fair front, only another turn of the screw of ordinary human virtue. No attempt, none the less, could well require more tact than just this attempt to supply, one's self, *all* the nature.

The governess's words are a lovely expression of the author's own problem, for she, like him, must render the incredible credible, the unnatural natural, by bringing all within the purview of private reason. The "fair front" thus obtained for the intensest of anomalies pictures them deceptively—but in an important sense quite fairly—as requiring "only another turn of the screw of ordinary human virtue" for their comprehension and control.

Such a turn of the screw is tactfully provided by the governess's self-enclosed narration, which assimilates everything to its own nature. That nature is not so much abnormal as normally, if extraordinarily, subjective; and the horror lies in our being trapped unwittingly in the tightening circle of an inescapable subjectivity. For, as Richard Chase writes:

> The universe of meanings is bigger than the governess's own distraught mind, and the drama of the tale lies in her attempt to foresee and interpret with her frantic consciousness everything that can happen to her. Of course, she cannot do this, and if there is a moral in the book, it is that the attempt to live in a totally cognized world, in which all ambiguities are rationalized and symbolized according to the bias of one's own mind, is madness.[11]

We may wish to believe that such madness can be dispelled by our breaking away from the hothouse atmosphere of the narrator's consciousness, just as we may console ourselves by accepting at face value the author's statement that his frightening tale is simply an "irresponsible" fiction. But we should remember that James's experiment represents an only slightly exaggerated example of what every consciousness, left to itself, is

---

11. *The American Novel and Its Tradition*, p. 240.

capable of. The "white face of damnation" so terrifyingly presented to little Miles is perhaps no more than a private fantasy of the governess, but it all too plausibly and permanently pushes him "over an abyss," carrying us at least a little of the way with him. We may all be so affected, as we may all be so affecting, James seems to say, for the annexed but independent kingdom of romance is within us all.

4. *Reflections in a Golden Bowl*

"I SEE it's *always* terrible for women," remarks Maggie Verver toward the end of *The Golden Bowl*, whereupon her Italian Prince, looking "down in his gravity," replies as for a slight correction: "Everything's terrible, *cara*—in the heart of man."[12] While this interchange serves to exhibit succinctly the intense self-involvement of James's American heroine, it also opens out immediately into deeper and more international water: into that mysterious sea of inscrutable human relations which washes all shores, alternately supporting and sinking ships of all nations, floating and flooding all human hearts. Such is the concern and imagery of James's last complete romance, though that term, we must now admit, is much less to be insisted on than is his palpable adherence to the fictional tradition we have been tracing. The figure here used to suggest that concern is no rhetorical extravagance, but simply an introduction to James's metaphoric version of the adventure tale.[13] Indeed, if the American romance can be at least partially defined as an attempt to find metaphors for the inner life, we may say that James's masterwork completes and culminates the genre with dazzling brilliance. *The Golden Bowl* is at once a rewriting of Poesque explorations and an infinitely subtle reworking of *The Marble Faun*, in which the mysteries of art again provide a terminology and a touchstone for the varieties of human experience. Let us begin with Poe, as James himself does.

Musing, in the first chapter of the book, on the Ververs and their "extraordinary American good faith," the Prince finds himself metaphor-

---

12. Especially interesting treatments of *The Golden Bowl* are in F. O. Matthiessen, *Henry James: The Major Phase* (New York, 1944); John Bayley, *The Characters of Love: A Study in the Literature of Personality* (New York, 1960); Dorothea Krook, *The Ordeal of Consciousness in Henry James* (Cambridge, 1962); and Laurence B. Holland, *The Expense of Vision*.

13. Some aspects of James's use of metaphors of travel and adventure are treated in John Paterson, "The Language of 'Adventure' in Henry James," *American Literature*, XXXII (1960), 291–301.

ically at sea.[14] In his most optimistic moments, that faith figures itself to his imagination as an aromatic bath in which he has had the extreme good fortune to find himself floating. But, on reflection, such an element makes him uneasy. He had tried to warn his intended, Maggie, about the possibility—the mere *possibility*—of his harboring an unfathomable inner self on which her confidence, like all innocent human good faith, might conceivably founder. The Prince's warning was perhaps only theoretical, for he honestly believed himself to be free of "dangers from within," although "his race . . . had had them handsomely enough, and he was somehow full of his race." At all events, his mere suggestion of deception had made Maggie's color rise. "He had perceived on the spot that any *serious* discussion of veracity, of loyalty, or rather of the want of them, practically took her unprepared, as if it were quite new to her. He had noticed it before: it was the English, the American sign that duplicity, like 'love,' had to be joked about. It couldn't be 'gone into.' " It is precisely this immeasurable American "innocence"—which paradoxically sees both "too much" and "too little"—that makes his bride-to-be and her father appear "incredibly romantic" to the Prince and constitutes his chief perplexity. Unlike Christopher Newman, whose more conventional romance adventure was viewed as an introduction to the darkly sinister, the Prince is on the brink of an experience with people whose strangeness takes the ambiguous form of pure candor. Like Newman, he is a metaphoric explorer—indeed, the negative image of his earlier American counterpart. Whereas Newman is supposed to remind us of the man who "first showed Americans the way to Europe," Prince Amerigo (named for the man who "discovered America—or got himself honoured as if he had") is setting out "to discover the Americans."[15] Accordingly, on the eve of his mar-

---

14. This chapter seems a good illustration of Hisayoshi Watanabe's argument that James's use of the pluperfect, especially in *The Golden Bowl*, tends to remove the action from the actual and the historical: "the actual, the palpable, seems to elude our grasp." Instead, James focuses on "the consciousness, the intelligence, the retrospection of his characters" ("Past Perfect Retrospection in the Style of Henry James," *American Literature*, XXXIV [1962], 165–181).

15. Also like Newman—and here one must notice how frequently the "mystery" of romance reduces in the hands of James to a suggestion of profound enigmas in human communication—whose problem is that of understanding "French conversation," the Prince finds himself at a linguistic disadvantage with his prospective relations: he speaks of "practising his American in order to converse properly, on equal terms as it were, with Mr. Verver," who "had a command of it . . . that put him at a disadvantage in any discussion."

riage the Prince's situation reminds him of that most bizarre of romances, *The Narrative of Arthur Gordon Pym*:

> The motives of such people were obscure—a little alarmingly so; they contributed to that element of the impenetrable which alone slightly qualified his sense of his good fortune. He remembered to have read as a boy a wonderful tale by Allan Poe, his prospective wife's countryman—which was a thing to show, by the way, what imagination Americans *could* have: the story of the shipwrecked Gordon Pym, who, drifting in a small boat further toward the North Pole—or was it the South?—than anyone had ever done, found at a given moment before him a thickness of white air that was like a dazzling curtain of light, concealing as darkness conceals, yet of the colour of milk or of snow. There were moments when he felt his own boat move upon some such mystery. The state of mind of his new friends, including Mrs. Assingham herself, had resemblances to a great white curtain. He had never known curtains but as purple even to blackness—but as producing where they hung a darkness intended and ominous. When they were so disposed as to shelter surprises the surprises were apt to be shocks.

James would complain, in the Preface to *The Altar of the Dead*, that the "would-be portentous climax" of Poe's tale fails because it lacks any connection to the history of Poe's protagonist: "the attempt is all at the horrific in itself," and the elements "hang in the void; whereby we see the effect lost, the imaginative effort wasted." But Poe's imaginative effort hardly seems wasted on the Prince. It is precisely the unexpected shock of Poe's ending that makes it an effective metaphor for the deepest mystery. As with the extravagantly disparate figures of metaphysical poetry, we are being forced to see connections between apparent opposites.

The extremity of the Prince's reaction to his situation, though at first surprising, is a measure of how profound an enigma may lurk behind the blandest of appearances. A voyage into the threatening dark is predictably frightening; but a voyage into absolute blankness holds unpredictable terrors. It took an American imagination to think of Poe's figure, the Prince seems to say; will it not require an American imagination to fathom its meaning? What lies behind the veil is "the quantity of confidence reposed in him" by the Ververs, but that quantity will have reflexive meaning for the Prince: it is not only their natures but a new view of his own nature that seems to await him. Like Christopher Newman, the Prince is exploring not only an alien mystery but also unknown depths in himself. Newman reacts under the pressure of the iniquitous, Amerigo under the pressure of a candid refusal to admit the existence of iniquities, but both pressures have equal power to reveal hidden aspects of human personality.

The metaphor of oceanic exploration introduced by the Prince in the first chapter of *The Golden Bowl* continues throughout the book as an oblique representation and interpretation of the action. The Prince desperately appeals to Fanny Assingham, the woman whose own marriage helped open "a kind of hymeneal Northwest Passage," to be his guide:

> "I'm starting on the great voyage—across the unknown sea; my ship's all rigged and appointed. . . . But what seems the matter with me is that I can't sail alone; my ship must be one of a pair, must have, in the waste of waters, a—what do you call it?—a consort. I don't ask you to stay on board with me, but I must keep your sail in sight for orientation."

That Fanny may not prove a reliable guide has, however, already been suggested by the Prince himself. She shares the Ververs' aversion to any hint of difficulties or dangers in human relations, and her "deep serenity" worries him, coming, as it does "for his fancy, from behind the white curtain." Now he notices that the seriousness of his own metaphoric imagination makes Fanny nervous and she tries to blunt its effect, treating "him in fine as if he were not uttering truths but making pretty figures for her diversion." She insists that his voyage is ending, not beginning: "You talk about ships, but they're not the comparison. Your tossings are over—you're practically *in* port. The port . . . of the Golden Isles." This conclusion offered by Amerigo's "fairy godmother" might serve as the finale to a fable whose protagonists are guaranteed to live happily ever after, but its shining assurances will prove deceptive for the Prince's Poesque travel narrative. Amerigo must be expected to remember Maggie's humorous admission that she and her father are "like a pair of pirates," and we shall shortly learn that the main business of Adam Verver's life is "to rifle the Golden Isles." Thus Fanny Assingham's serene attempt to squelch Amerigo's seagoing metaphor amounts to the suggestion that he relinquish his quest for deeper knowledge of the Ververs and himself, and unreflectively submit to the comfortable spiritual exploitation all too innocently practiced by Adam and Maggie.

The Prince, however, plunges ahead, finding in Charlotte Stant the true "consort" of his voyage. "We're beyond her," Charlotte says of Fanny, as she convinces Amerigo that the unfathomable "sweet simplicity" of their *sposi* commits them to exploring together in secret the deepest water of their passional natures. Because the Ververs have a mortal fear of sexual involvement, the Prince and Charlotte decide that they have a "sacred" obligation to keep such knowledge and experience from their *sposi* by taking it all upon themselves. They therefore make a solemn "pledge" that carries them far beyond the lee shore:

> "It's sacred," she breathed back to him. They vowed it, gave it out and took it in, drawn, by their intensity, more closely together. Then of a sudden, through this tightened circle, as at the issue of a narrow strait into the sea beyond, everything broke up, broke down, gave way, melted and mingled.

Later, after the Prince returns from completing his journey with Charlotte during the "Easter revels" at Matcham and Gloucester, the Princess herself will confirm the force of his metaphor: "She had seen him last but five days since, yet he had stood there before her as if restored from some far country, some long voyage, some combination of dangers or fatigues."

Restored the Prince—and Charlotte—may indeed be, but their explorations are fated to end in a less gratifying fashion. Thanks to Maggie, Charlotte will be "removed, transported, doomed" to a living death in American City, and Amerigo will find himself facing a remarkably Pym-like conclusion. "I see nothing but *you*," he will concede to Maggie, with "strangely lighted" eyes, on the last page of the book, thus admitting that the Princess has succeeded in carrying him off permanently to that realm "beyond everything" where he must become, like her, "a creature consciously floating and shining in a warm summer sea, some element of dazzling sapphire and silver, a creature cradled upon depths, buoyant among dangers, in which fear or folly, or sinking otherwise than in play, was impossible." It is love's limbo, the realm of a love "the most abysmal and unutterable," into which Maggie draws the Prince, where the exclusion of dangers—"fear or folly"—for the sake of theoretical perfection signals the impossibility that love will ever again be allowed to express itself in a truly human way.

James's debt to Poe in the metaphoric texture of *The Golden Bowl* cannot, of course, be called much more than a flicker of recognition, since *The Narrative of Arthur Gordon Pym* supplies at most an ounce of raw material for a distinctly Jamesian product. Nevertheless, this mere touch of Poe suffices to add many notes of romance strangeness and depth to

James's book without disturbing its realistic premises.[16] So far, James seems to have paid careful attention to Hawthorne's advice, in the preface to *The House of the Seven Gables*, that it is the part of wisdom in a romancer "to mingle the Marvellous rather as a slight, delicate, and evanescent flavor, than as any portion of the actual substance of the dish offered to the Public." But the major imaginative extravagance in James's book clearly ignores this caveat, requiring—as do most of the works of Hawthorne himself—the further license provided by Hawthorne's next sentence: "He can hardly be said, however, to commit a literary crime, even if he disregard this caution." The device of the golden bowl itself represents, if not a literary crime, at least a novelistic misdemeanor, for by continually violating the boundary between fantasy and reality, between the metaphoric and the concretely present, it distinctly casts an aura of the marvelous and the preternatural over the "actual substance" of the whole book, providing a range of applications and implications scarcely less ample than that suggested by the scarlet letter or the white whale.[17]

The golden bowl defies delimitation of meaning. In its largest sense it is the totality of James's book, physically and metaphorically—the whole mold into which these elements of human experience are poured. It is "art" itself, literally as well as figuratively: both artifact and idea, a presence and a significance, an image and an interpretation, an object and a subject, both that which is performed and that which performs. It in-

---

16. "There is nothing Poësque about its sinister and mysterious notes," writes Joseph Warren Beach, "and yet there is some suggestion of the earlier American writer in the strange figures of speech and the romantic accessories that raise the whole to a high imaginative level" (*The Method of Henry James*, p. 265).

17. A recent English opinion, in some ways typical of non-American responses to the "poetry" of James's last books, is D. W. Jefferson's allegation that to claim centrality for the device of the bowl is to bring "James into quite the wrong relationship with his great predecessor [Hawthorne] and with the allegorical tradition in American literature. . . . To attach great importance to such a feature of James's art . . . is a way of belittling him. It deflects attention from the incomparably more interesting things in the book, and from its generally expansive and varied quality" (*Henry James and the Modern Reader* [Edinburgh, 1964], pp. 23–25). Although Jefferson objects to "uniting James with the American literary heritage" by stressing "allegory and symbol," it seems to me that, losing such a link, we lose a great deal indeed. Moreover, to separate the "interesting things" in any James book from its metaphoric texture or symbolic structure is to run the risk of producing just the sort of disjointed criticism that has often hindered the understanding of Hawthorne and Melville.

fluences the action of the book and comments on that action; it represents individual characters and relationships between and among characters; it serves as a touchstone for measuring personality and as a philosopher's stone for transmuting personality. It functions in the book as the grail of every quest for meaning, a vessel useful for communion with oneself or with others, a ritual cup suitable for celebrations both diabolical and divine.

Presiding over this thoroughly magical item is one of James's queerest creations, the Bloomsbury antiquario—Miriam's model brought truly to life. Introduced to us in Chapter VI with an air of intense and conscious mystery which underlines the importance of his bowl, this strange creature without a name carries credentials familiar to readers of romance. Presumably (but not very credibly) Jewish; speaking and understanding, it would seem, all languages, but of no determinate nationality; "singularly, intensely coercive" and endowed with "an extraordinary pair of eyes"—this great "curiosity" is the arch artificer/deceiver, whose shop is the witches' kitchen of art. "Of decent old gold, old silver, old bronze, of old chased and jewelled artistry, were the objects" first laid out on the counter by his "slim light fingers, with neat nails," which "touched them at moments, briefly, nervously, tenderly, as those of a chess-player rest, a few seconds, over the board, on a figure he thinks he may move and then may not: small florid ancientries, ornaments, pendants, lockets, brooches, buckles, pretexts for dim brilliants, bloodless rubies, pearls either too large or too opaque for value. . . ." On and on goes James's list of the conjurer's toys with which this wizard tries to engage the interest of the Prince and Charlotte, but it becomes clear that only his greatest trick will be able "to tempt them":

> He placed the box on the counter, pushed back a pair of small hooks, lifted the lid and removed from its nest a drinking-vessel larger than a common cup, yet not of exorbitant size, and formed, to appearance, either of old fine gold or of some material once richly gilt. He handled it with tenderness, with ceremony, making a place for it on a small satin mat. "My Golden Bowl," he observed—and it sounded on his lips as if it said everything. He left the important object—for as "important" it did somehow present itself—to produce its certain effect.

The effect that the bowl produces on us as Charlotte discusses it, first with the antiquario and then with Amerigo, is certainly that of exquisite mystification. The product of "a lost time" and "a lost art," it is both "precious" and "cheap"—perhaps pure gold, but perhaps again mere gilt; apparently a perfect crystal, but possibly deeply faulted. Everything and nothing, the bowl seems, in short, to represent the enchanted glass (the crystal ball) of art, whose value and significance lie purely in the mind and spirit of the beholder.

Mute as Keats's Urn, it nevertheless speaks many meanings, one of which, like that of the Cenci portrait in *The Marble Faun*, concerns the universal prevalence of *flaws* in a fallen world. This lesson centers chiefly, of course, in the person of the Prince, the European *"morceau de musée"* of uncertain value which Adam effectively purchases for Maggie. (The metaphoric connection between the Prince and the bowl is confirmed in the next chapter when Adam remarks to Amerigo that "for living with, you're a pure and perfect crystal," whereupon the Prince replies, "Oh, if I'm a crystal I'm delighted that I'm a perfect one, for I believe that they sometimes have cracks and flaws.") A related meaning concerns the complexities of giving and receiving in human love relationships. But we must first recall the actual circumstances leading up to the introduction of the bowl (although it will hardly be possible to keep actuality and metaphor from intermingling).

On the eve of the Prince's marriage to Maggie Verver, Charlotte invites him to join her in searching for a wedding gift for Maggie, but this ostensible purpose of the expedition is frustrated by Charlotte's being too "poor" to purchase the bowl. The ironic corollary is clear: Charlotte's lack of a fortune, by preventing her from marrying the Prince, has allowed her, as it were, to give him to Maggie. The golden bowl, unpurchased by Charlotte but finally purchased by Maggie, thus symbolizes the Prince as Charlotte's dubious "gift" to her friend—dubious, because the Prince is "flawed" by his past love and residual desire for Charlotte. Indeed, one might say that the real purpose of Charlotte's expedition is, in fact, to celebrate and renew, although presumably for the last time, her past intimacy with the Prince, and this celebration is also symbolized by the bowl. Accordingly, the bowl comes at least partially to stand for both a particular dilemma facing Charlotte and a general one confronting all of the book's protagonists: "Does one make a present . . . of an object that contains to one's knowledge a flaw?"

From Charlotte's point of view the bowl is "cracked" because, as a gift, it would represent an ambiguous intention. Would it be a sign of truly golden love and good will toward Maggie or the guilt (gilt) offering of an uneasy conscience? The antiquario, a worldly-wise spokesman for the fallen angels of postlapsarian humanity, provides some answers for Charlotte's question: "But if it's something you can't find out isn't that as good as if it were nothing?" Charlotte insists, however, that the truth will out. "Well, if one knows of it one has only to mention it. The good faith . . . is always there." What is meant as a love offering, however imperfect, he suggests, will be one, if the confession of doubt is balanced by a sincere avowal of good intention.

Such wisdom, however, puts a burden on Charlotte. How can she be certain of her own good faith or anyone else's? When the shopman admits that the bowl might be smashed "upon a marble floor," she thinks of the past and future ("they were a connection, marble floors; a connection with many things: with her old Rome, and with *his*; with the palaces of his past, and, a little, of hers; with the possibilities of his future, with the sumptuosities of his marriage, with the wealth of the Ververs"), and she fears the dangers posed by knowledge of old intimacy or by the growth of new feelings. Still, the value of the antiquario's outlook is strong: he has made her see that if one worries too much about the "flaws," one's sense of beauty will be poisoned. Human love, she realizes, is necessarily predicated on imperfection, acknowledged or suspected. "Thank goodness then that if there *be* a crack we know it!" she tells the Prince. "But if we may perish by cracks in things that we don't know—!" and, James tells us, "she smiled with the sadness of it"—"We can never then give each other anything."

Amerigo, however, does not presently share Charlotte's opinion. Eager to make a fresh start in everything, he is determined to forget the past and thus shrugs off the sense of guilt and renewed intimacy thrust upon him by the bowl. Rejecting the "omen" implied in it, he refuses to make Charlotte a gift of the bowl (and it is the only thing she wants), promising that when she marries he will present her with a "perfect" gift—meaning, clearly, an object devoid of reference to their past or present complicity and thus suitable for celebrating the act that will, presumably, divide them even further and insure the integrity of his new life. But, of course, there can be no real gift without "flaws," for the true act of giving must involve the sharing of one's imperfect human love, and a "perfect" gift would be an empty one. When Amerigo's "gift" is finally presented to Charlotte (after the marriage which, ironically, first draws them more closely together and then separates them forever, initially completing but finally destroying his happiness), it turns out, as we should expect, to be nothing other than (metaphorically) the golden bowl, his own beautiful but tarnished humanity.

Preparing to consummate his love for Charlotte at Gloucester, the Prince conceives of his "freedom" as being "as perfect and rounded and lustrous as some huge precious pearl." This is illusory, however. The spirit hovering over their splendid moment together is not that of ideal perfection and freedom from danger, but rather that of the Bloomsbury antiquario's artifact, bespeaking contingency, imperfection, tragedy. "I feel the day like a great gold cup that we must somehow drain together," Amerigo says rather carelessly, intending only to confirm his sense of security. But Charlotte realizes that his own imagination has betrayed the truth of their situation. "Do you remember," she asks, "apropos of great gold cups, the beautiful one, the real one, that I offered you so long ago and that you wouldn't have?"

> "Oh, yes!"—but it took, with a slight surprise on the Prince's part, some small recollecting. "The treacherous cracked thing you wanted to palm off on me, and the little swindling Jew who understood Italian and who backed you up! But I feel this an occasion," he immediately added, "and I hope you don't mean," he smiled, "that *as* an occasion it's also cracked."

The Prince has touched on precisely Charlotte's meaning, and she takes him up: "Don't you think too much of 'cracks,' and aren't you too afraid of them? I risk the cracks." Whereupon Amerigo charmingly but uncomprehendingly advises Charlotte to "risk them as much as you like for yourself, but don't risk them for me." He speaks this, James tells us, "in all the gaiety of his just barely-tremulous serenity"—a sufficient sign for Charlotte that the subject had best be dropped. But, for us at least, her point has been made. Like every occasion of human love, this one is indeed "cracked," an imperfect mixture of good and evil, pleasure and pain, strength and weakness. One cannot have the golden bowl without risk.[18]

That risk—the possibility of causing suffering and of suffering in return—is made manifest when the "queer little foreign man" once again appears to flourish his magic symbol, this time for Maggie's sake. "That

---

18. In "Henry James's Last Portrait of a Lady: Charlotte Stant in *The Golden Bowl*," *American Literature*, XXVIII (1957), 449–468, Jean Kimball comments on Charlotte's attitude toward the crack as compared to the Prince's and Maggie's. Kimball argues persuasively for viewing Charlotte as the tragic heroine of the book.

cup there has turned witness," she announces to Fanny Assingham in the course of a long and pregnant discussion of the object. Fanny finds the bowl beautiful as a work of art, though "ugly" as a "document"—"brave and firm and rich, with its bold deep hollow . . . an enviable ornament, a possession really desirable," without the "queer torment about it" which has totally filled Maggie's imagination. And that is exactly the difficulty. Maggie sees the bowl *only* as a "witness" of evil intentions on the part of Charlotte and the Prince, not as a complex symbolic representation of the imperfect nature of human relations in general. "Ah to thrust such things on *us*, to do them here between us and with us day after day and in return, in return—!" In return, we should add, for the Ververs' own flawed love for their respective *sposi*. Maggie, however, sees herself only as sinned against, and not as sinning.

Fanny tries to convince Maggie that her "idea" of the bowl is cracked, is indeed nothing but a "crack," since her uncertain "knowledge" of the Prince's liaison with Charlotte has crowded out all sense of his basic generosity and blinded her to his thwarted affection. As a demonstration of her argument, Fanny smashes the golden bowl, trying to obliterate from reality the object that has inspired in Maggie only a deformed interpretation and an impulse of horror. "Whatever you meant by it—and I don't want to know *now*—has ceased to exist," Fanny concludes. Nevertheless, the damage has been done, the shock has been too great. This experience of moral ambiguity renders the Princess, not more, but less human. Her tortured awareness of evil causes a reaction that amounts to a refinement of cruelty: the desire to reconstruct for herself, and for the other protagonists, an illusion of prelapsarian innocence. "The golden bowl—as it *was* to have been," is what she wants. "The bowl with all happiness in it. The bowl without the crack." She insists on human relationships without admission of pain, secure from any confession of weakness or threat of discomposure. But this is impossible. Consequently, the "perfect" golden bowl that she refashions in her own way is a fraud, offering only the appearance of marriage and a poor imitation of friendship. By insisting on a bowl without flaws, she creates a situation of glittering falsity for everyone.

It is important to recall that *The Golden Bowl* (James's book) is also "cracked"—told in two parts from the two points of view, respectively, of the Prince and the Princess. Truth, James seems to have been suggesting along with Melville, has "ragged edges," and neat representations lie. Nevertheless, it is on a note of superficial neatness—that of the golden bowl without a seam—that James's tale draws to a conclusion, as his grand controlling metaphor swells to enclose all the action, marking the success of Maggie's plan:

> Charlotte throned, as who should say, between her hostess and her host, the whole scene having crystallised, as soon as she took her place, to the right quiet lustre; the harmony wasn't less sustained for being superficial, and the only approach to a break in it was while Amerigo remained standing long enough for his father-in-law, vaguely wondering, to appeal to him, invite or address him, and then in default of any such word selected for presentation to the other visitor a plate of *petits fours*.

This is the final horror of Adam and Maggie's "passion for perfection at any price," an insistence that superficial harmony be maintained at the cost of ignoring human suffering and emotional truth.

In the drawing room of a thoroughly modern and recognizable world, amid the clatter of tea things and the munching of *petits fours*, James has conducted us to the deepest abyss of the human heart.[19] His theme, as R. P. Blackmur points out, is ancient and inexhaustible: man's inhumanity to man, to himself as well as to others.[20] The last scene of *The Golden Bowl* is attenuated but nevertheless tragic. Having "doomed" Charlotte, a woman who has learned painfully the human uses of compromising with evil, to the sterile aesthetic vacuum of American City—where her capacity for and knowledge of love, her compassionate understanding of the heart, will be submerged in her new role as nursemaid and museum guide—Maggie is left alone with Amerigo. (Miriam, we might say, has been packed off with Kenyon and Donatello left to Hilda, each relegated to a world he neither understands nor enjoys.) She has destroyed everything except her glorious idea of success, and as the book ends, she is shown turning away from her thoroughly tamed old-world Prince, who now sees nothing but her, in "pity and dread"—pity for the accomplishment of his fate, and dread of her own. Despite the good breeding that prevents the escape of any cries of pain, fear, or alarm, the scene is one final illustration of the truth of romance—one last proof of Amerigo's statement that "everything's terrible . . . in the heart of man."

---

19. "The underlying movement of the novel is problematic, dark and frightened, for all the urbanity of its surfaces," notes Francis Fergusson ("*The Golden Bowl* Revisited," *Sewanee Review*, LXIII [1955], 26).

20. See his "Introduction" to *The Golden Bowl* (New York, 1963).

AFTERWORD

Perry Miller, in a brilliant posthumously published essay, observed: "It would strain the limits of space and patience were I to call the role [*sic*] of all the dark ladies in the American Romances who, from *The Last of the Mohicans* to the eve of the Civil War, expired for a love that could not be requited, or of the glowering Byrons of the forest who stalked majestically into the sunset. Here and there a writer might attempt a bit of variety by leaving out one or another of the standard cast of characters, or by allowing the heroine to exhibit a brown instead of a golden head. By and large they remained faithful to the conventions, for in their eyes these were not conventions but indispensable symbols for setting forth the true burden of Romance in America, which was not at all the love story. What all of them were basically concerned with was the continent, the heritage of America, the wilderness."[1]

I hope that the roll of heroes, heroines, and themes called in the foregoing chapters has not strained the limits so wisely observed by Miller. I hope, too, that it has succeeded in demonstrating with some cogency how persistently many of the conventions and patterns of romance evinced themselves from Cooper through James, and how richly and complexly these imaginative habits of romance have borne their weight of meaning. That meaning, in Miller's formulation, mainly concerned the spirit of the New World and especially of titanic Nature. "With a machinery for mounting the action furnished by the formula," he continues, "American writers could devote themselves heart and soul to portraying the uniqueness, the glory, the ordeal of America."

I have tried to show that, from the very beginning, the fictional quest for knowledge of the wilderness was synonymous—as in the Emersonian

---

1. This and all further references to Miller are from "The Romance and the Novel," in *Nature's Nation* (Cambridge, Mass., 1967), pp. 241–278.

equation[2]—with the desire and need to explore the self. "The ordeal of America," the special agony and unique glory of being an American romancer, was conceived as lying in the responsibility to question the fundamental conditions of human existence and the inner nature of man. William Carlos Williams' *In the American Grain* long ago made just such a claim, metaphorically linking the physical exploration of the continent with a more personal search, for our seemingly least American writer, Edgar Allan Poe: "His greatness is in that he turned his back and faced inland, to originality, with the identical gesture of a Boone." Poe shared in the national destiny, Williams insisted, by requiring himself to live on the limits, to plumb new depths and reach new conclusions, both human and stylistic: "to originate a style that does spring from the local conditions, not of trees and mountains, but of the 'soul'—here starved, stricken by loss of liberty, ready to die—he is *forced in certain directions for his subjects*." These darkly emphasized *"certain directions"* identify Poe as a typical, not an eccentric, American writer, whose job it was to demonstrate "that literature is *serious*, not a matter of courtesy but of truth."[3] Constance Rourke was to make a claim for Poe's adherence to the popular comic tradition in America that reaches an identical conclusion. Along with Hawthorne and Melville, she argued, Poe "invaded . . . and in some measure conquered" the area "of the inner mind or consciousness" which the comic tradition had made its own.[4]

Perry Miller's generally rigid limitation of American romance to a concern with nature on this continent leads him to conclude that the form was largely outmoded for writers of the post-Civil War period. Associating romance with an exaggerated belief in *Naturphilosophie*, which predictably declined, and with a virgin land that was "steadily being first defiled and then destroyed by the inexorable march of civilization," he sees Hawthorne and Melville as pronouncing their own "funeral oration," providing the "culmination" of a tradition and not a renaissance. To a writer such as Henry James (who "beheld the revolution accomplished by George Eliot" and learned from her "that the adventures and histories of her characters—that is to say, 'the author's subject-matter all'—were determined by [their] feelings and the quality of their

---

2. "In fine, the ancient precept, 'Know thyself,' and the modern precept, 'Study nature,' become at last one maxim." (From "The American Scholar.")

3. *In the American Grain* (New York, 1956), pp. 226, 227, 216.

4. *American Humor: A Study of the National Character* (New York, 1953), pp. 148–149.

minds") what relevance, Miller asks, could there be in the conventions and characters of orthodox romance, in the featureless heroes of a Cooper or even in the "demonic rebellions" of Hawthorne's dark ladies?

The relevance of these particular aspects of romance was perhaps at best indirect for James. But Miller's error, I think, lies in an overly restrictive definition of romance tradition that fails to perceive certain fundamental and organic links among our authors. If the great lesson James learned was that his true subject lay in the geographically unlocatable realm between society (or nature) and the responding consciousness, one must concede he had as much to learn from Melville or Hawthorne as from George Eliot. Hawthorne, as Charles Feidelson has noted, was anxious "to fix the status of the romance in an almost metaphysical sense. . . . What seems at first a wholly personal problem, resulting from Hawthorne's peculiar temperament, turns out to be a reflection of the problem of the times. The Actual and the Imaginary can meet only in a theory or habit of perception."[5] As a result, the province of romance—indeed, its very subject matter—often involved a scrupulous questioning and testing of motives, materials, and methods. And such a theory or habit and the literary program it engendered were as germane to James's craft and criticism of fiction as they were to the work of his compatriots. Here, not surprisingly, a key passage from Emerson's "Experience" suggests the central mood and problem of the times: "Sleep lingers all our lifetime about our eyes, as night hovers all day in the boughs of the fir-tree. All things swim and glitter. Our life is not so much threatened as our perception."

It was precisely this threat to consciousness that became a perpetual challenge for American writers of the nineteenth century and beyond. From Cooper's Natty Bumppo, who learned from the Indian to look hard that he might see and understand, to James's epistemologically obsessed heroes and heroines, "an almost chemical analysis of the soul and consciousness" (in Lawrence's phrase[6]) has preoccupied our authors and forced them continually to re-examine their own premises. What began as a literal and ended as a metaphoric need to peer into and pierce through the wilderness constitutes the true burden of the romance in America and a major strand of our literary heritage.

---

5. *Symbolism and American Literature* (Chicago, 1953), p. 7.

6. *Studies in Classic American Literature*, reprinted in *The Shock of Recognition*, edited by Edmund Wilson (New York, 1955), p. 967.

INDEX